# JUMP Math K

**Book K** Part 2 of 2

T0302625

## Contents



Put your name or picture here!

jump math™

MULTIPLYING POTENTIAL.

**JUMP Math**
One Yonge Street, Suite 1014
Toronto, Ontario M5E 1E5
Canada
www.jumpmath.org

Writers: Dr. Heather Betel, Dr. Francisco Kibedi, Julie Lorinc
Editors: Megan Burns, Liane Tsui, Julie Takasaki, Natalie Francis, Jackie Dulson, Janice Dyer, Rita Vanden Heuvel
Layout and Illustrations: Linh Lam, Fely Guinasao-Fernandes, Sawyer Paul
Cover Design: Blakeley Words+Pictures
Cover Photograph: © Photo Pegah

ISBN 978-1-927457-72-6

Fifth printing October 2024

Printed and bound in Canada

*A note to educators, parents, and everyone who believes that numeracy is as important as literacy for a fully functioning society*

# Welcome to JUMP Math

Entering the world of JUMP Math means believing that every child has the capacity to be fully numerate and to love math. Founder and mathematician John Mighton has used this premise to develop his innovative teaching method. The resulting resources isolate and describe concepts so clearly and incrementally that everyone can understand them.

JUMP Math is comprised of Teacher Resources, Digital Lesson Slides, student Assessment & Practice Books, assessment tools, outreach programs, and professional development. All of this is presented on the JUMP Math website: **www.jumpmath.org**.

The Teacher Resource is available on the website for free use. Read the introduction to the Teacher Resource before you begin using these materials. This will ensure that you understand both the philosophy and the methodology of JUMP Math. The Assessment & Practice Books are designed for use by students, with adult guidance. Each student will have unique needs and it is important to provide the student with the appropriate support and encouragement as they work through the material.

Allow students to discover the concepts by themselves as much as possible. Mathematical discoveries can be made in small, incremental steps. The discovery of a new step is like untangling the parts of a puzzle. It is exciting and rewarding.

Students will need to answer the questions marked with a in a notebook. Grid paper notebooks should always be on hand for answering extra questions or when additional room for calculation is needed.

# Contents

## PART 1

### Unit 1: Counting and Cardinality: Numbers 1 to 5



### Unit 2: Counting and Cardinality: Comparing Numbers 1 to 5



### Unit 3: Geometry: Flat Shapes

## Unit 4: Counting and Cardinality: Numbers 6 to 10



## Unit 5: Counting and Cardinality: Comparing within 10



## Unit 6: Measurement and Data: Categories and Sorting



# PART 2

## Unit 7: Operations and Algebraic Thinking: Addition within 5

## Unit 11: Operations and Algebraic Thinking: Subtraction within 5



## Unit 12: Operations and Algebraic Thinking: Subtraction within 10



## Unit 13: Operations and Algebraic Thinking: Fluency within 5



## Unit 14: Measurement and Data: Measurement

# OAK-1 Counting to 70

Trace.

1.

60 61 62

63 64 65

66 67 68

69 70

2.

6 6 6 6 6 6 6

Write 6.

3.

# OAK-2 Counting On to 5

☐ Connect the dots.

1.

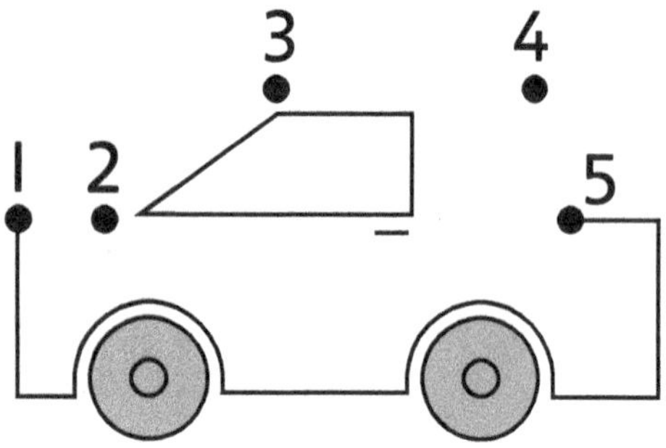


2.

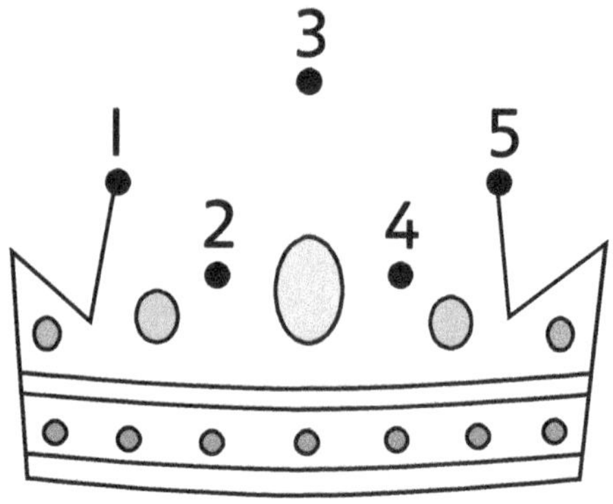


3.

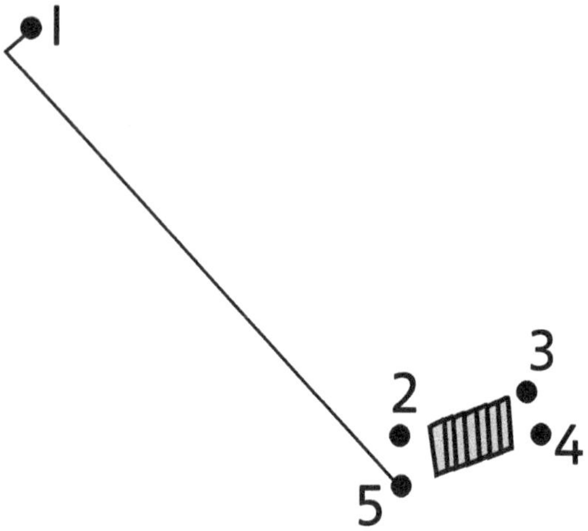


4.

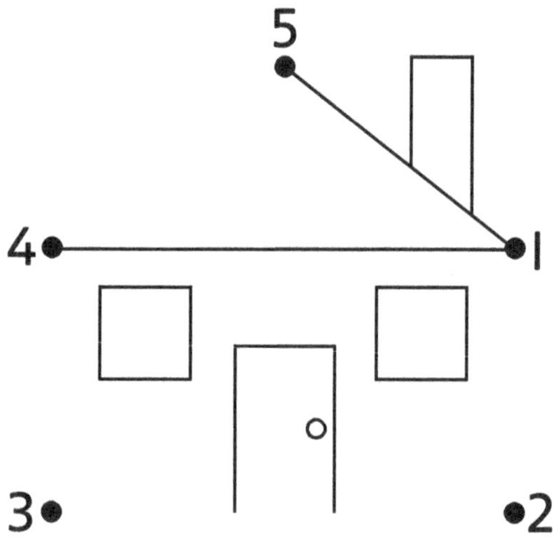


5.

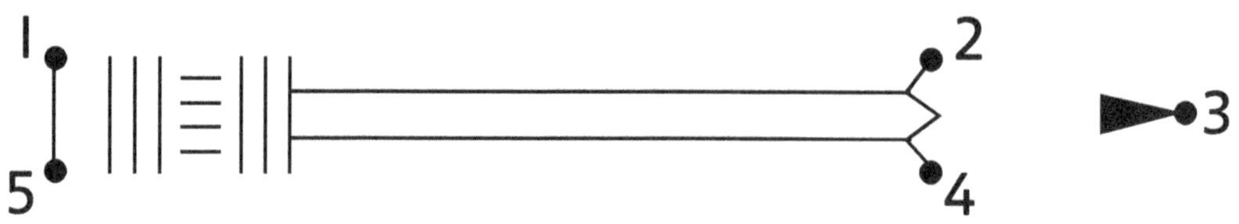

☐ Count on to 5.

6. 4 5

7. 3 4 5

8. 2

9. 1

10. 1

## ☐ Count on to 5.

**11.**

3 4 5

**12.**

2

**13.**

4

**14.**

1

# OAK-3 Acting Out Addition

☐ How many children in all?

1.

3 **plus** I more

makes ______

2.

2 plus 3 more

makes ______

☐ Count how many at the start.

☐ Count how many **more**.

☐ How many children in all?

**3.**

2 plus ______

makes ______

**4.**

______ plus ______

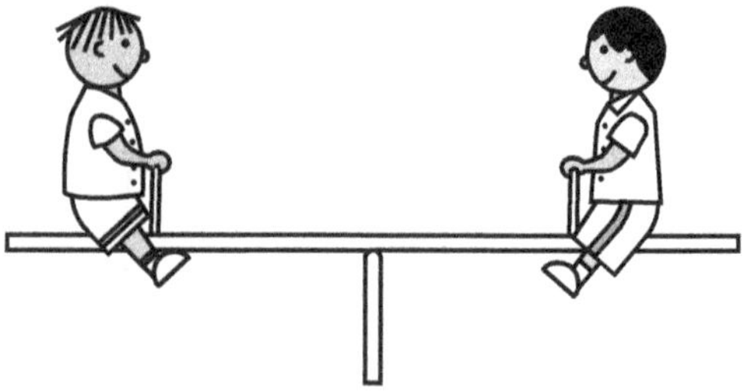

makes ______

# OAK-4 Adding with Objects

☐ Use blocks to show how many at the start.

☐ Use blocks to show how many **more**.

☐ How many in all?

**1.**

1  plus 2 more 

_______ 

**2.**

4  plus 1 more 

_______ 

☐ Use blocks to show how many at the start.

☐ Use blocks to show how many **more**.

☐ How many in all?

**3.**

I  plus 3 more 

______ 

**4.**

I cat + 3 more cats

______ 

☐ Use blocks to show how many.

☐ How many in all?

**5.**

2 dogs + 2 more dogs

| | |
|---|---|
| | |

**6.**

3 cats + 2 more cats

| | |
|---|---|
| | |

# OAK-5 Adding with Pictures

☐ How many in all?

**1.**

2 frogs + I more frog

equals ______ frogs

**2.**

I fish + 3 more fish

equals ______ fish

## ☐ How many in all?

**3.**

2 dogs + 2 more dogs

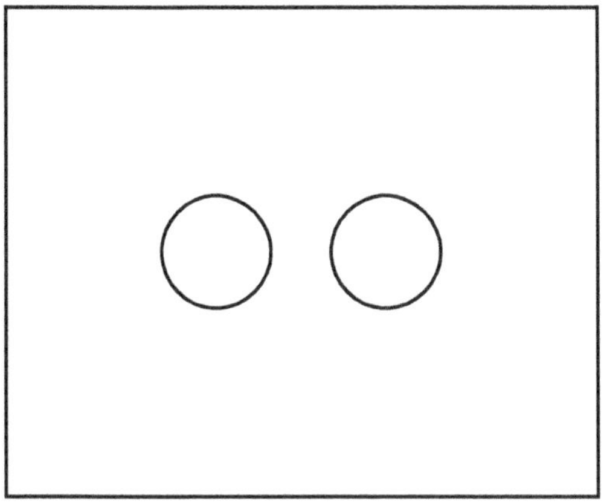

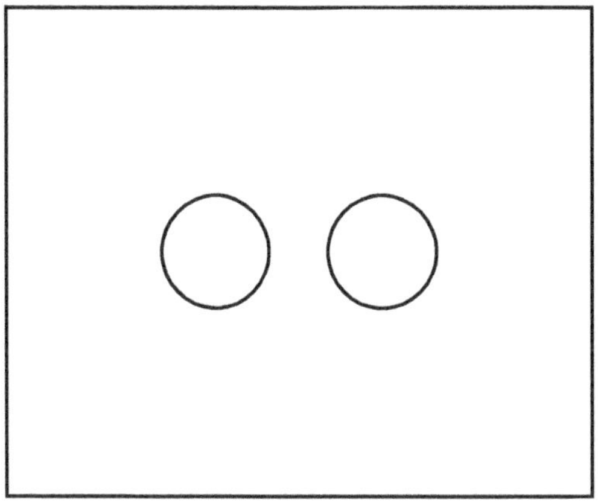

= ______ 

**4.**

I cat + 4 more cats

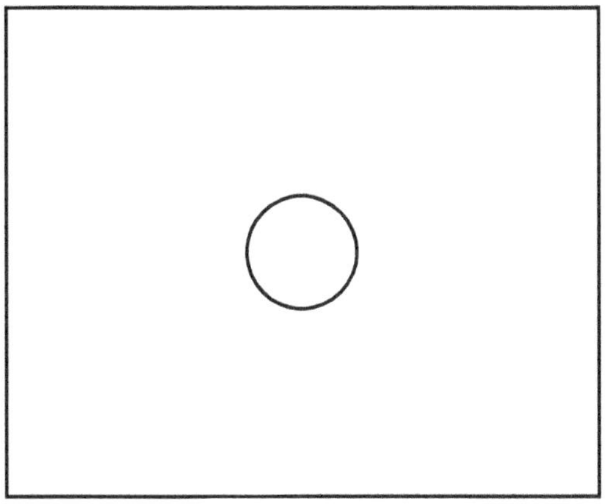

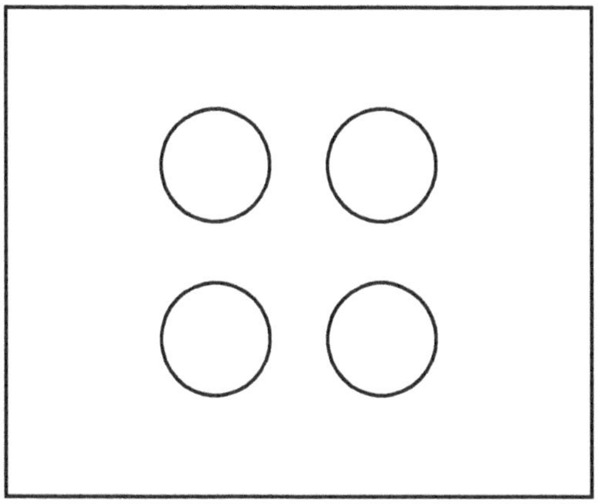

= ______ 

☐ Draw ◯ to show how many.

☐ How many in all?

5.

3 cats + 1 more cat

= ______ 

6.

2 dogs + 1 more dog

= ______ 

# OAK-6 Putting Together with Objects

☐ Use blocks to show how many .
☐ Use blocks to show how many .
☐ How many in all?

**1.**

3  + 1 

= ______ bugs

**2.**

2 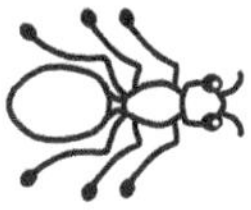 + 2 

= ______ bugs

☐ Use blocks to show how many of each.

☐ How many in all?

**3.**

1  + 3 

= ______ cars

**4.**

3  + 2 

= ______ pets

☐ Use blocks to show how many of each.

☐ How many in all?

**5.**

2  + 3 

= ______ cups

**6.**

4  + 1 

= ______ pets

# OAK-7 Putting Together with Pictures (I)

☐ How many in all?

**1.**

I tree + 3 trees

= ______ trees

**2.**

2 girls + 2 boys

= ______ children

☐ How many in all?

3.

2  + 3 

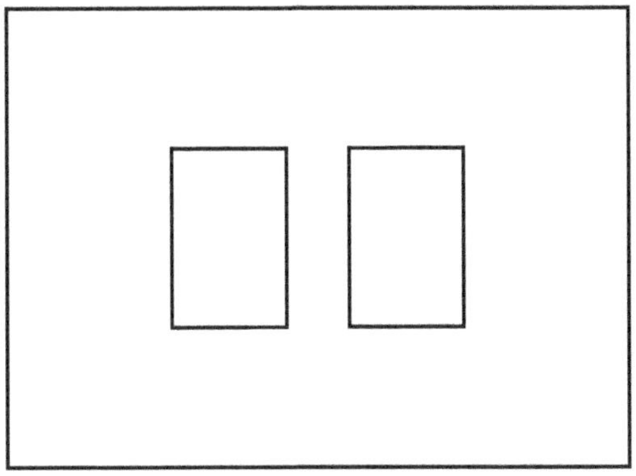 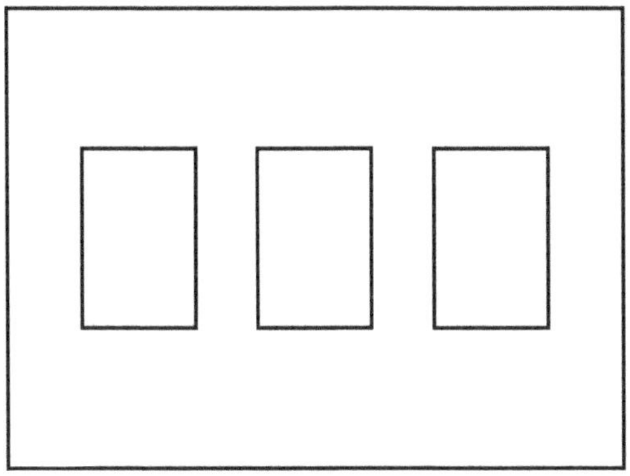

= ______ dogs

4.

4  + 1 

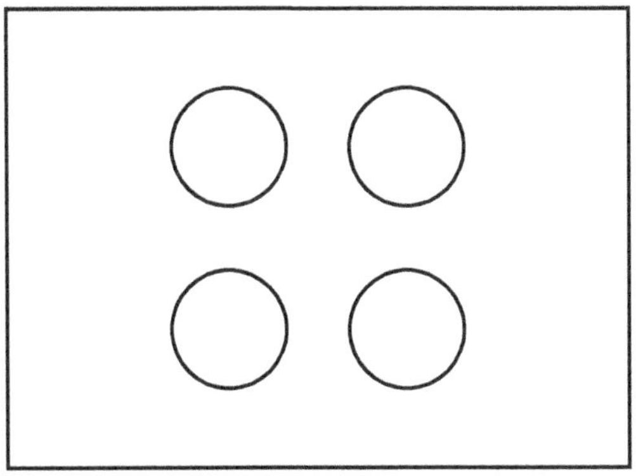 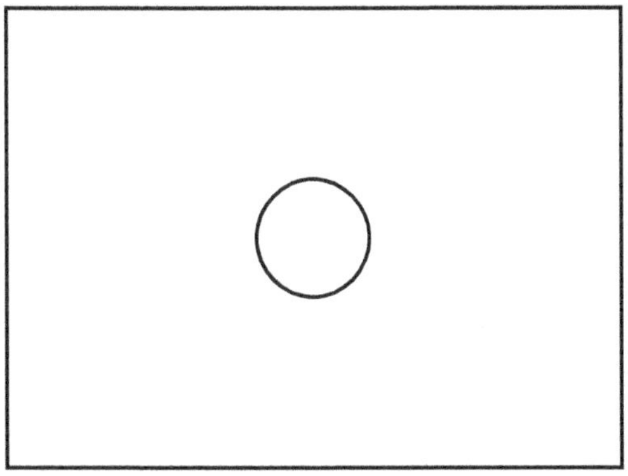

= ______ pets

☐ Draw ◯ to show how many.

☐ How many in all?

**5.**

3  + 1 

= ______ balls

**6.**

1  + 2 

= ______ pets

☐ How many of each?

☐ How many in all?

**7.**

____ + ____

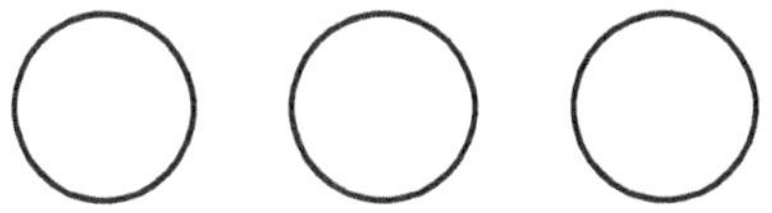

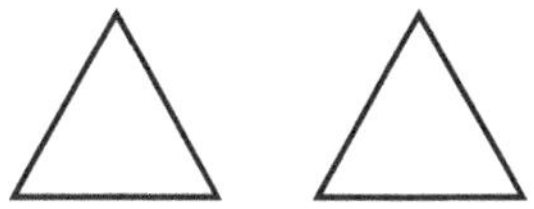

= ____ shapes

**8.**

____ + ____

= ____ pets

# OAK-8 Putting Together with Pictures (2)

☐ How many in all?

**1.**

2 cats + 3 dogs = ______ pets

**2.**

2 fish + 1 fish = ______ fish

**3.**

2 boys + 2 girls = ______ children

**4.**

1 ball + 3 balls = ______ balls

☐ How many in all?

**5.**

I tree + 2 trees = ______ trees

**6.**

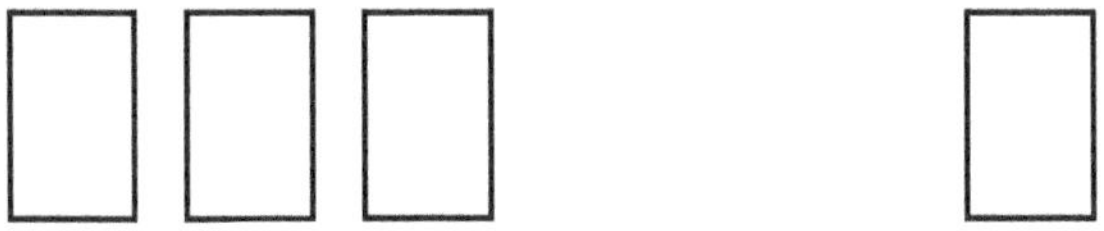

3 flags + I flag = ______ flags

**7.**

2 frogs + 3 fish = ______ pets

**8.**

I boy + 4 girls = ______ children

☐ Draw ◯ to show how many.

☐ How many in all?

9.

I big bug + I small bug = ______ bugs

10.

4 girls + I boy = ______ children

11.

2 trees + 2 trees = ______ trees

12.

3 cats + 2 dogs = ______ pets

# OAK-9 Decomposing 5

☐ What addition do you see?

**1.**

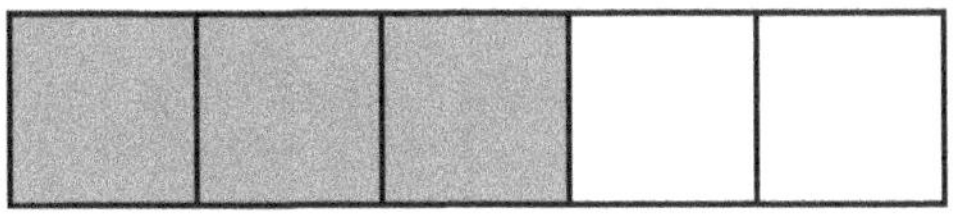

_____ + _____

**2.**

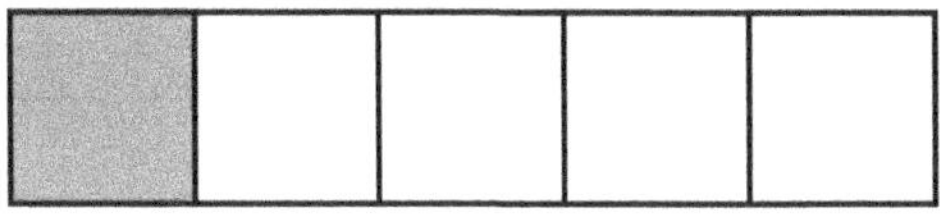

_____ + _____

**3.**

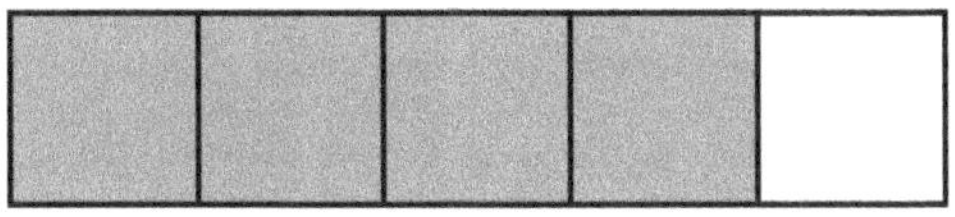

_____ + _____

**4. BONUS**

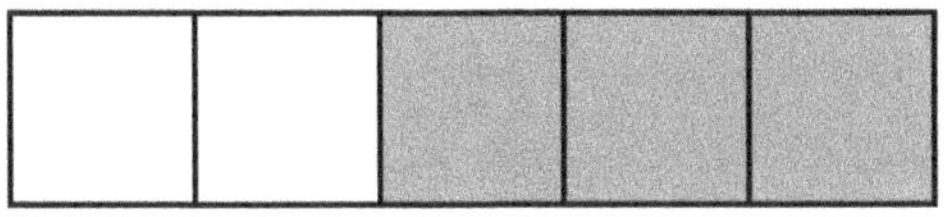

_____ + _____

☐ Color to show the addition.

**5.**

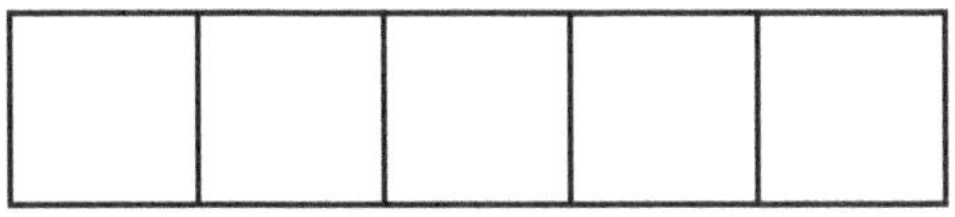

2 + 3

**6.**

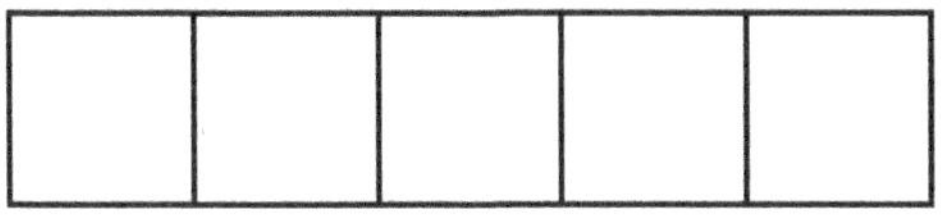

3 + 2

**7.**

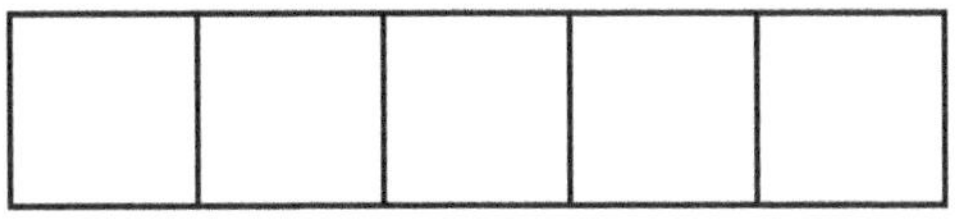

1 + 4

**8.**

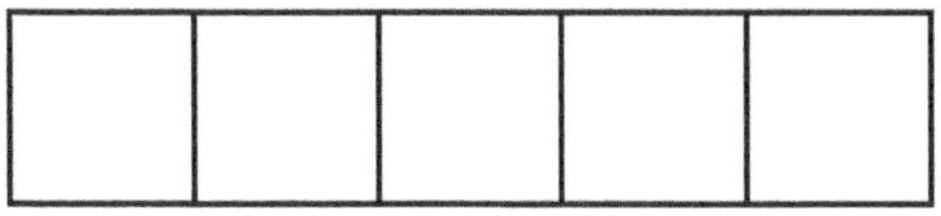

4 + 1

☐ Color to show an addition.

☐ Write the addition.

9.

| | | | | |
|---|---|---|---|---|
| | | | | |

5 = ____ + ____

10.

| | | | | |
|---|---|---|---|---|
| | | | | |

5 = ____ + ____

11.

| | | | | |
|---|---|---|---|---|
| | | | | |

5 = ____ + ____

# OAK-10 Decomposing Up to 5

☐ Circle to show the addition.

1.

1 + 4

2.

2 + 3

3.

3 + 2

4.

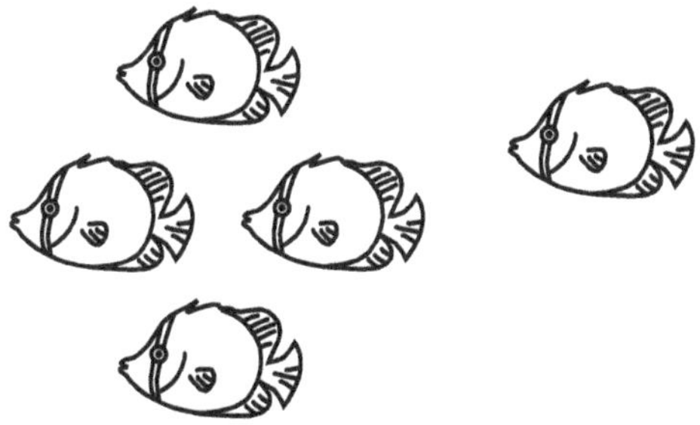

4 + 1

5.

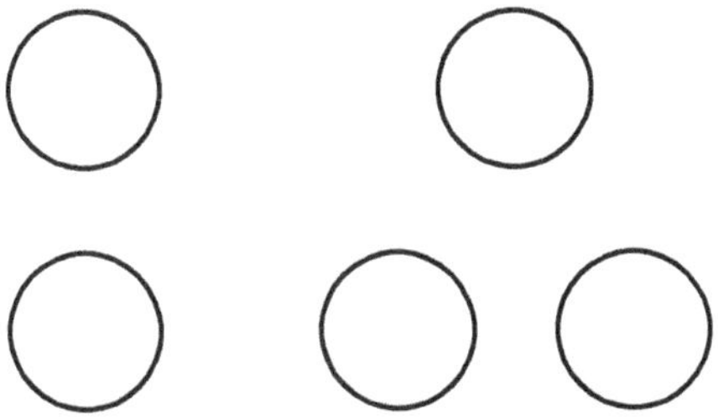

2 + 3

6.

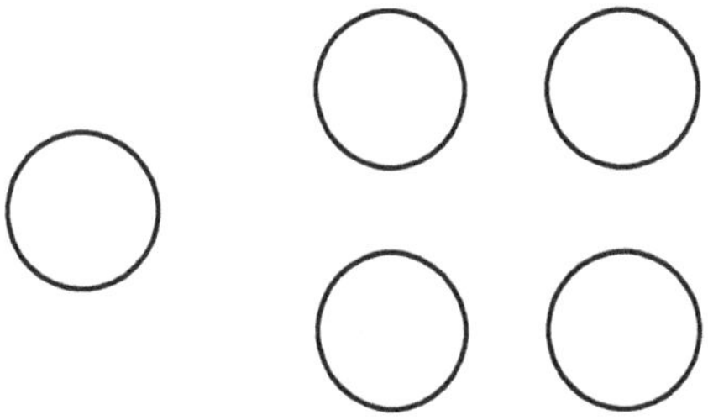

1 + 4

☐ What addition do you see?

7.

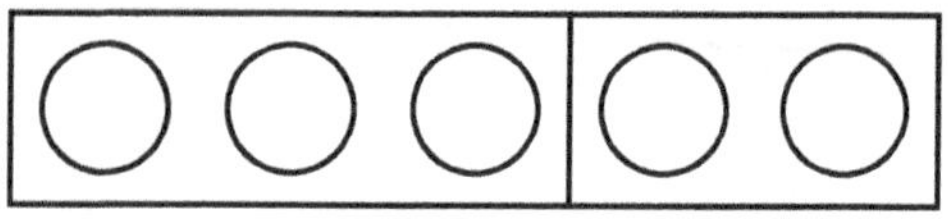

5 = ____ + ____

8.

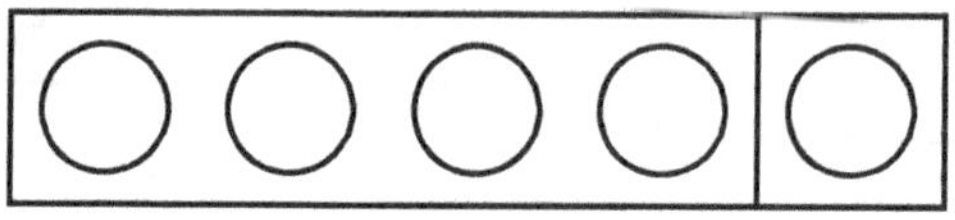

5 = ____ + ____

☐ Draw a line to show the addition.

9.

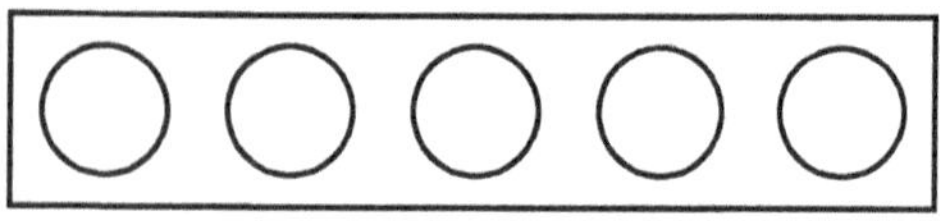

5 = 2 + 3

10.

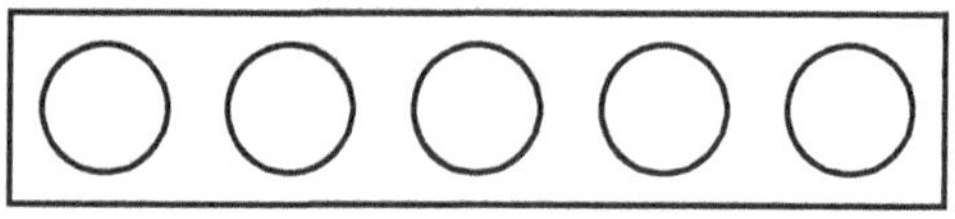

5 = 1 + 4

11.

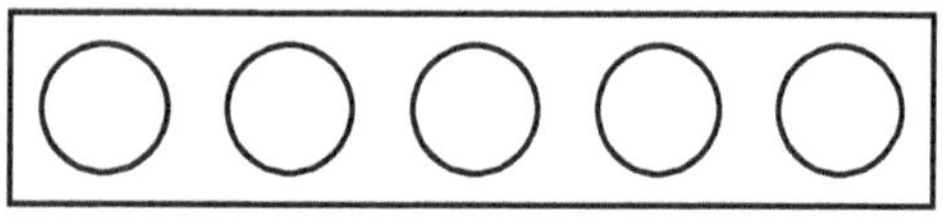

5 = 4 + 1

12.

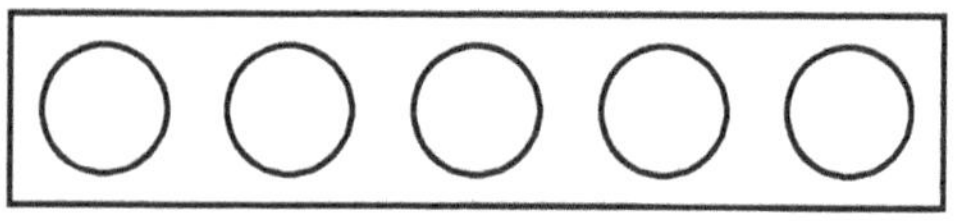

5 = 3 + 2

☐ What addition do you see?

13.

4 = ____ + ____

14.

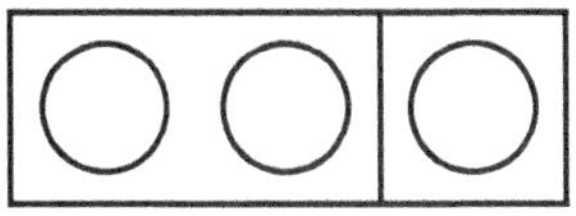

3 = ____ + ____

☐ Draw a line to show the addition.

15.

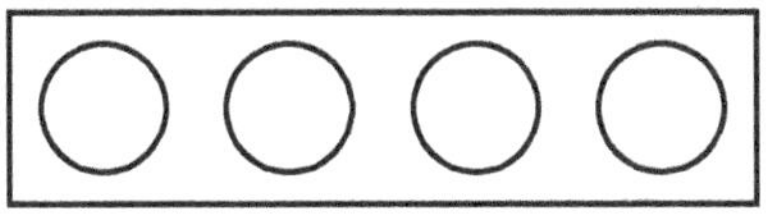

4 = 3 + 1

16.

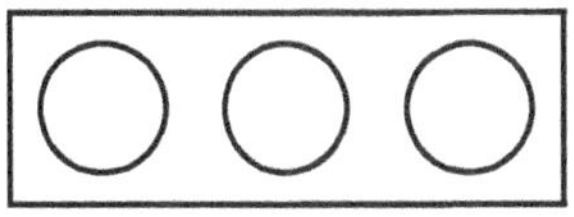

3 = 1 + 2

17.

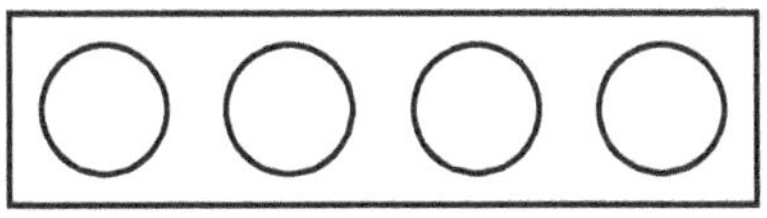

4 = 2 + 2

18.

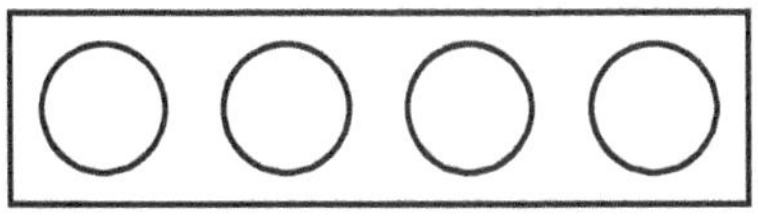

4 = 1 + 3

# OAK-11 Adding

☐ Add.

1.

 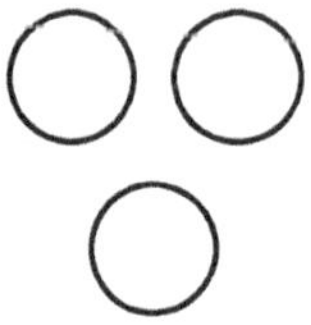

1 + 3 = ____

2.

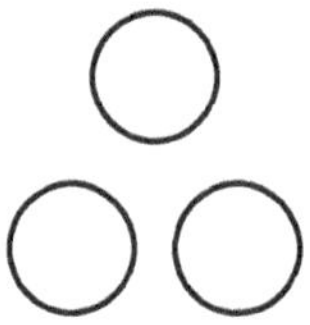 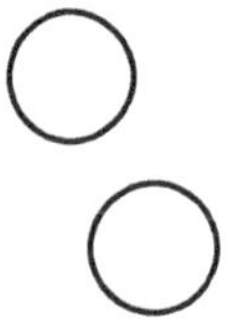

3 + 2 = ____

3.

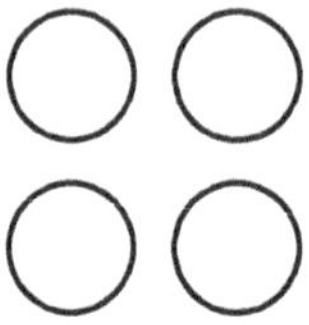 

4 + 1 = ____

4.

2 + 2 = ____

☐ Draw circles to add.

5.

$2 + 1 = \_\_\_$

6.

$1 + 1 = \_\_\_$

7.

$2 + 3 = \_\_\_$

8.

$1 + 4 = \_\_\_$

# OAK-12 Adding 0 and 1

☐ Draw circles to add.

1. 1 + 1 = ____

2. 3 + 1 = ____

3. 2 + 1 = ____

4. 4 + 1 = ____

☐ Add.

5. 4 + 1 = ____

6. 2 + 1 = ____

7. 3 + 1 = ____

8. 1 + 1 = ____

☐ Draw circles to add.

9.

$1 + 0 =$ ______

10.

$5 + 0 =$ ______

11.

$3 + 0 =$ ______

12.

$4 + 0 =$ ______

13. BONUS

$0 + 2 =$ ______

14. BONUS

$0 + 0 =$ ______

☐ Add.

15.

$2 + 0 =$ ______

16.

$3 + 0 =$ ______

# OAK-13 Counting to 80

☐ Trace.

1.

70 71 72

73 74 75

76 77 78

79 80

2.

7 7 7 7 7 7 7

☐ Write 7.

3.

# OAK-14 Counting On to 10

☐ Connect the dots.

1.

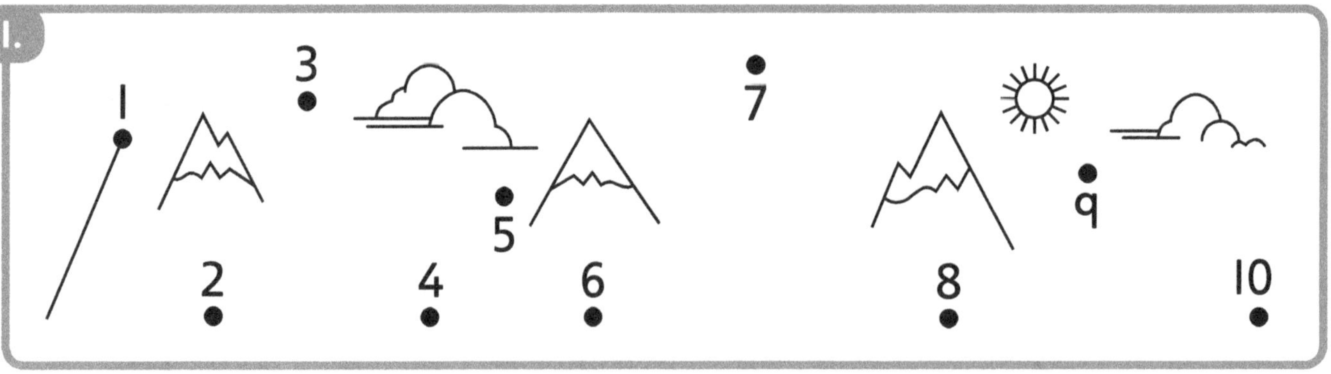


2.

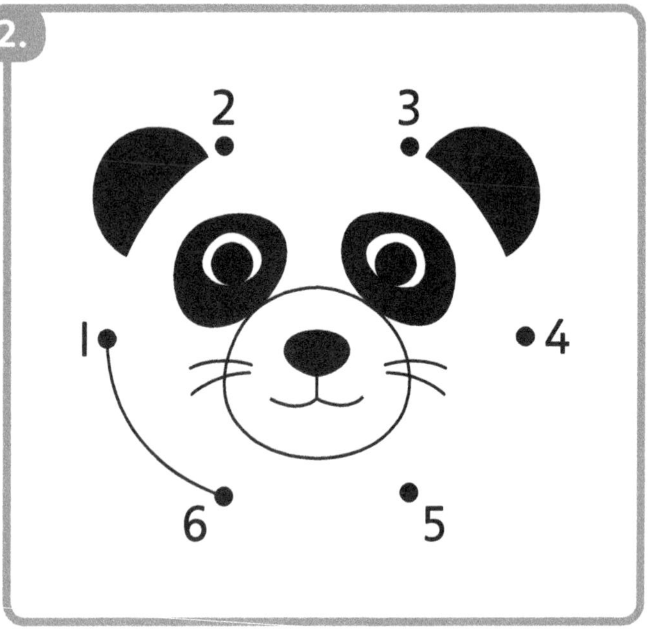


3.

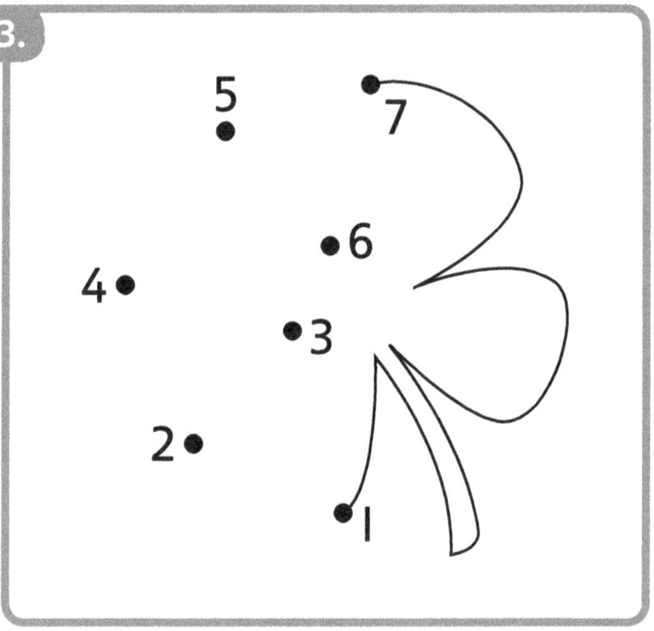


4.

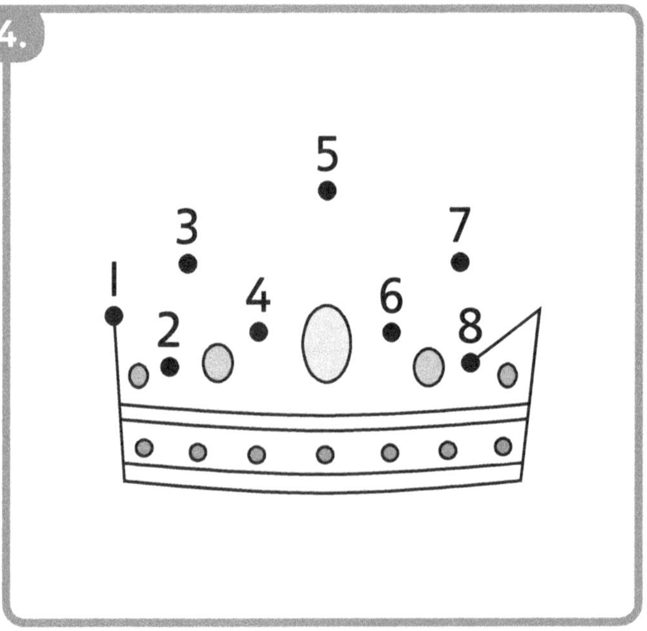


5.

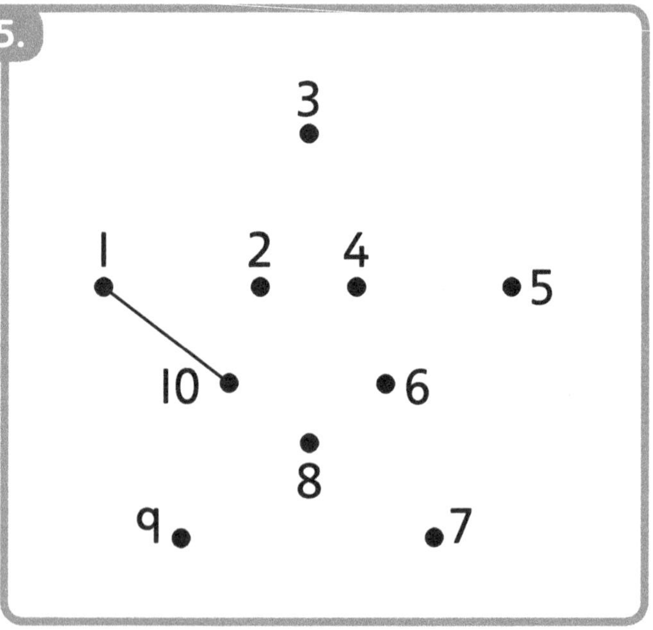

☐ Count on to 10.

6.

1 2 3 4 5 6 7 8 9 10

7.

3 4 5 6 7 8 9 10

8.

6

9.

4

Draw ◯ to show how many.

10.

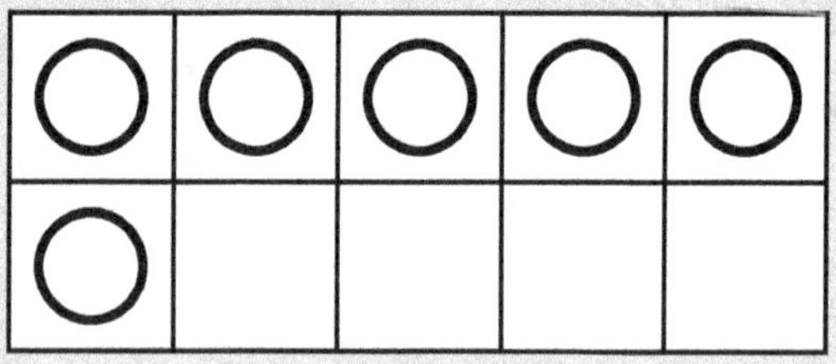

6

11.

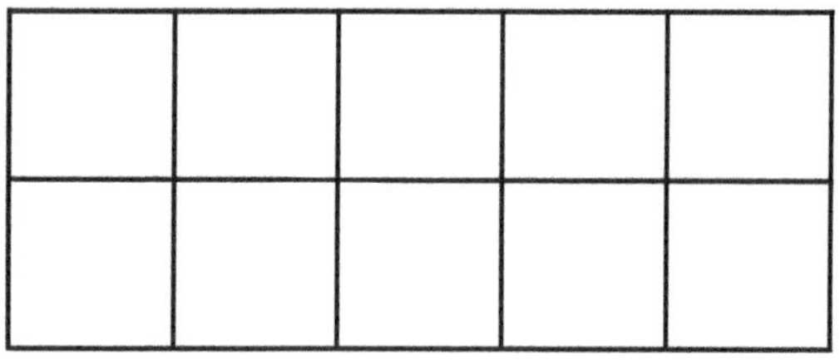

8

12.

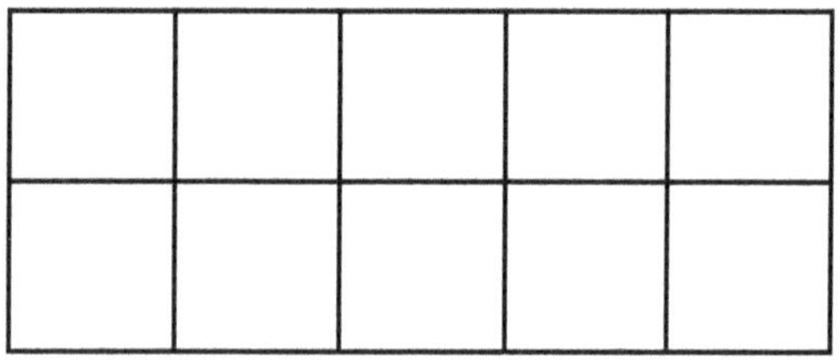

7

13.

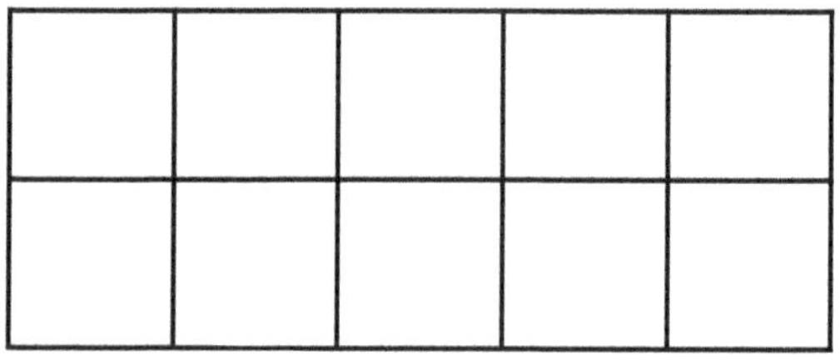

5

14.

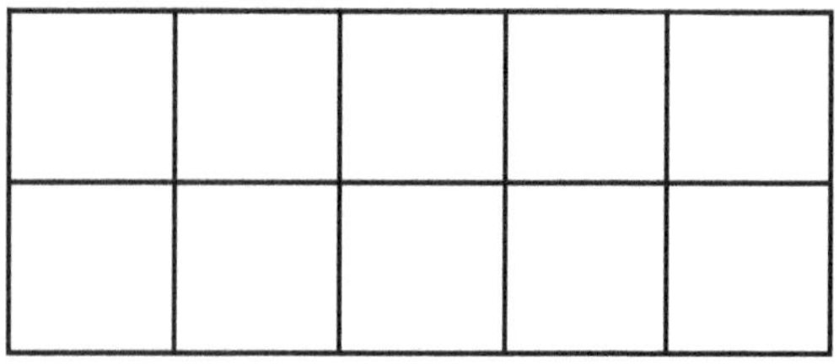

3

15.

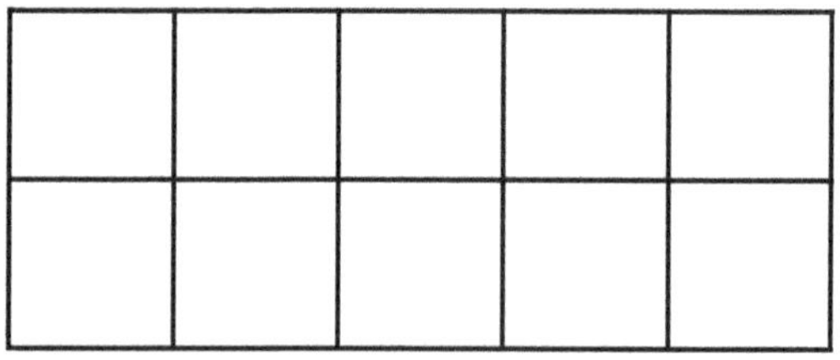

q

# OAK-15 Acting Out Addition to 10

☐ How many in all?

**1.**

4 plus 3 more

4 + 3 = ______ bunnies

**2.**

2 and 5

2 + 5 = ______ pets

☐ How many in all?

3.

6 and 2

6 + 2 = ______ fish

4.

2 plus 7 more

2 + 7 = ______ children

# OAK-16 Adding to 10 with Objects (1)

☐ Use cubes to show how many.

☐ Add.

**1.**

3  + 4 more  = ______

**2.**

5  + 1  = ______

**3.**

2 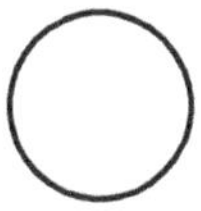 + 4 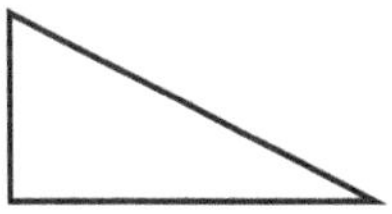 = ______

☐ Use cubes to show how many.

☐ Add.

**4.**

4  + 5 more  = ______

**5.**

3  + 3 more  = ______

**6.**

4  + 2 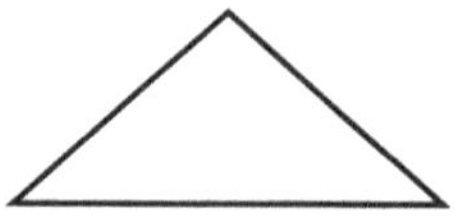 = ______

☐ Use cubes to show how many.

☐ Add.

**7.**

| | | | | | | | | | |
|---|---|---|---|---|---|---|---|---|---|
| | | | | | | | | | |

4  + 3  = ______

**8.**

| | | | | | | | | | |
|---|---|---|---|---|---|---|---|---|---|
| | | | | | | | | | |

2  + 5 more  = ______

**9.**

| | | | | | | | | | |
|---|---|---|---|---|---|---|---|---|---|
| | | | | | | | | | |

5 ☐ + 3 more ☐ = ______

# OAK-17 Adding to 10 with Pictures (1)

☐ Color ☐ to show how many.

☐ Add.

**1.**

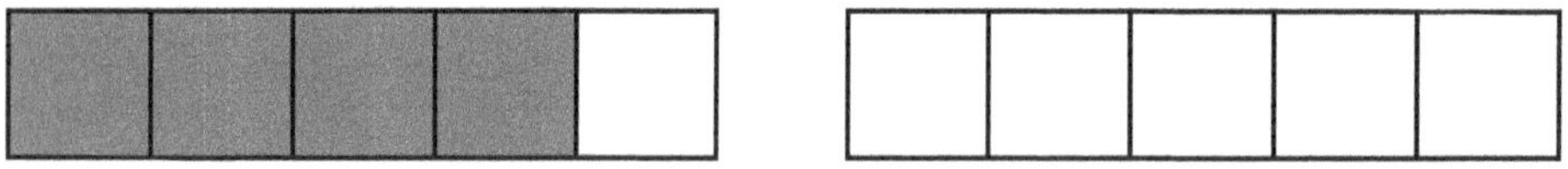

4  + 3 more  = ______

**2.**

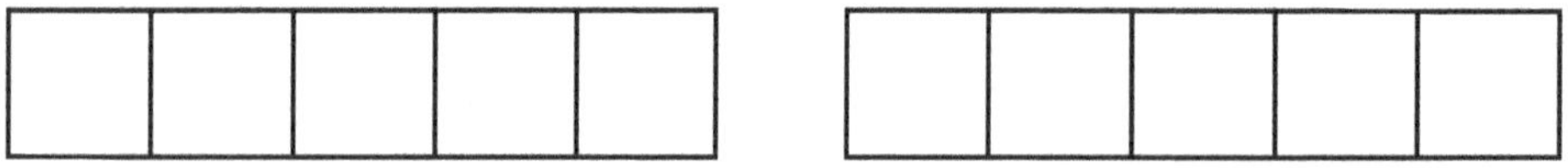

4  + 2  = ______

**3.**

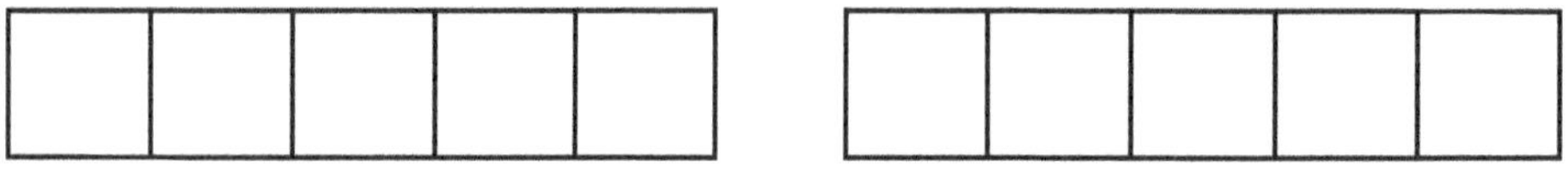

1 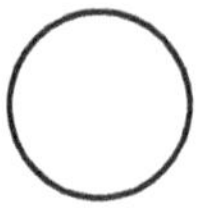 + 5 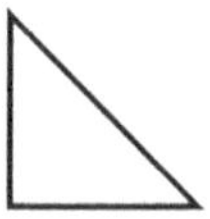 = ______

☐ Color ☐ to show how many.

☐ Add.

**4.**

3  + 3 more  = ____

**5.**

5  + 4  = ____

**6.**

2 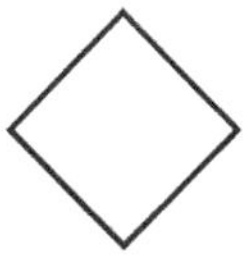 + 4 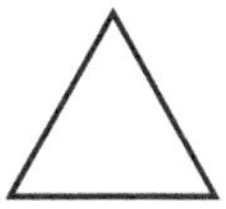 = ____

☐ Color ☐ to show how many.

☐ Add.

**7.**

5  + 2  = ____

**8.**

3  + 4 more  = ____

**9.**

3  + 5 more  = ____

☐ Color  to show the numbers.

☐ Add.

**10.**

4 + 3 = ____

**11.**

2 + 5 = ____

# OAK-18 Adding to 10 with Objects (2)

- [ ] Use cubes to show how many.
- [ ] Add.

**1.**

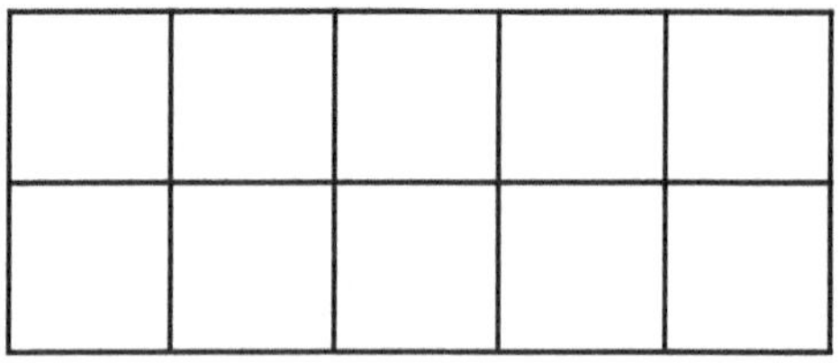

6  + 2 more  = ______

**2.**

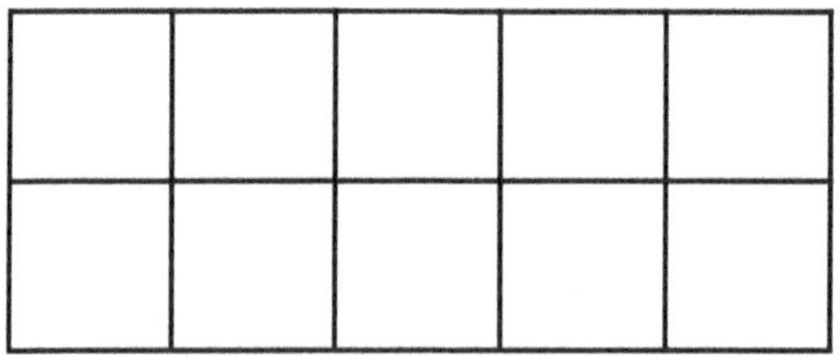

7  + 3  = ______

**3.**

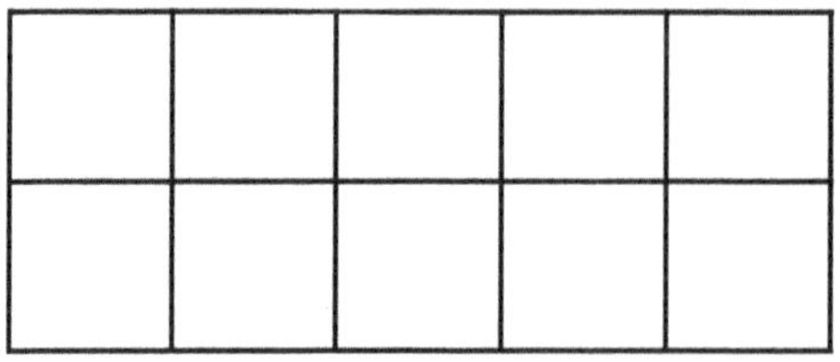

6 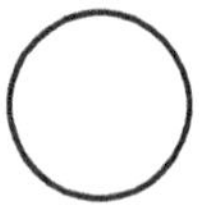 + 1 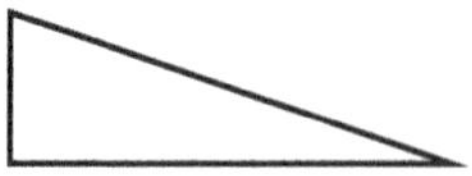 = ______

☐ Use cubes to show how many.

☐ Add.

**4.**

| | | | | |
|---|---|---|---|---|
| | | | | |

6  + 3 more  = ______

**5.**

| | | | | |
|---|---|---|---|---|
| | | | | |

1  + 7  = ______

**6.**

| | | | | |
|---|---|---|---|---|
| | | | | |

8  + 1 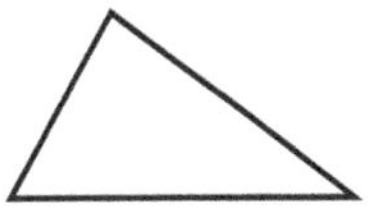 = ______

☐ Use cubes to show how many.

☐ Add.

**7.**

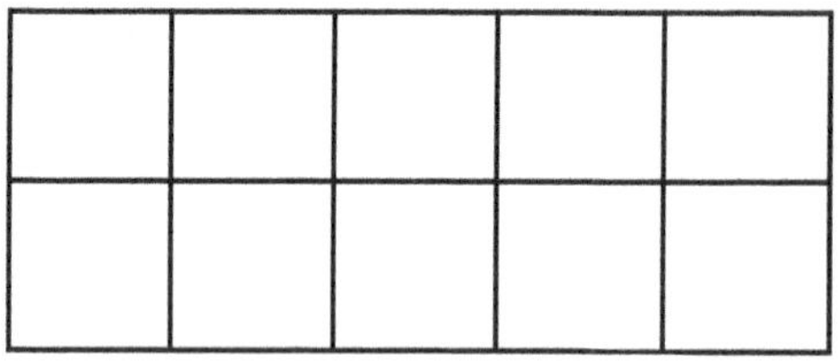

3  + 6  = ______

**8.**

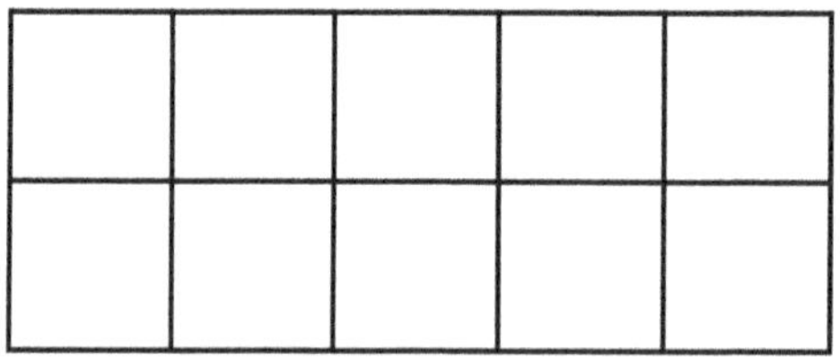

7  + 2 more  = ______

**9.**

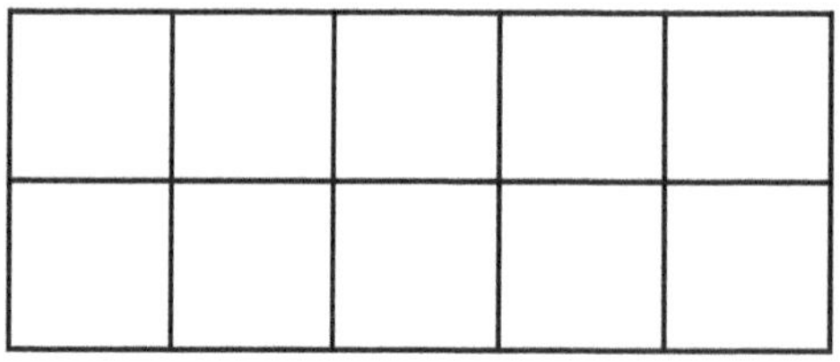

1  + 9 more  = ______

# OAK-19 Adding to 10 with Pictures (2)

☐ Color ☐ to show the numbers. Use 2 colors.

☐ Add.

**1.**

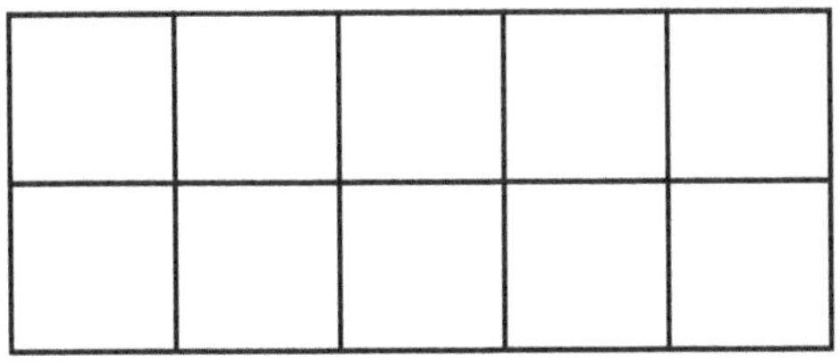

6  + 3 more  = ______

**2.**

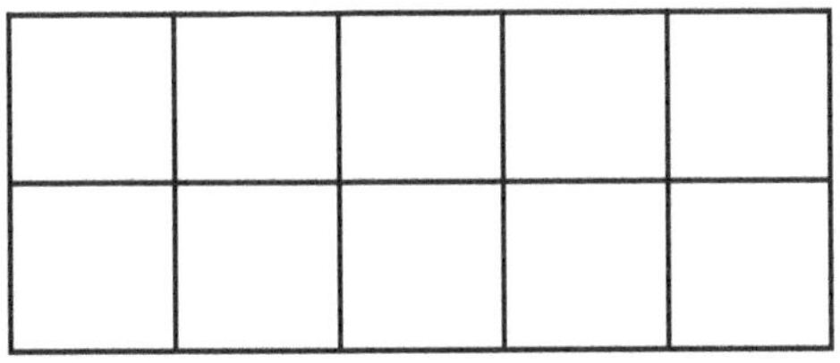

7  + 2  = ______

**3.**

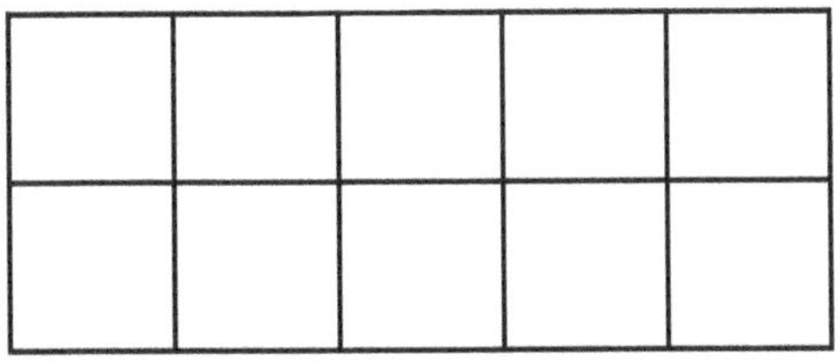

6 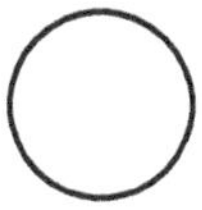 + 4 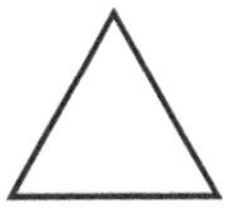 = ______

☐ Color ☐ to show the numbers. Use 2 colors.

☐ Add.

**4.**

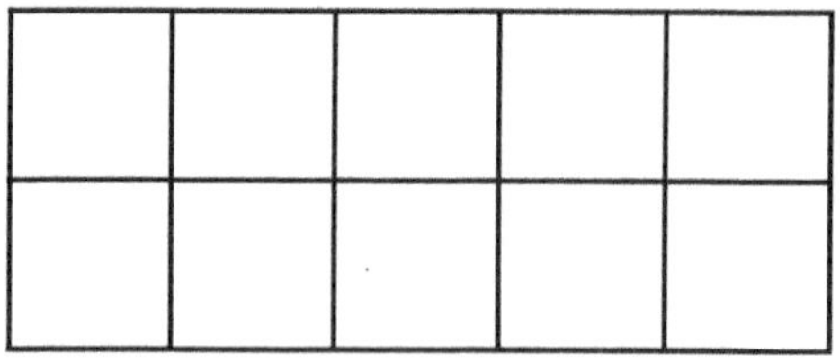

6  + I more  = ______

**5.**

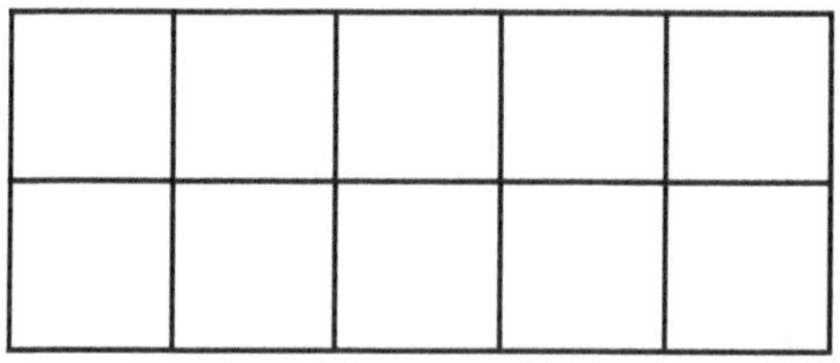

I  + 8  = ______

**6.**

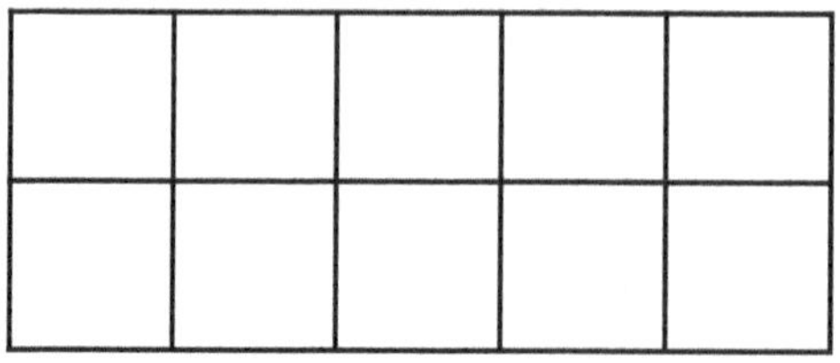

3  + 6 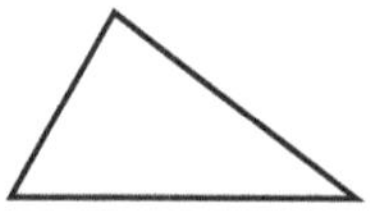 = ______

☐ Color ☐ to show the numbers. Use 2 colors.

☐ Add.

**7.**

| | | | | |
|---|---|---|---|---|
| | | | | |

2  + 7  = ______

**8.**

| | | | | |
|---|---|---|---|---|
| | | | | |

1 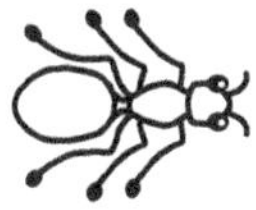 + 6 more 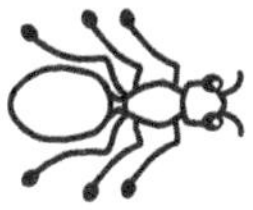 = ______

**9.**

| | | | | |
|---|---|---|---|---|
| | | | | |

9 ☐ + 1 more ☐ = ______

☐ Color  to show how many.

☐ Add.

**10.**

4 + 3 = ______

**11.**

6 + 1 = ______

**12.**

2 + 5 = ______

**13.**

7 + 3 = ______

# OAK-20 Decomposing 10

☐ What addition do you see?

**1.**

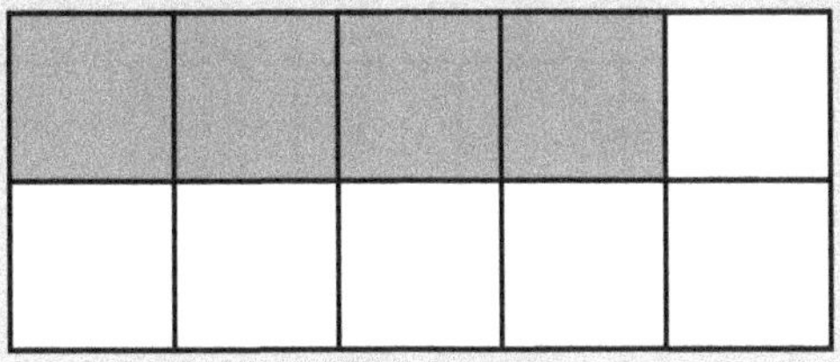

10 = 4 + 6

**2.**

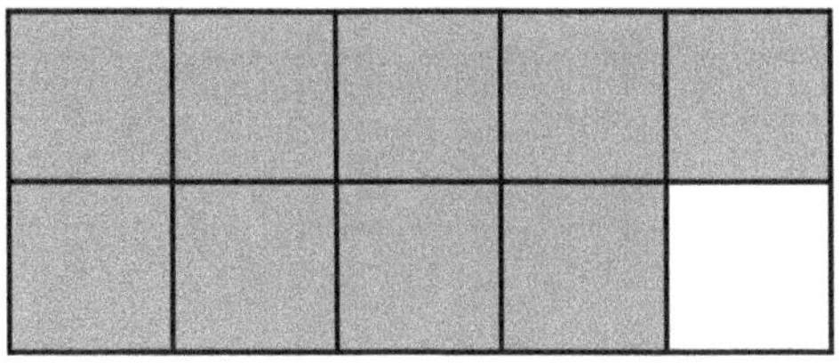

10 = ____ + ____

**3.**

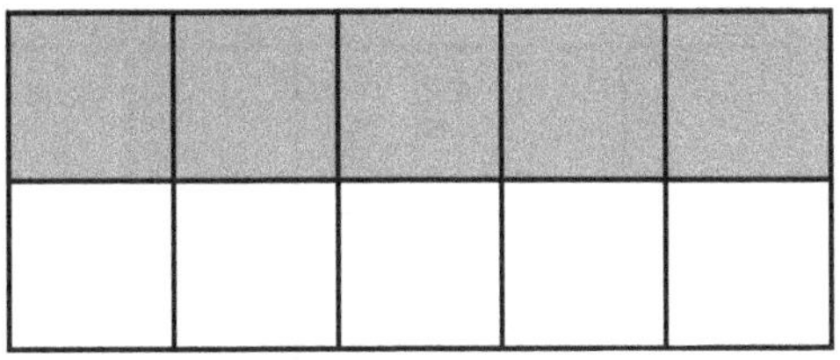

10 = ____ + ____

**4.**

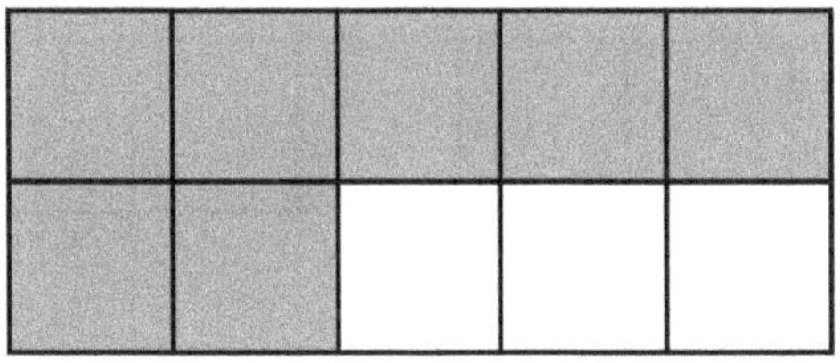

10 = ____ + ____

**5. BONUS**

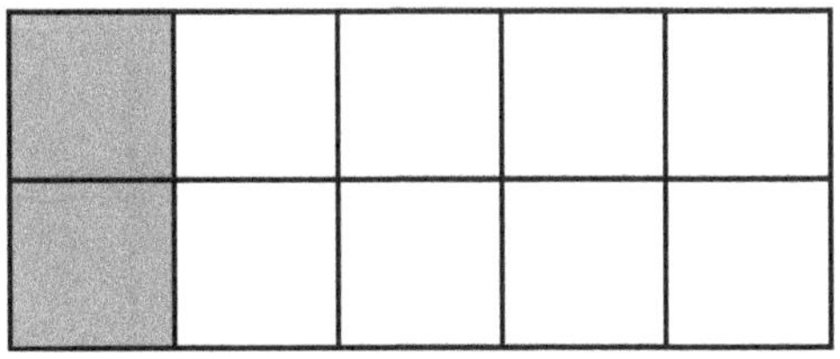

10 = ____ + ____

**6. BONUS**

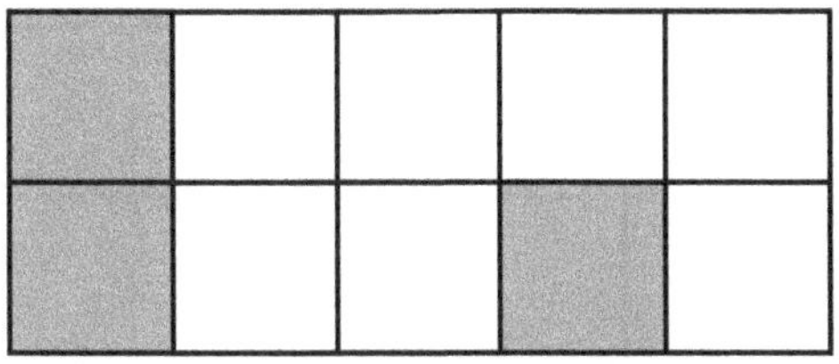

10 = ____ + ____

☐ Use 2 colors to show an addition.

☐ Write the addition.

**7.**

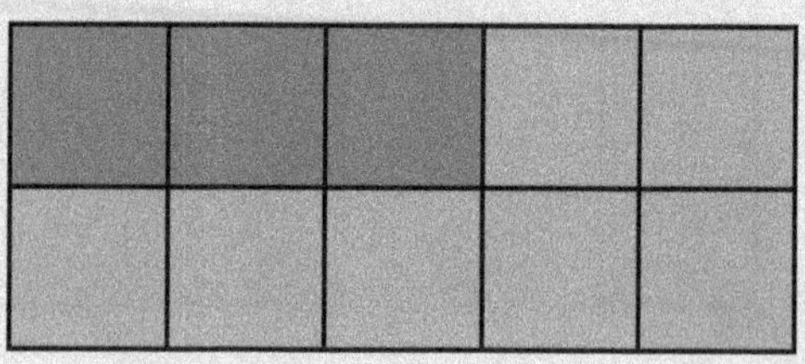

10 = 3 + 7

**8.**

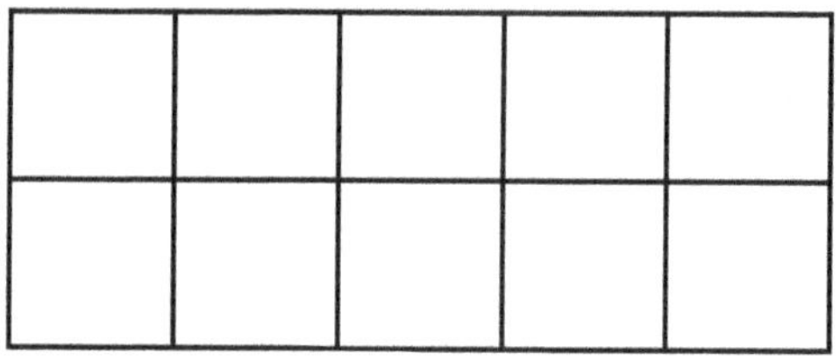

10 = ____ + ____

**9.**

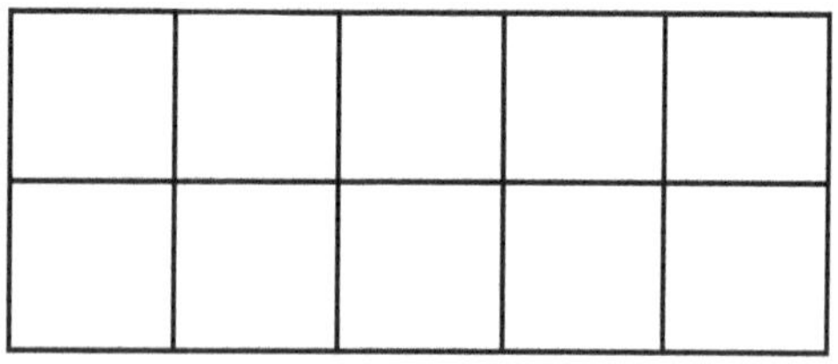

10 = ____ + ____

**10.**

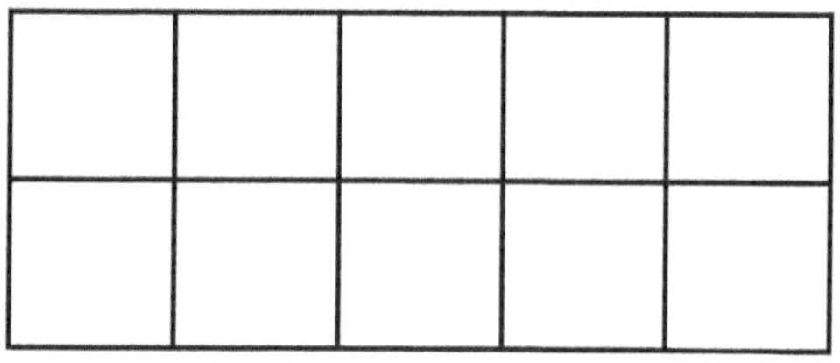

10 = ____ + ____

**11.**

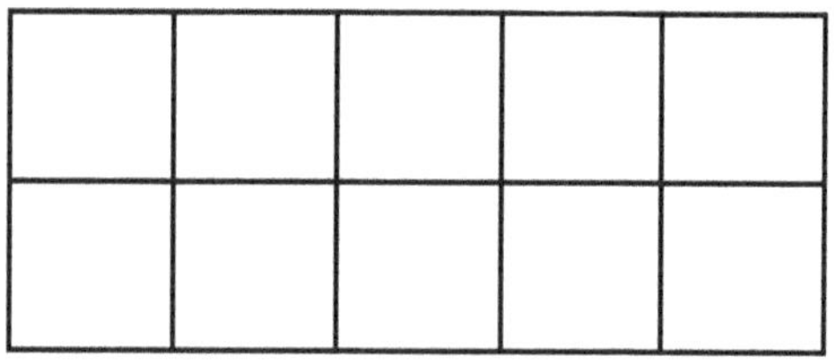

10 = ____ + ____

**12.**

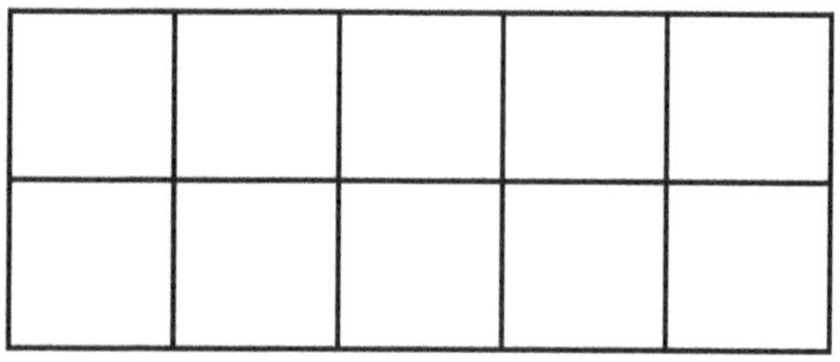

10 = ____ + ____

☐ Use 2 colors to show the addition.

**13.**

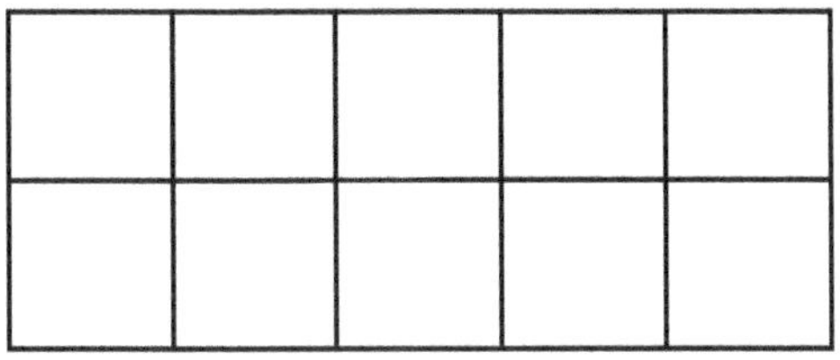

10 = 6 + 4

**14.**

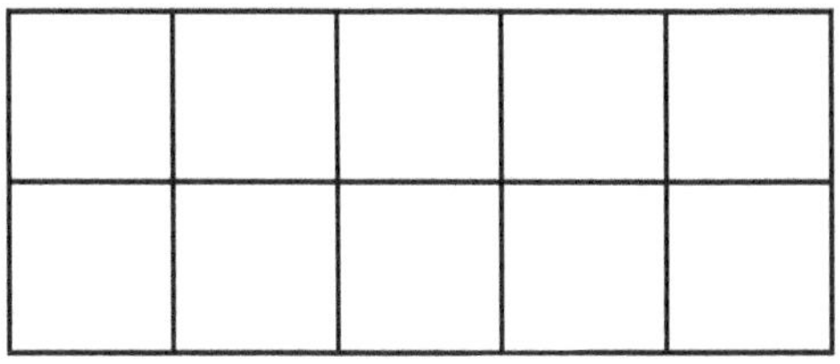

10 = 1 + 9

**15.**

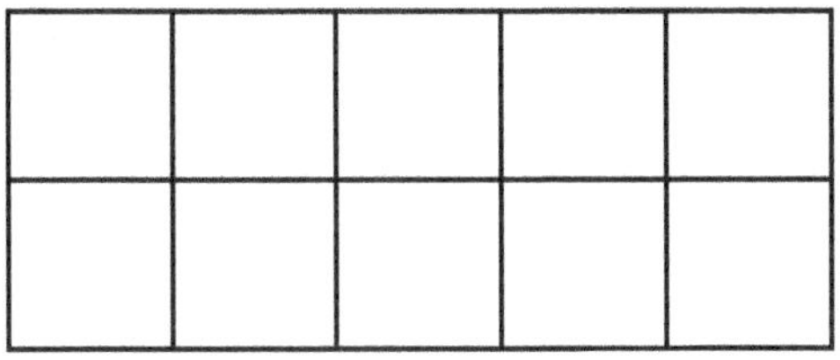

10 = 8 + 2

**16.**

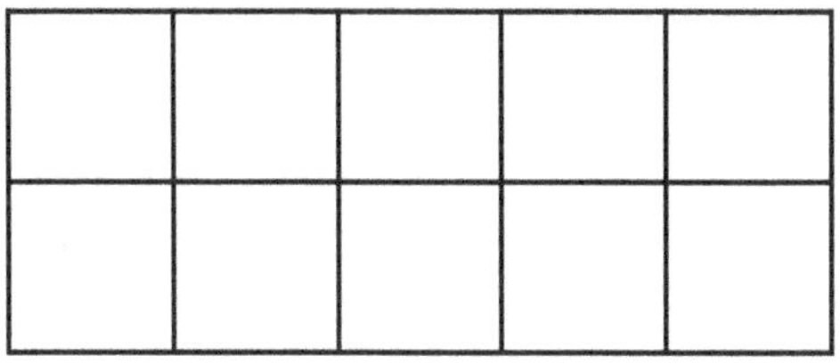

10 = 5 + 5

**17.**

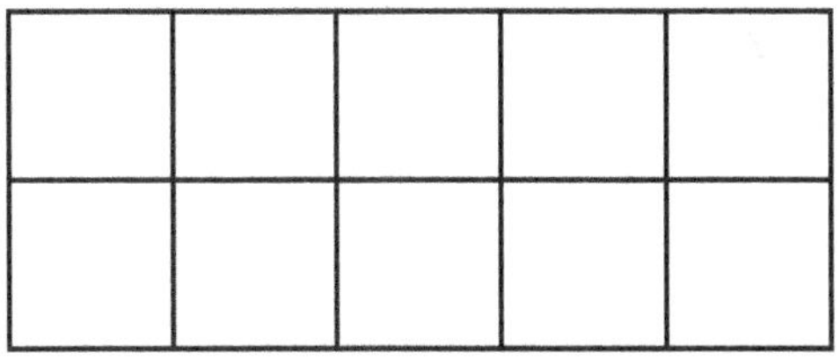

10 = 3 + 7

**18. BONUS**

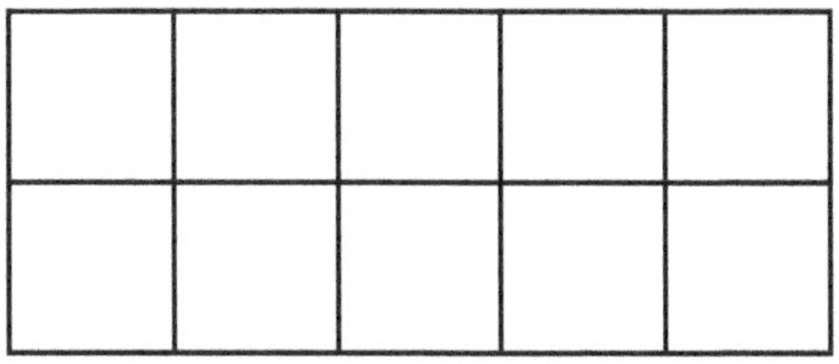

10 = 0 + 10

# OAK-21 Decomposing Up to 10

☐ What addition do you see?

1.

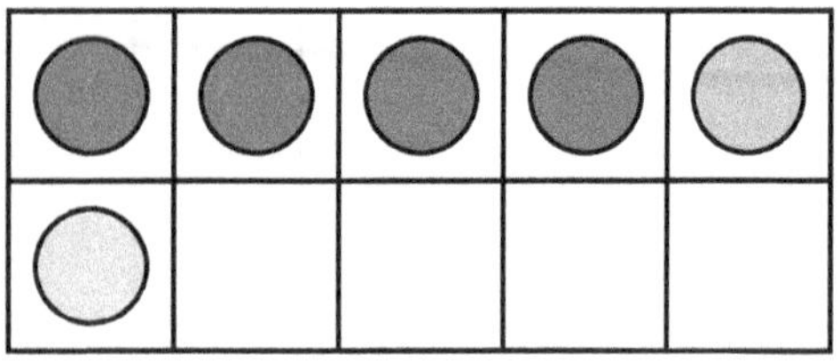

6 = 4 + ____

2.

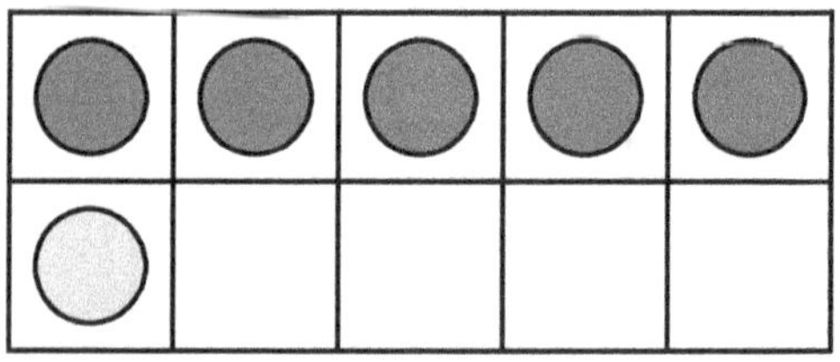

6 = ____ + ____

3.

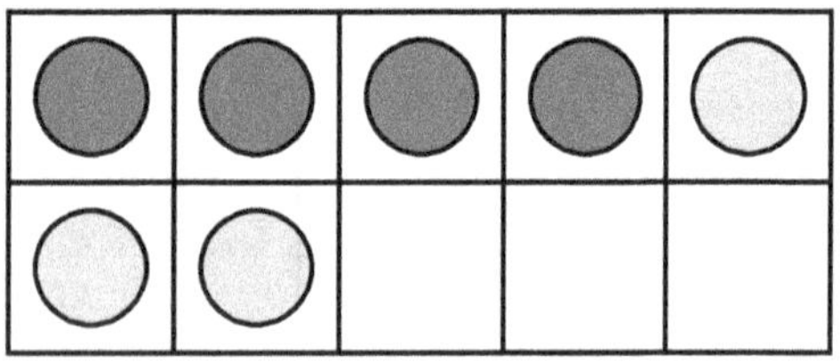

7 = ____ + ____

4.

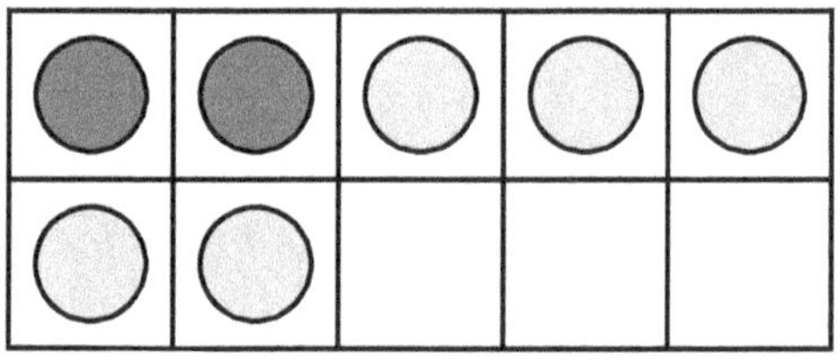

7 = ____ + ____

5.

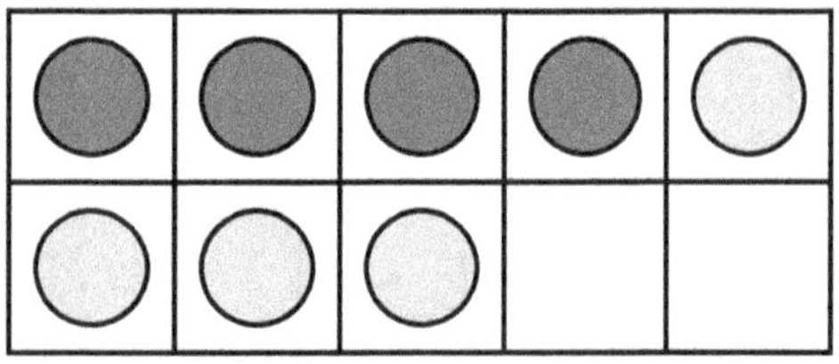

8 = ____ + ____

6.

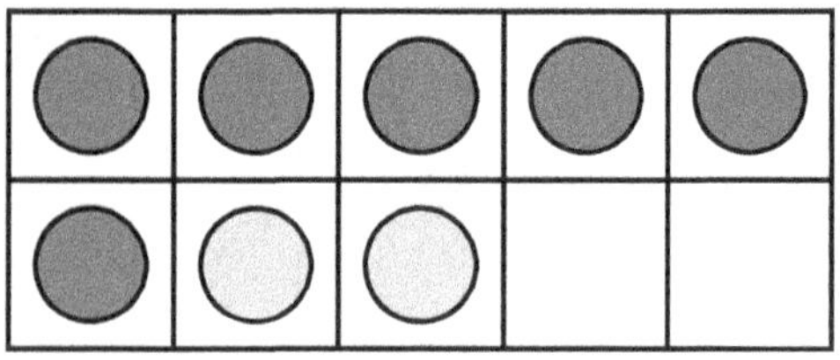

8 = ____ + ____

## ☐ What addition do you see?

**7.**

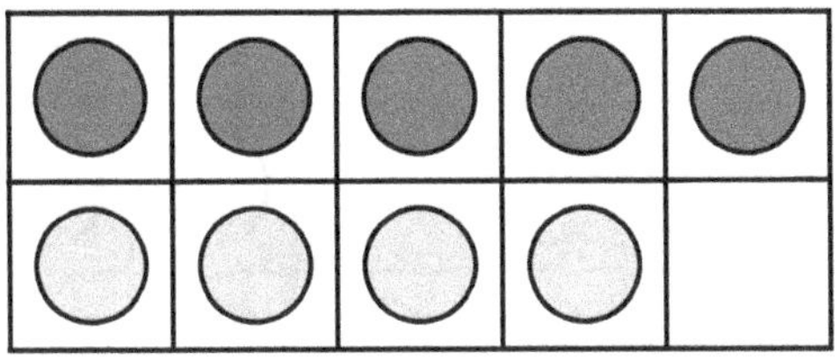

9 = _____ + _____

**8.**

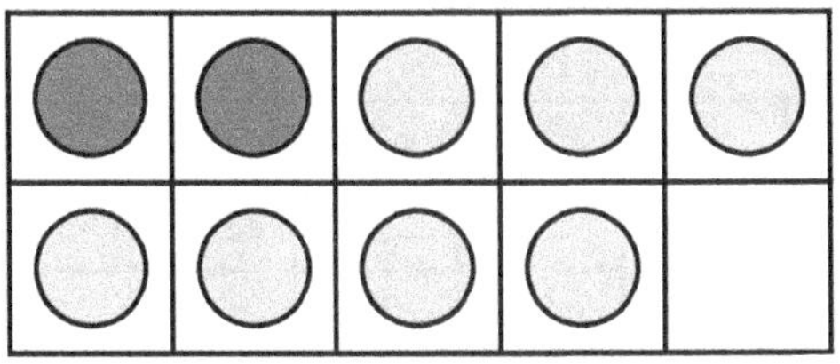

9 = _____ + _____

**9.**

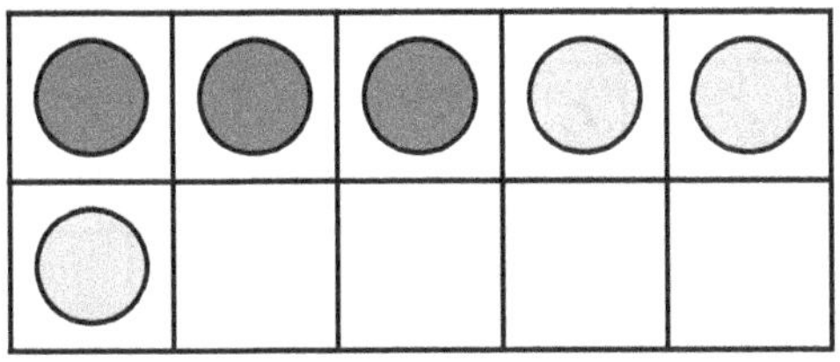

6 = _____ + _____

**10.**

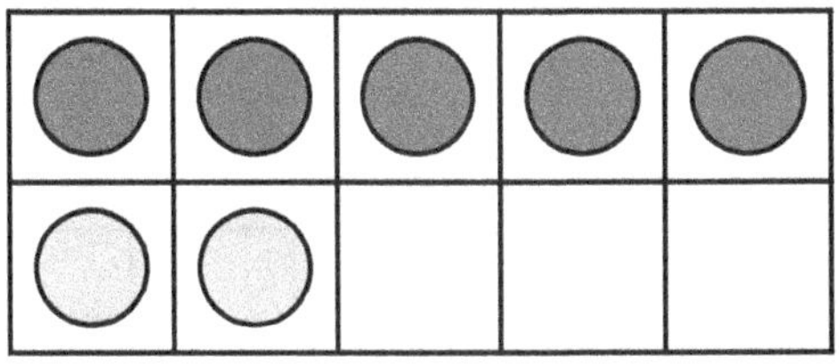

7 = _____ + _____

**11.**

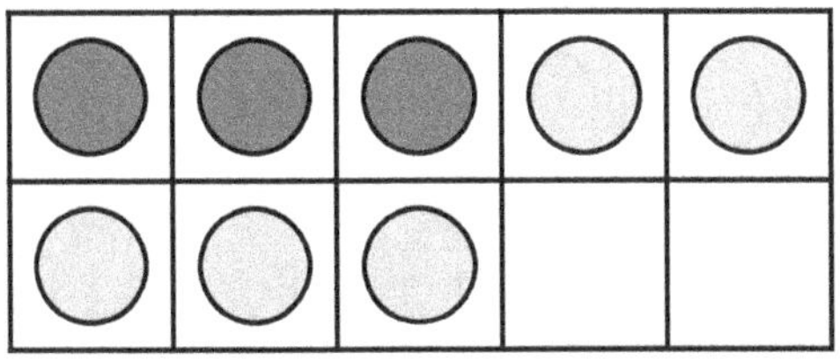

8 = _____ + _____

**12.**

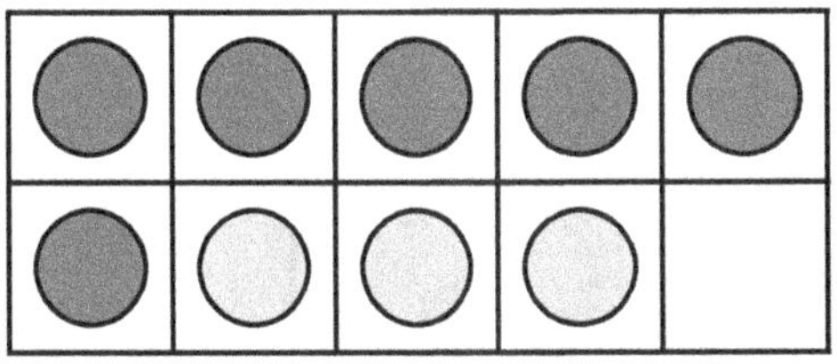

9 = _____ + _____

☐ Use 2 colors to show an addition.

☐ Write the addition.

**13.**

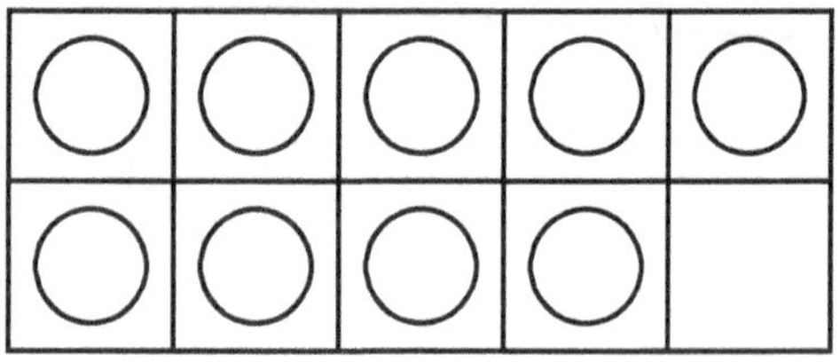

9 = ______ + ______

**14.**

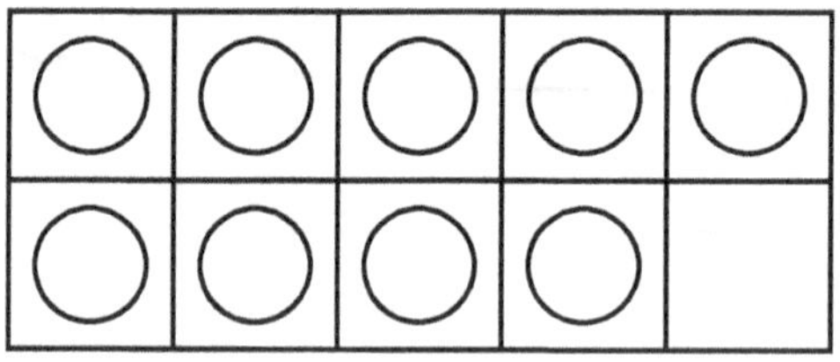

9 = ______ + ______

**15.**

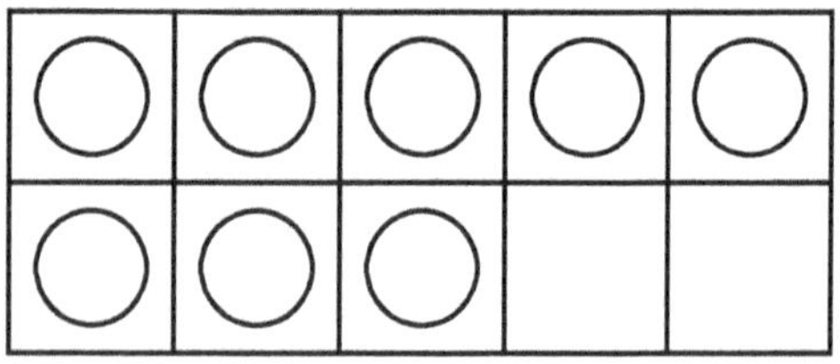

8 = ______ + ______

**16.**

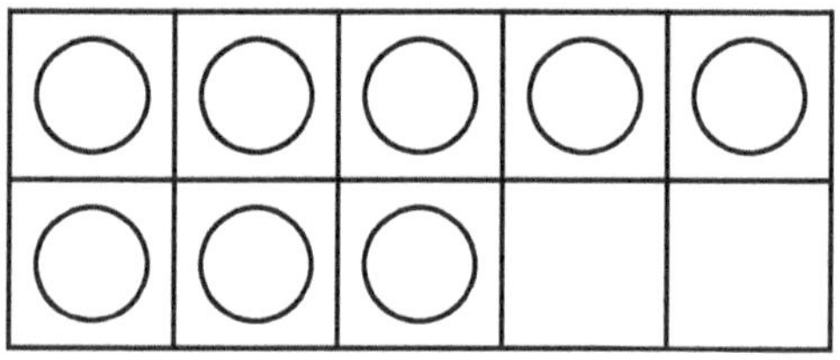

8 = ______ + ______

**17.**

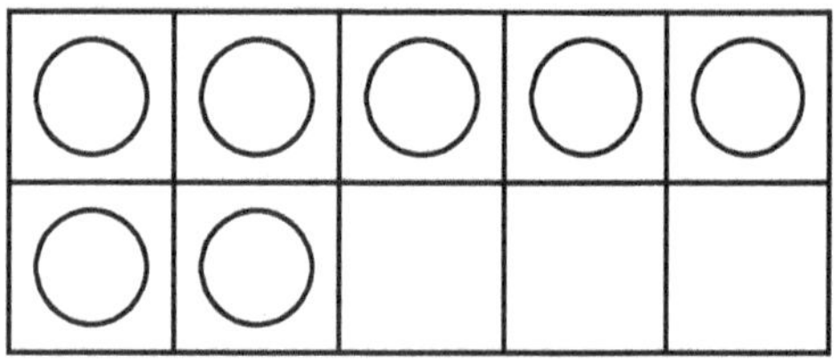

7 = ______ + ______

**18.**

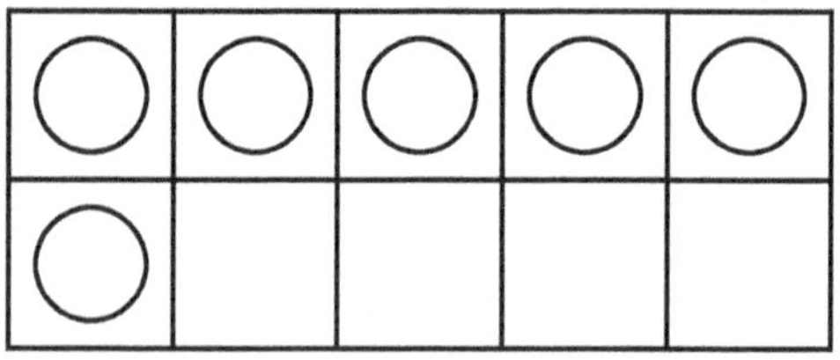

6 = ______ + ______

# OAK-22 Adding within 10

☐ Add.

**1.**

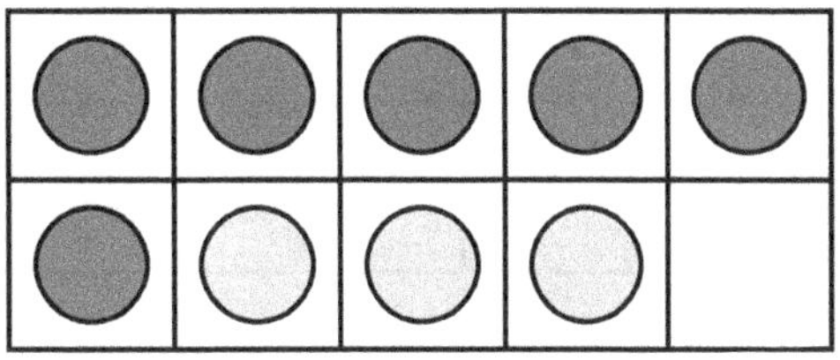

6 + 3 = ______

**2.**

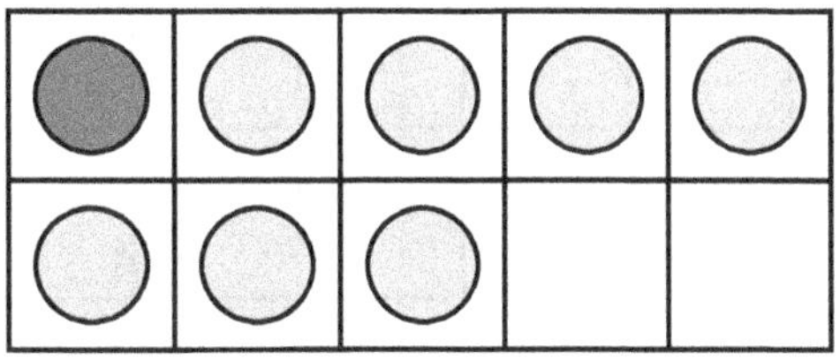

1 + 7 = ______

**3.**

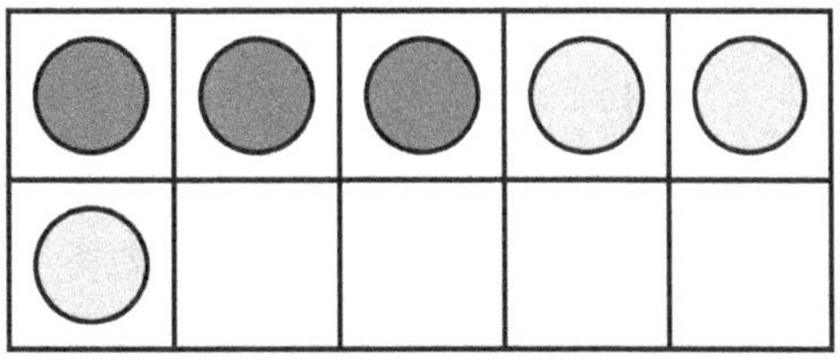

3 + 3 = ______

☐ Add.

4.

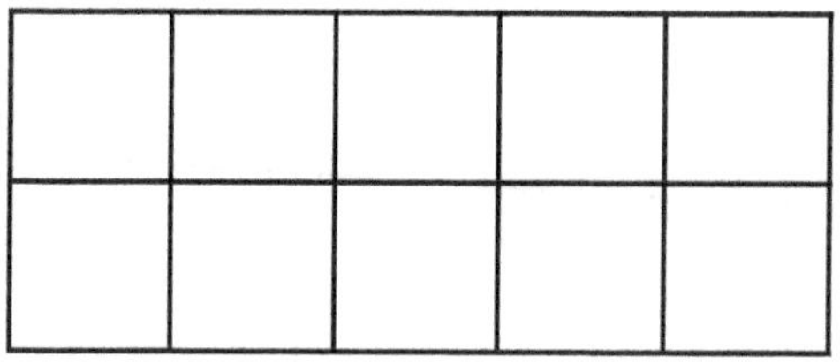

5 + 3 = ____

5.

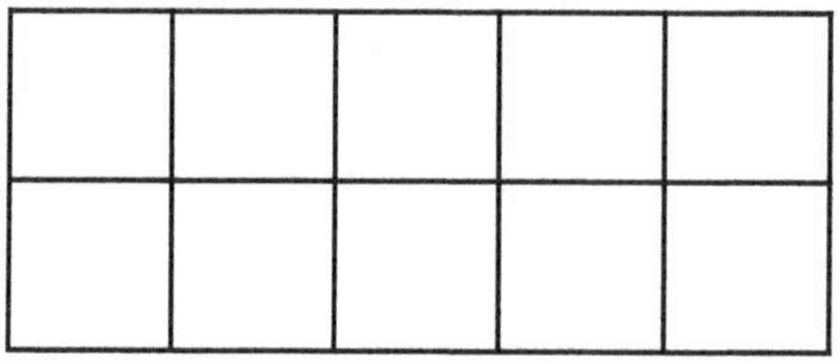

3 + 4 = ____

6.

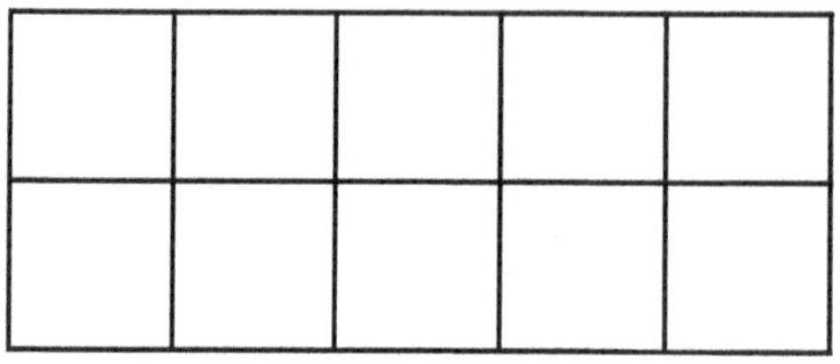

1 + 8 = ____

☐ Add.

7.

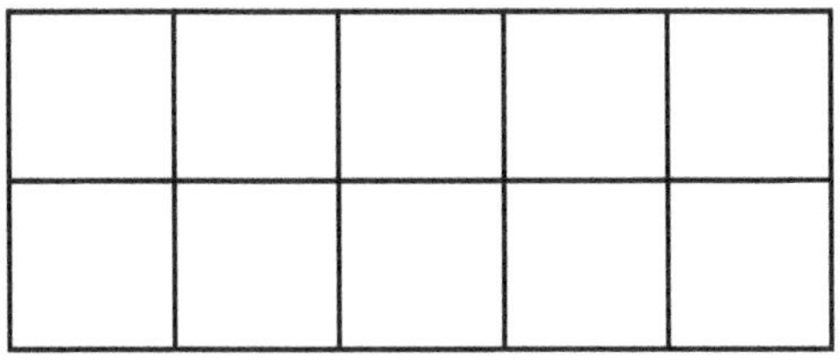

6 + 1 = ____

8.

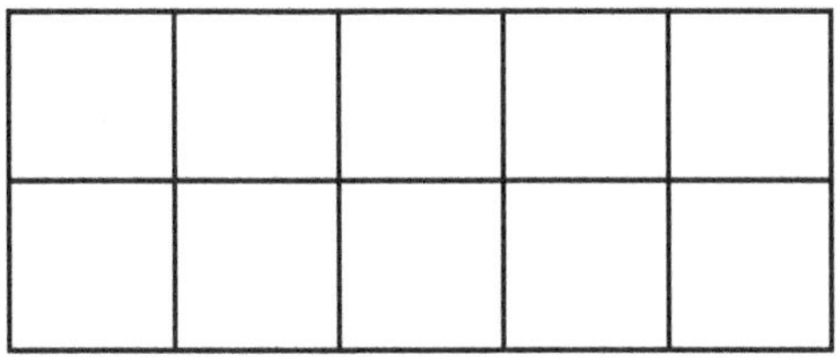

2 + 4 = ____

9.

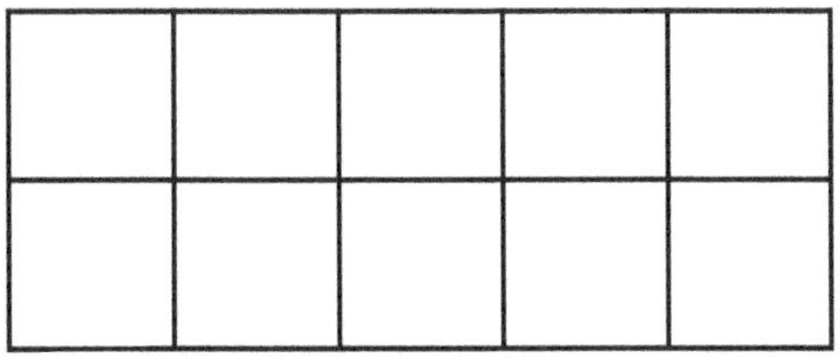

4 + 4 = ____

☐ Add.

10.

4 + 3 = ____

11.

1 + 6 = ____

12.

2 + 7 = ____

# OAK-23 Counting Out 10

☐ Draw more circles to make 5 in all.

1.

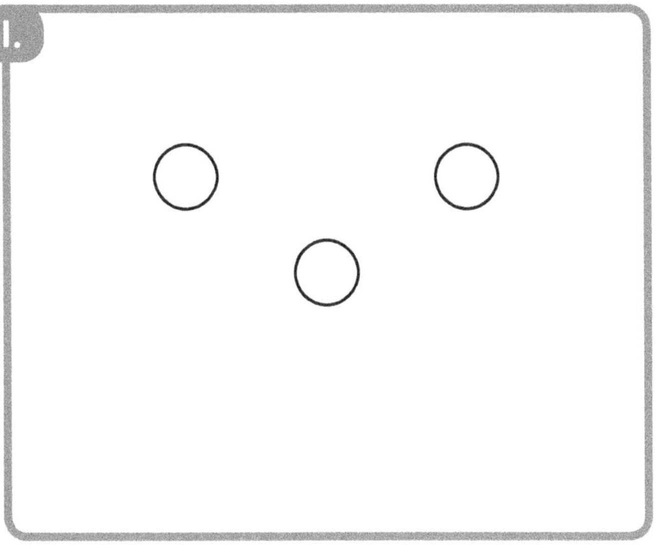

2.

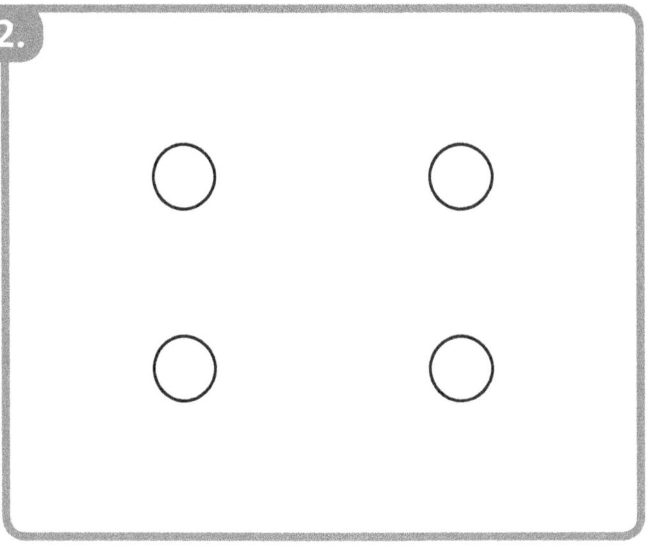

3.

4.

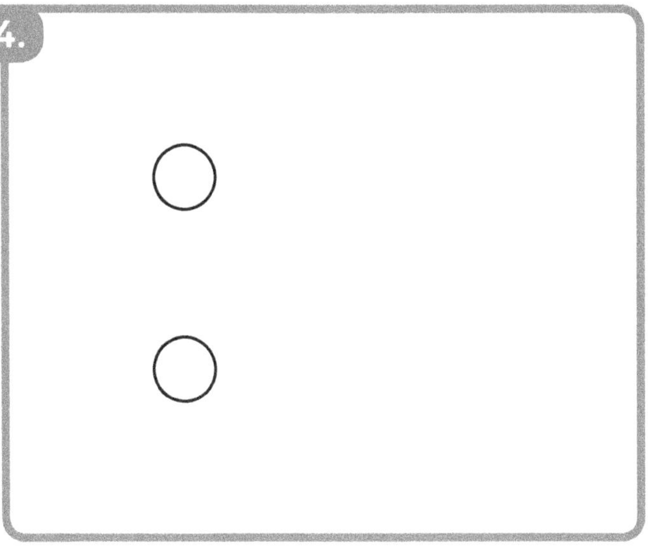

5.

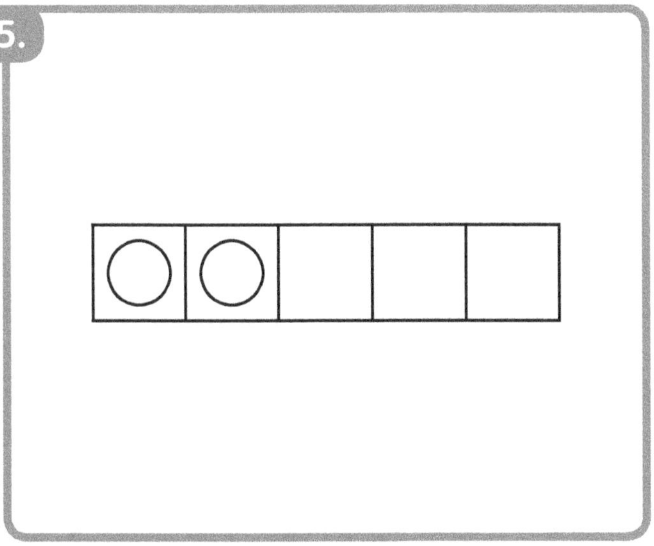

6.

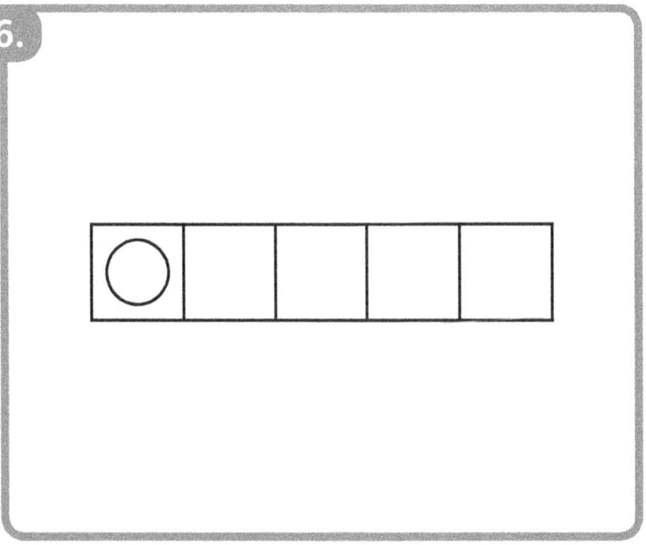

☐ Draw more circles to make 10 in all.

7.

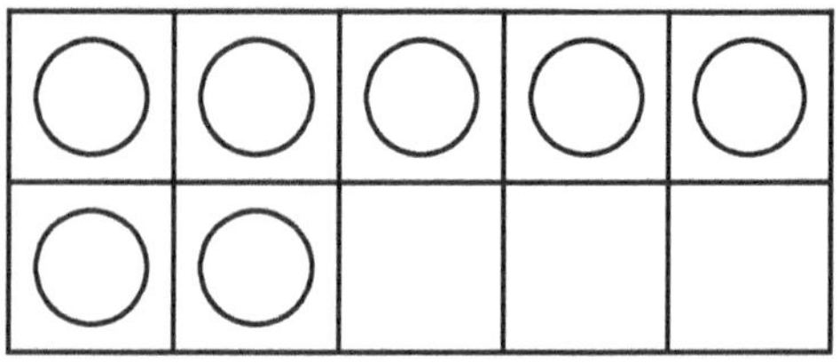

8.

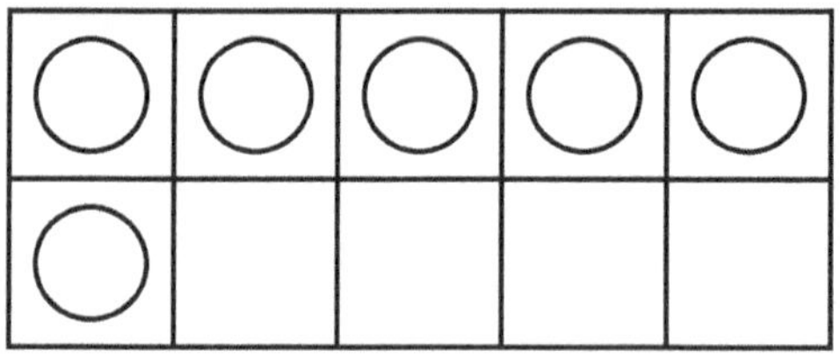

9.

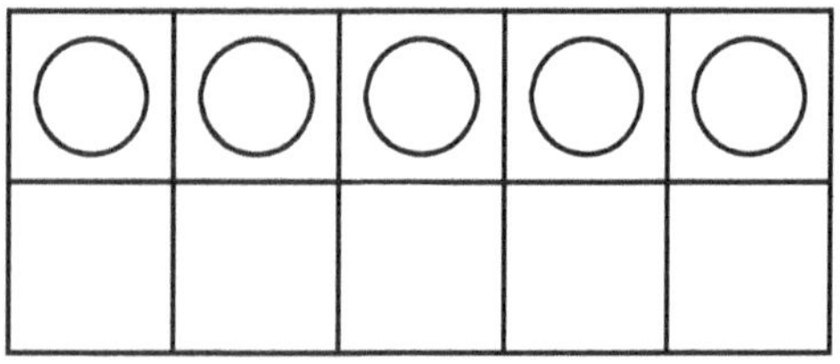

10.

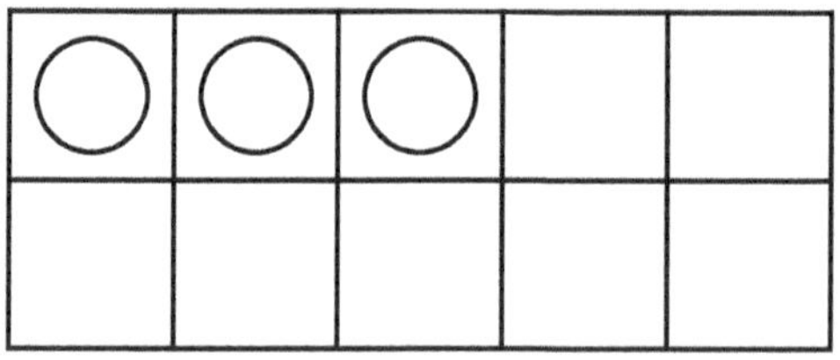

11.

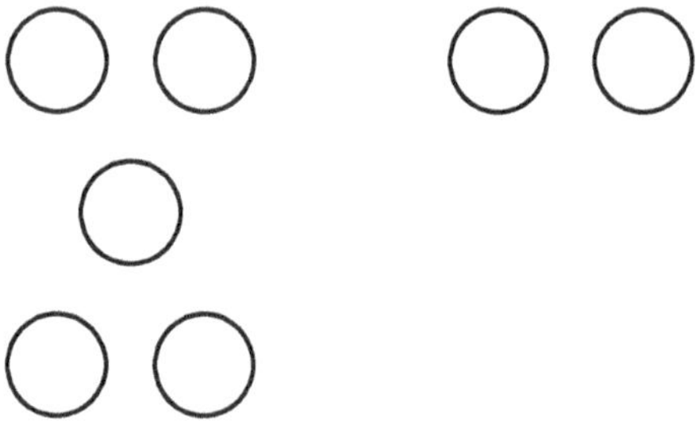

12.

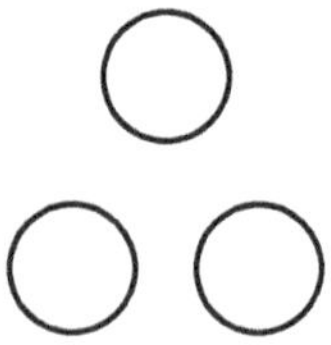

# OAK-24 Making 10

- [ ] Draw more circles to make 10 in all.
- [ ] Count the extra circles.

1.

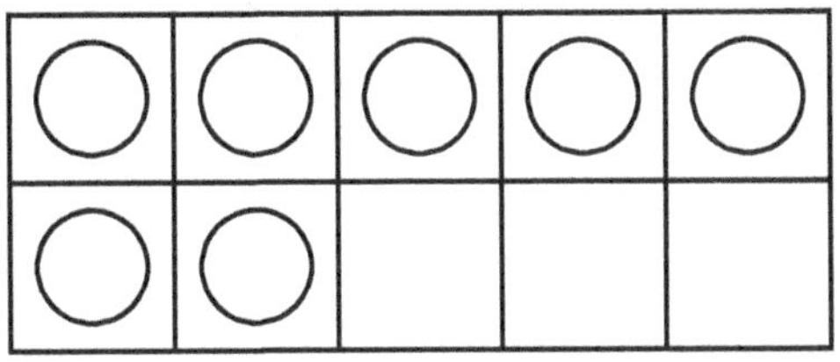

7 and ______ make 10

2.

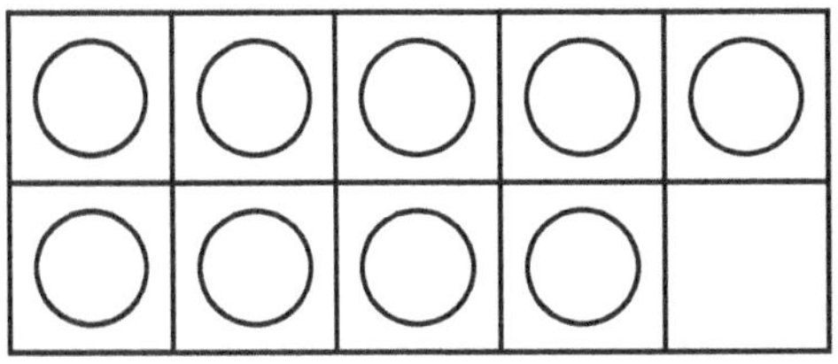

9 and ______ make 10

3.

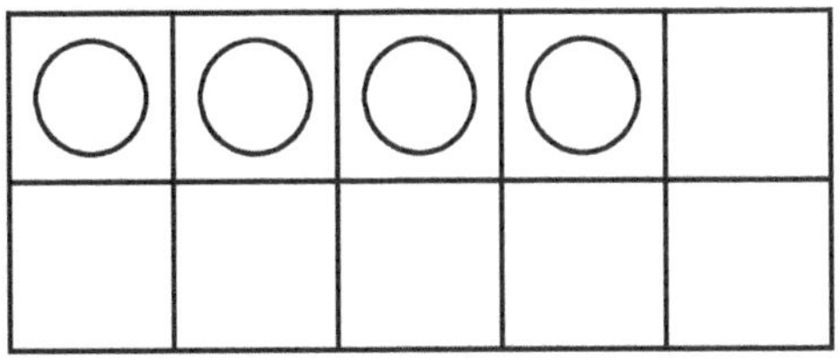

4 and ______ make 10

4.

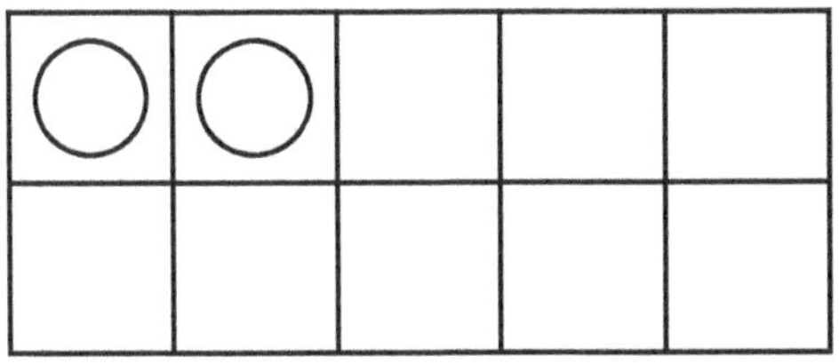

2 and ______ make 10

5.

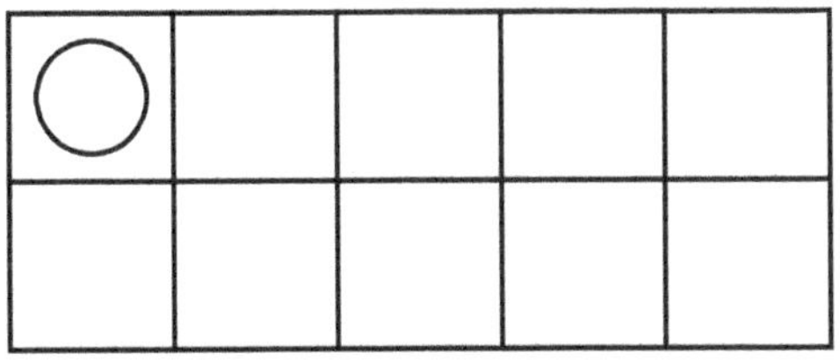

1 and ______ make 10

6.

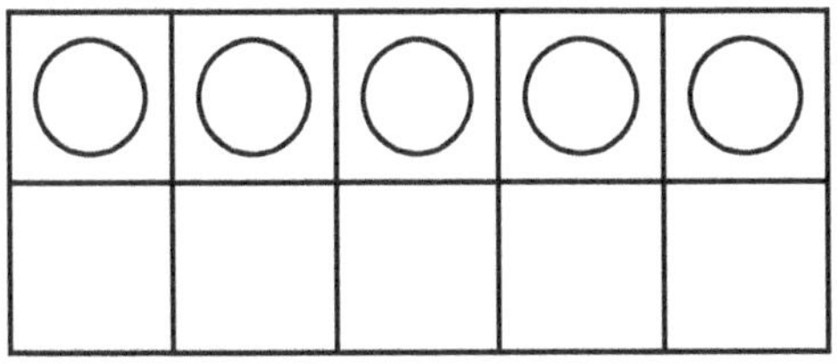

5 and ______ make 10

- [ ] Draw more circles to make 10 in all.
- [ ] Count the extra circles.

**7.**

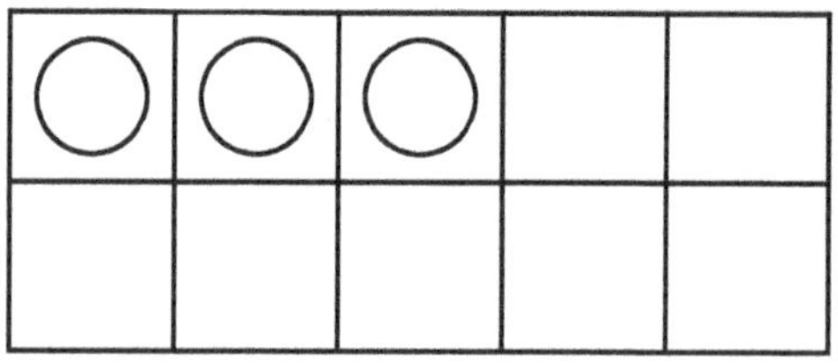

3 and _____ make 10

**8.**

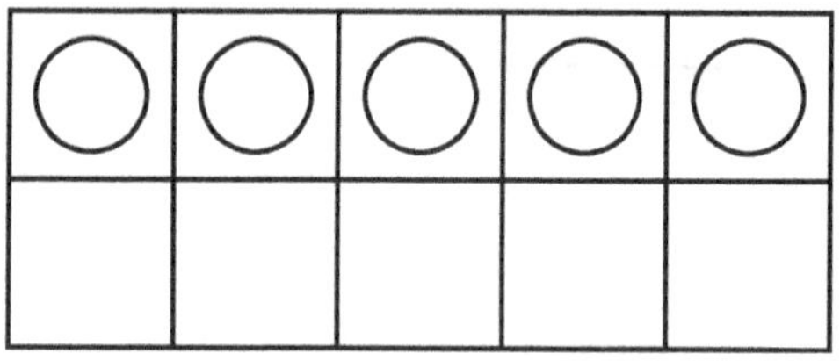

5 and _____ make 10

**9.**

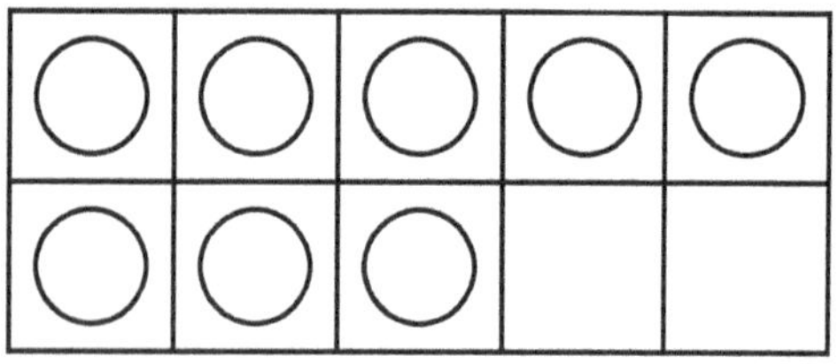

8 and _____ make 10

**10.**

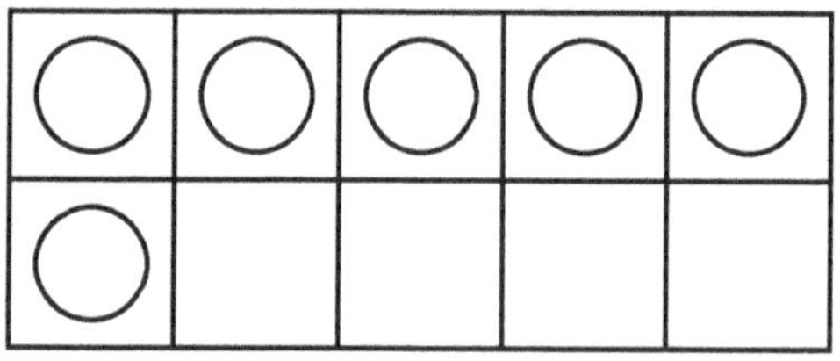

6 and _____ make 10

**11.**

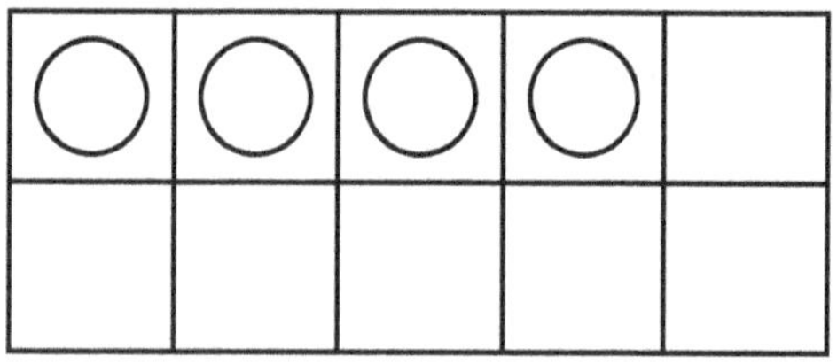

4 and _____ make 10

**12. BONUS**

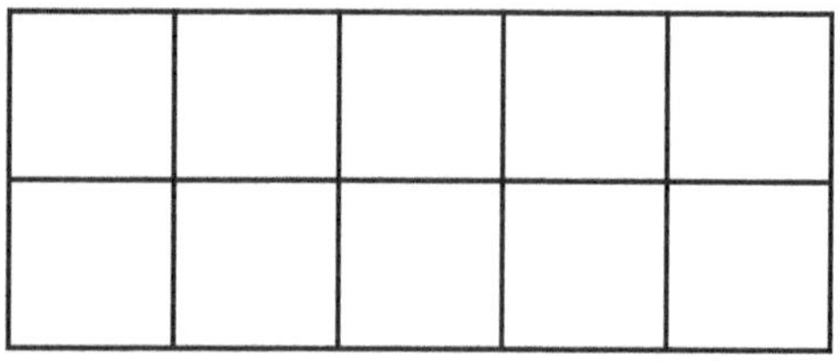

0 and _____ make 10

- [ ] Draw red circles to show the first number.
- [ ] Draw blue circles to make 10 in all.
- [ ] Count the blue circles.

**13.**

| | | | | |
|---|---|---|---|---|
| | | | | |

7 and ______ make 10

**14.**

| | | | | |
|---|---|---|---|---|
| | | | | |

2 and ______ make 10

**15.**

| | | | | |
|---|---|---|---|---|
| | | | | |

1 and ______ make 10

**16.**

| | | | | |
|---|---|---|---|---|
| | | | | |

4 and ______ make 10

**17.**

| | | | | |
|---|---|---|---|---|
| | | | | |

5 and ______ make 10

**18. BONUS**

| | | | | |
|---|---|---|---|---|
| | | | | |

10 and ______ make 10

# GK-15 Counting to 90

☐ Trace.

1.

80 81 82

83 84 85

86 87 88

89 90

2.

8 8 8 8 8 8 8

☐ Write 8.

3.

# GK-16 Spheres and Cubes

☐ Count the .

**1.**

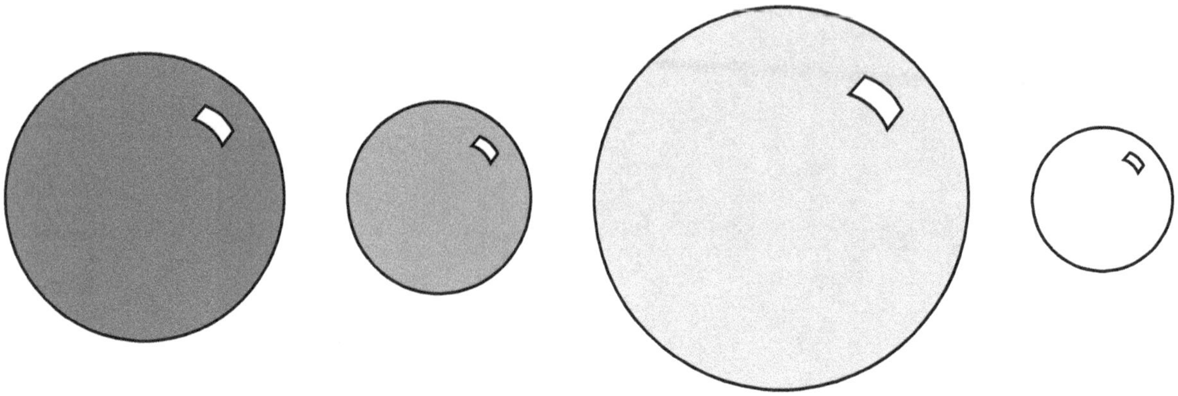

**2.**

☐ Color the .

☐ Draw × on the other shapes.

3.

☐ Count the 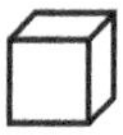.

4.

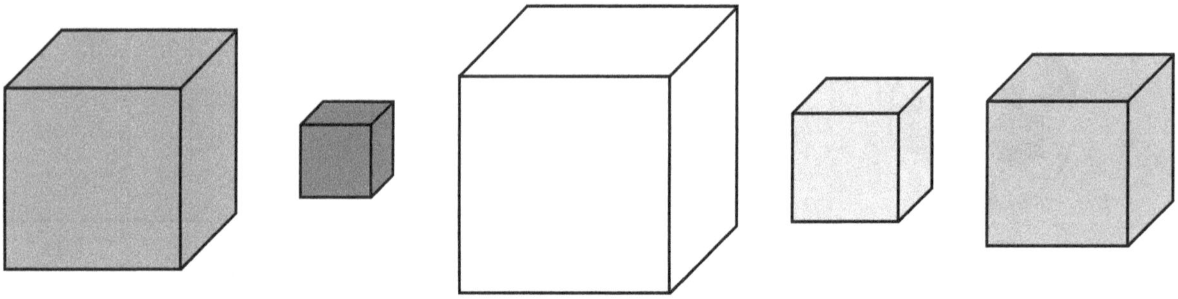

5.

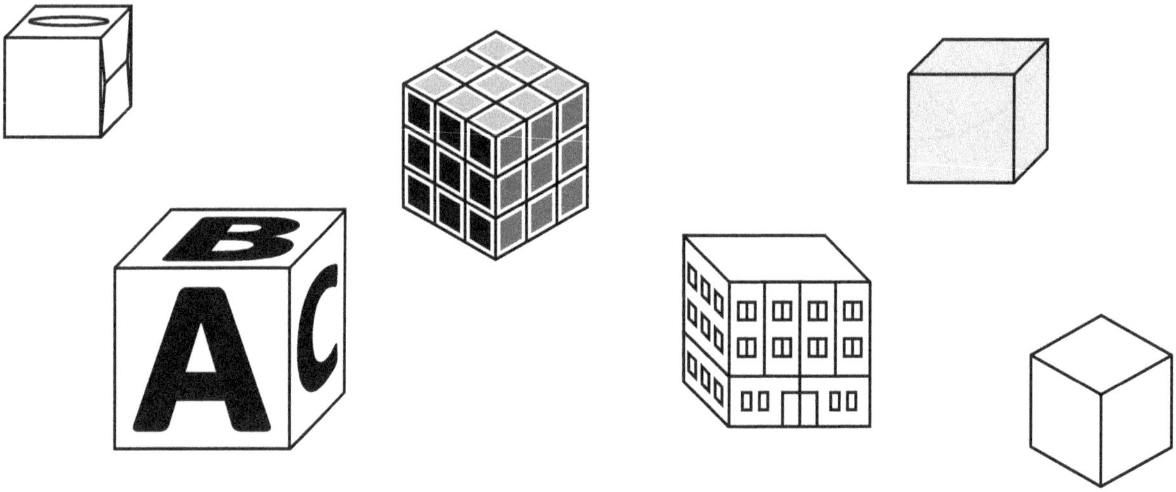

## ▢ Count the 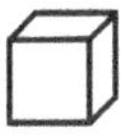.

6.

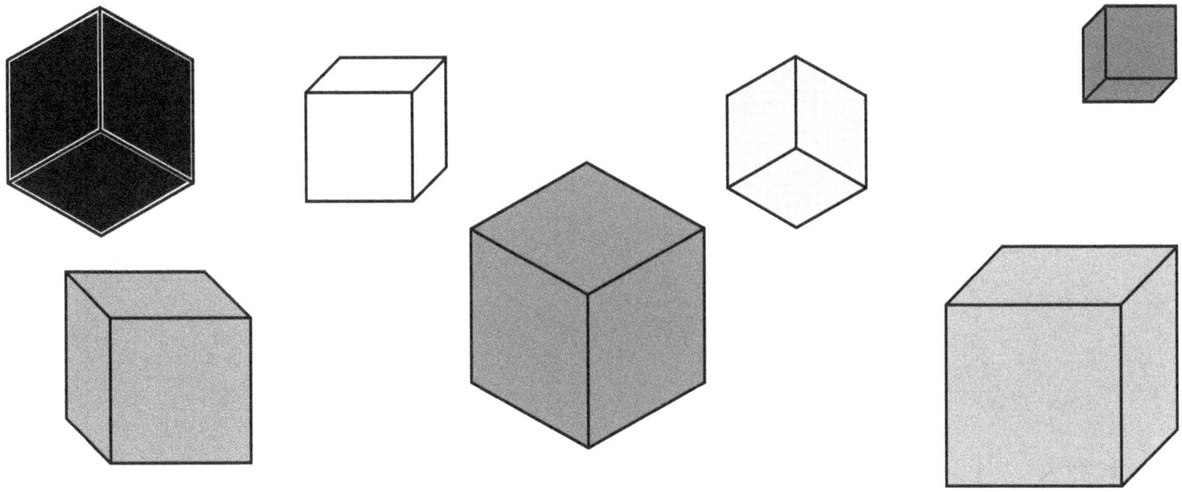

7.

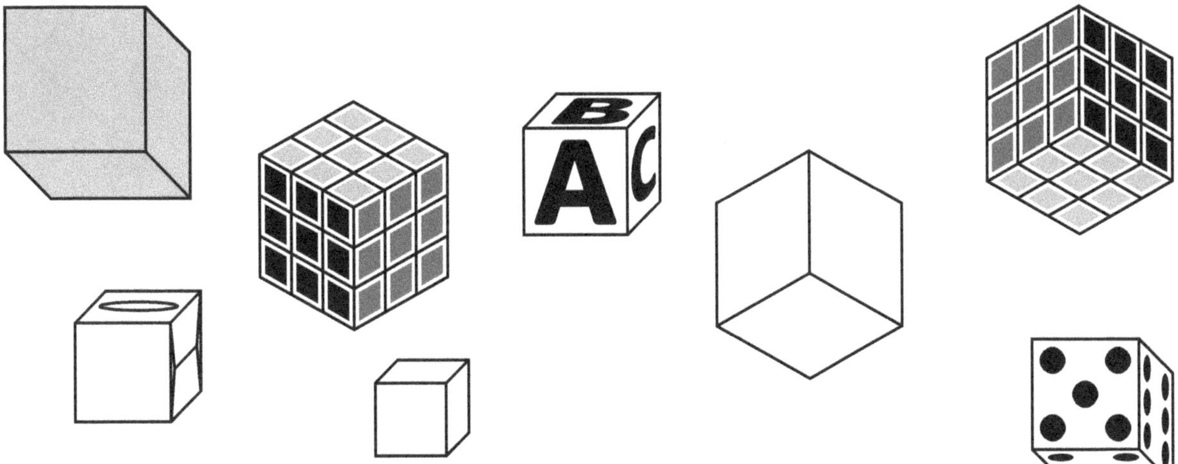

☐ Color the .

☐ Draw X on the other shapes.

8.

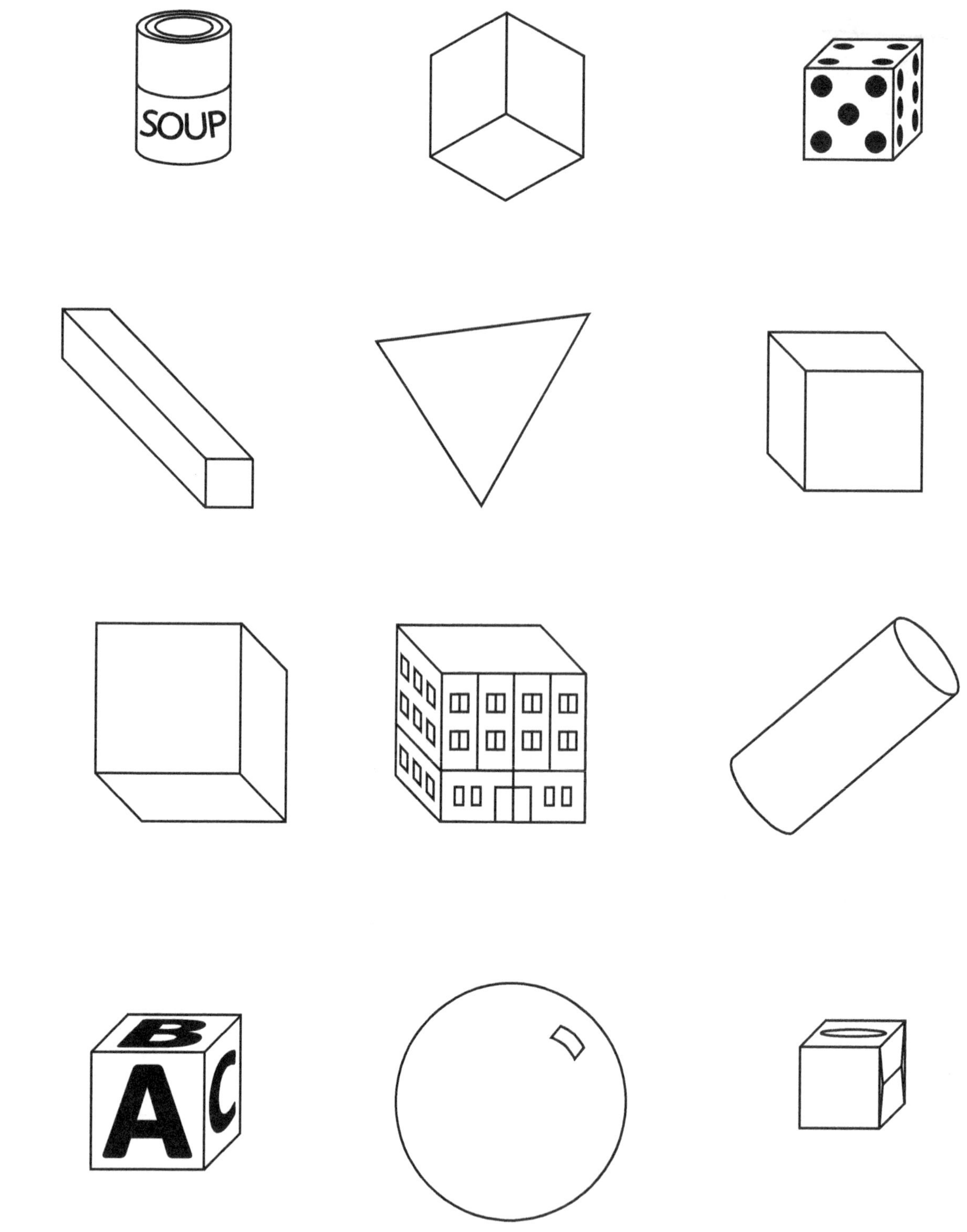

# GK-17 Cylinders and Cones

☐ Count the .

**1.**

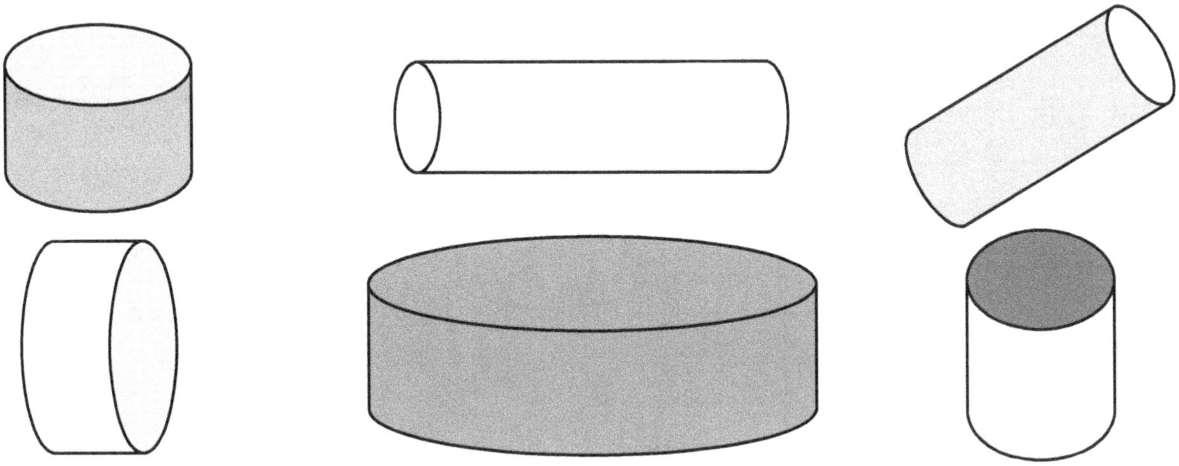

**2.**

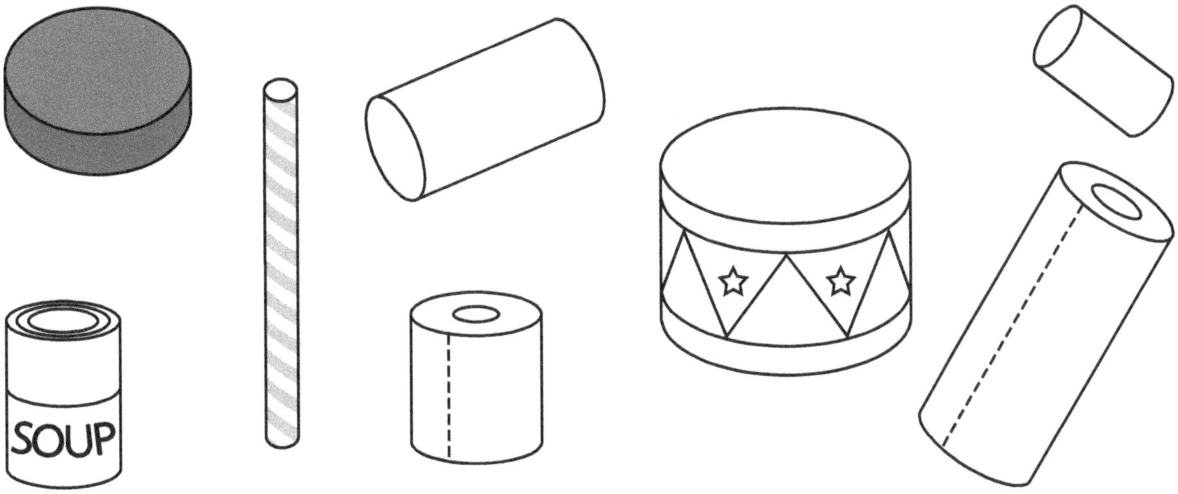

☐ Color the ⌭.

☐ Draw X on the other shapes.

**3.**

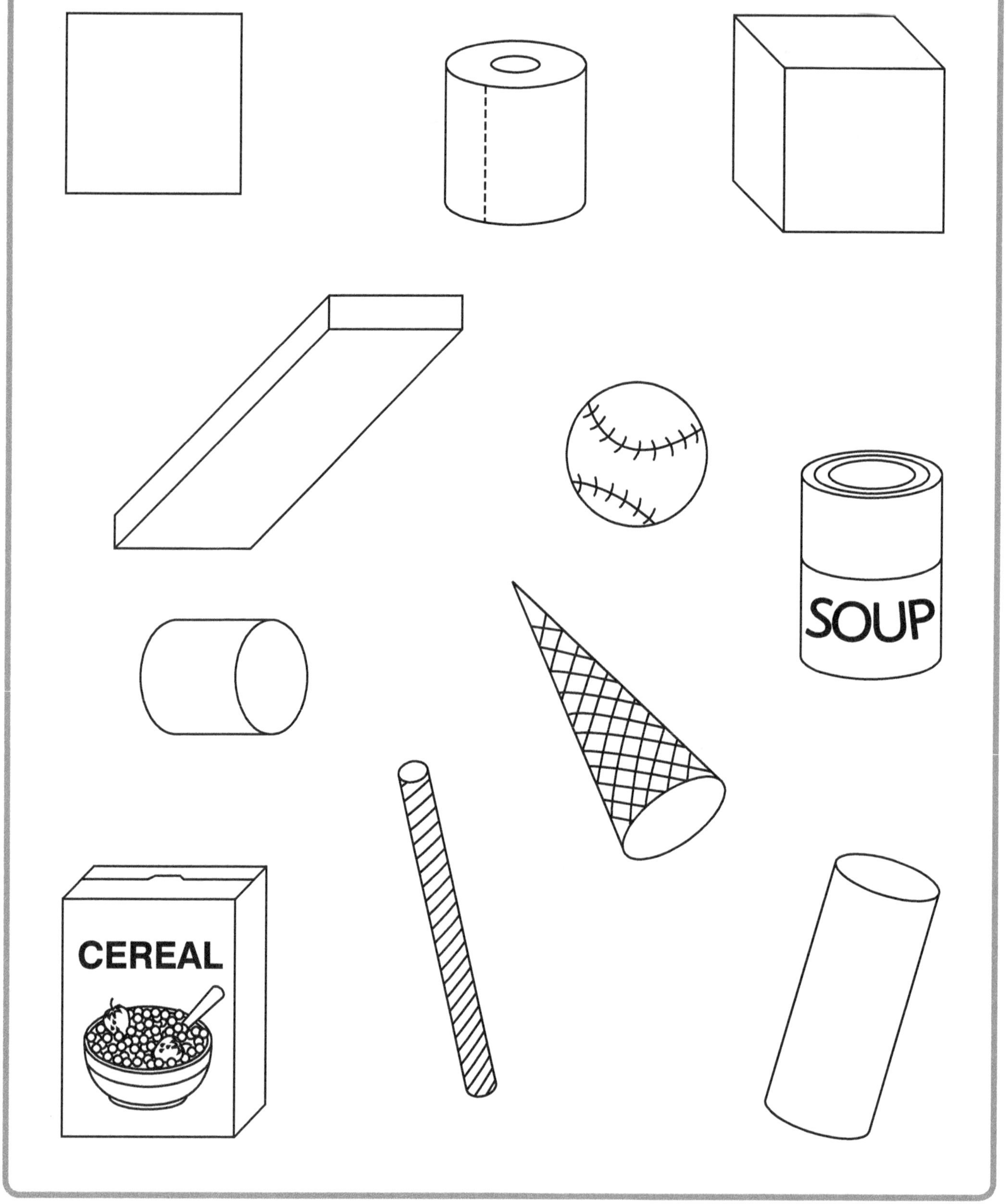

☐ Count the △.

4.

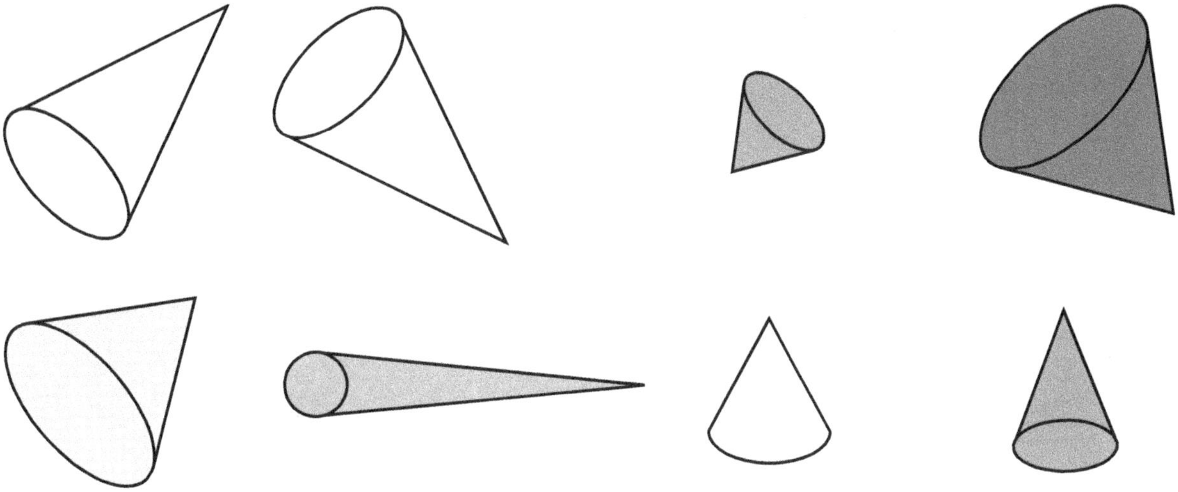

5.

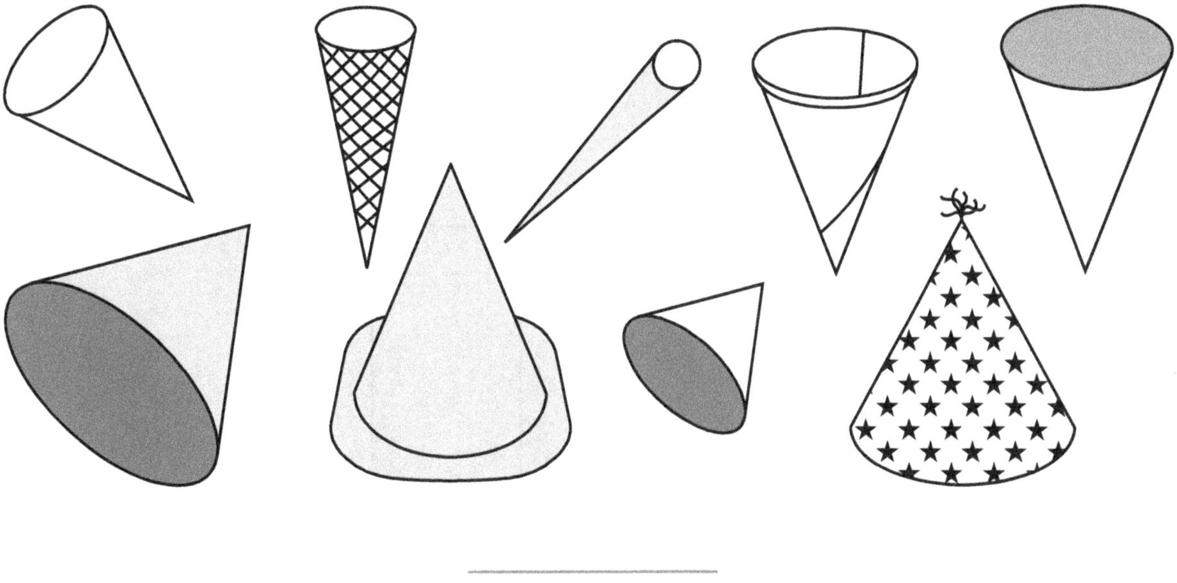

☐ Color the △.

☐ Draw ✕ on the other shapes.

6.

# GK-18 Faces and Corners

☐ Color the solid shapes.

☐ Draw X on the flat shapes.

1.

Color ☺ for the same. Color ☹ for not the same.

2.

3.

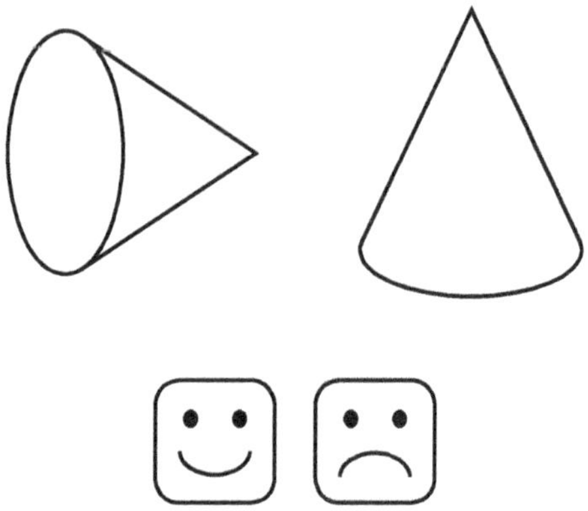

4.

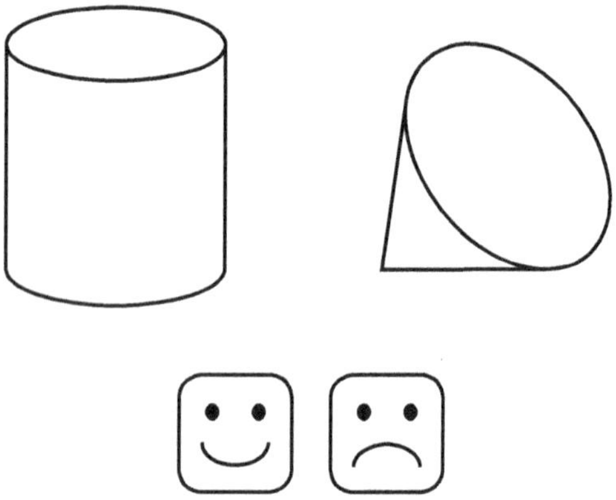

5.

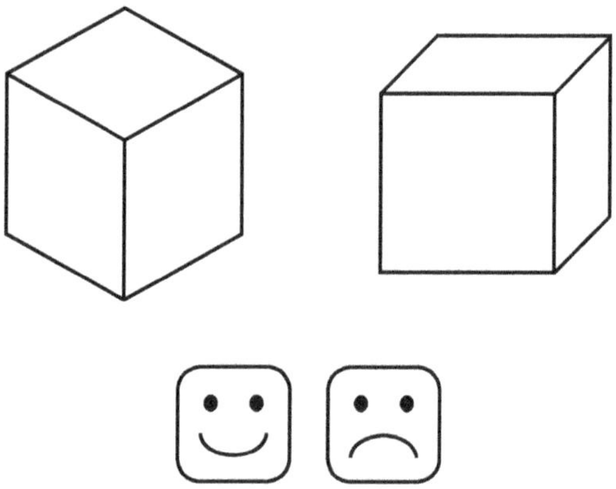

6.

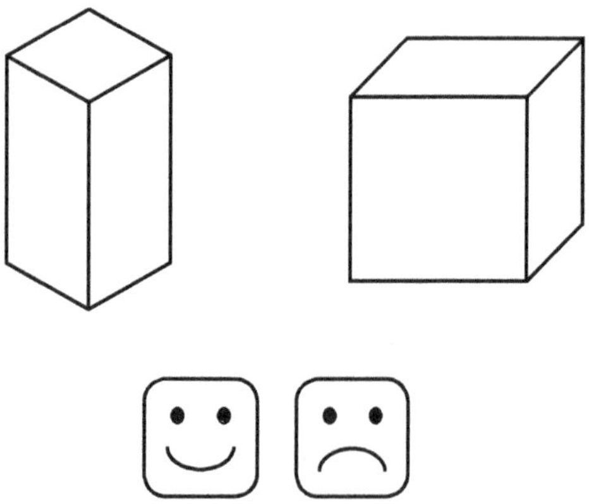

7.

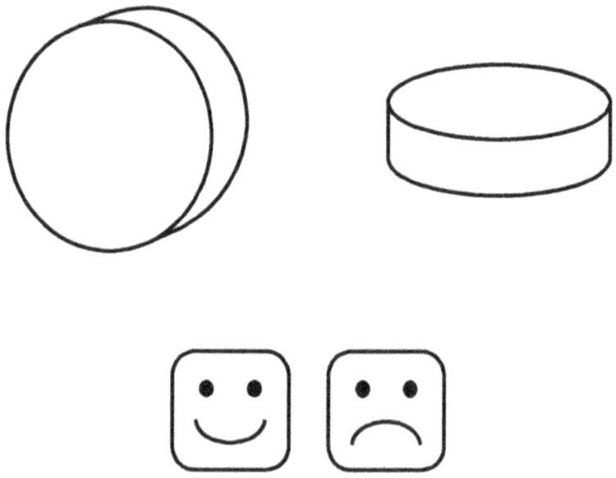

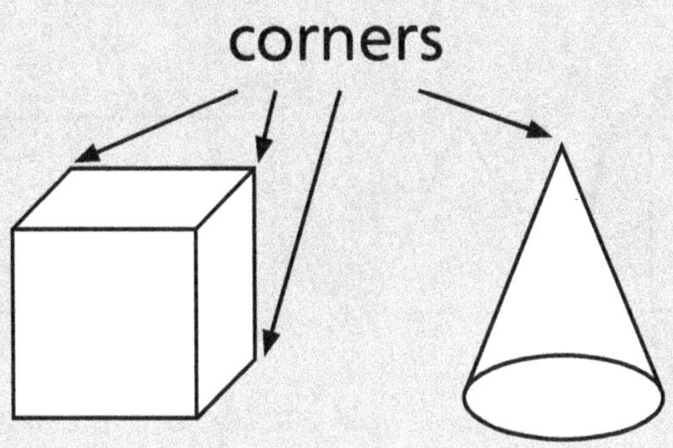


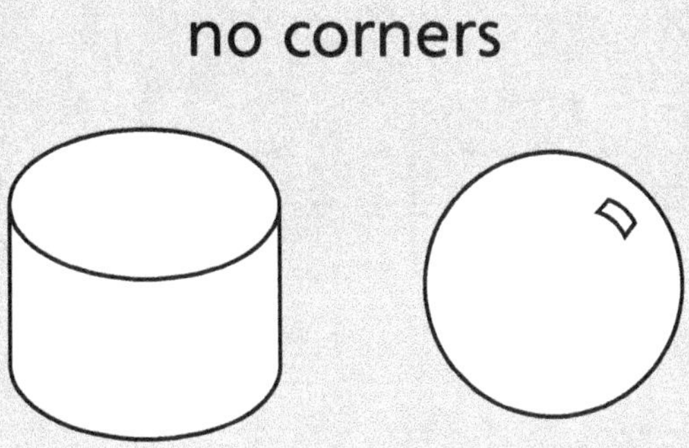


☐ Draw a ● on each corner you see.

8.

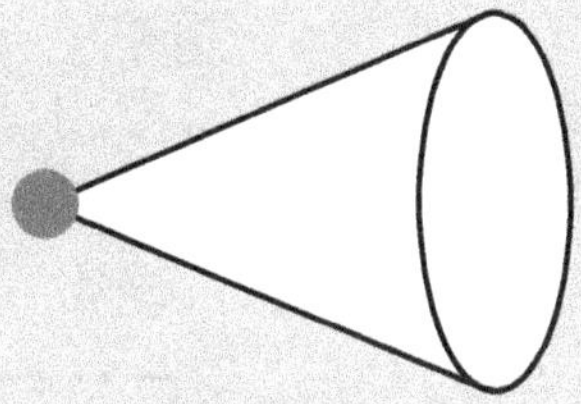

9.

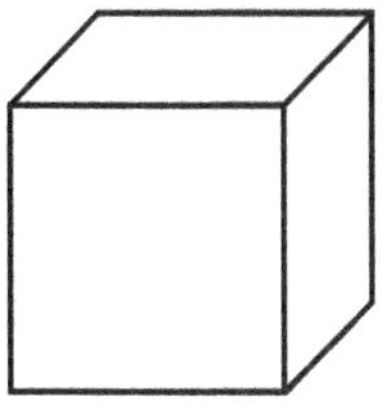

10.

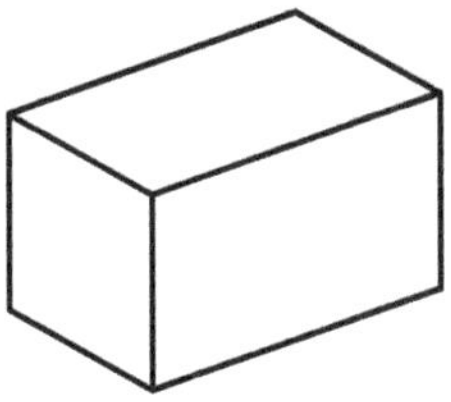

11.

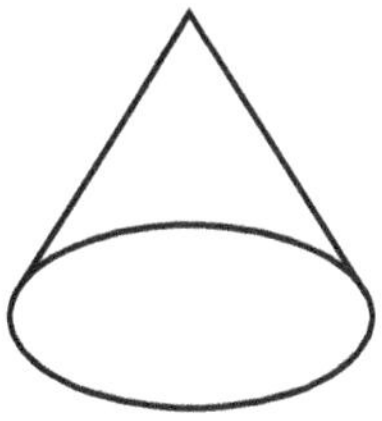

☐ Circle the shapes that have no corners.

12.

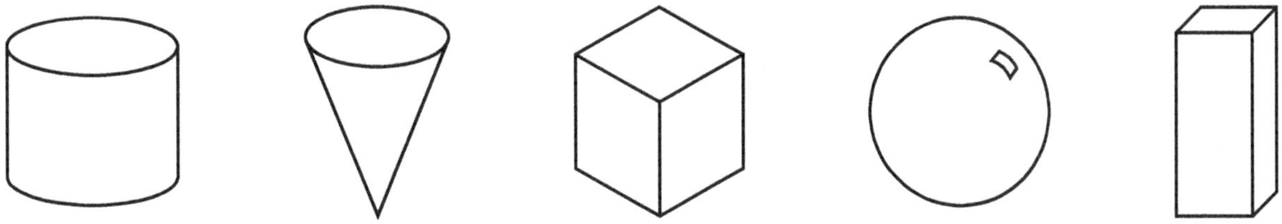

☐ Which shape is shaded? Circle it.

13.

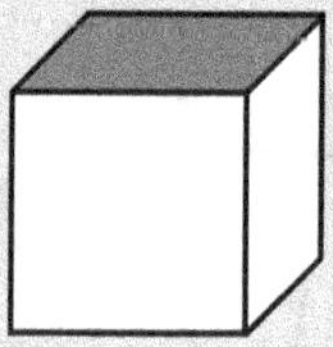

14.

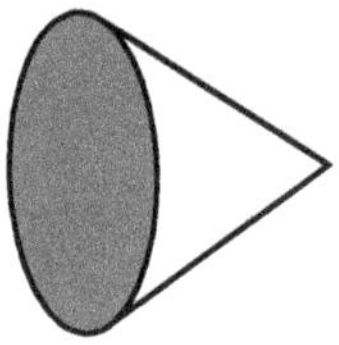

15.

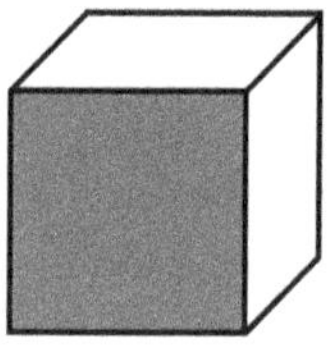

16.

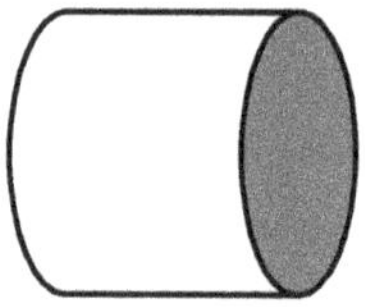

17.

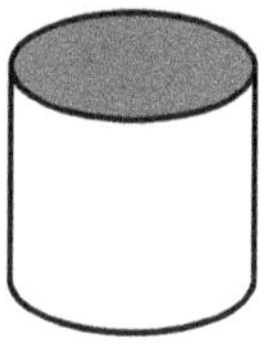

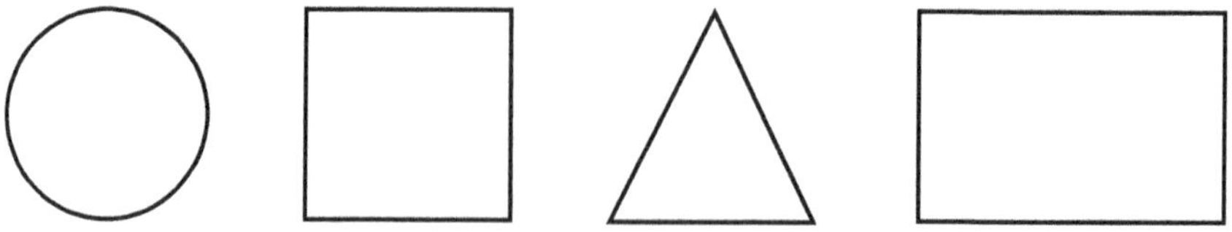

# GK-19 In Front and Behind

- [ ] Color the animals **in front of** the  orange.
- [ ] Color the animals **behind** the  blue.

1.

2.

3.

☐ Color the shapes in front of the  orange.

☐ Color the shapes behind the  blue.

4.

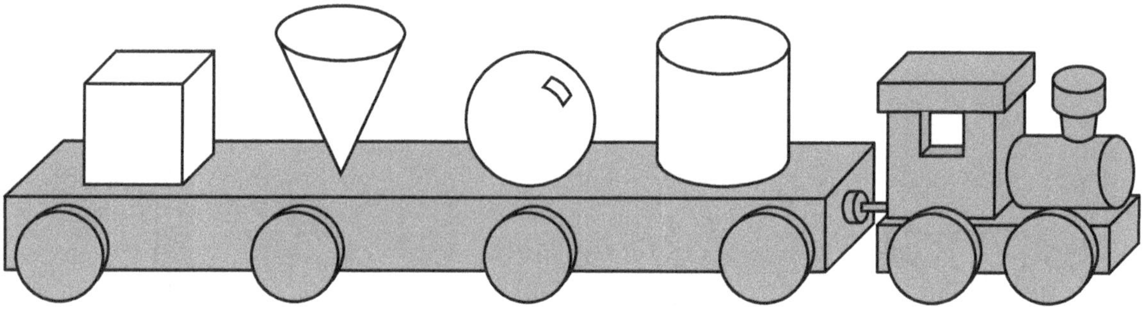

5.

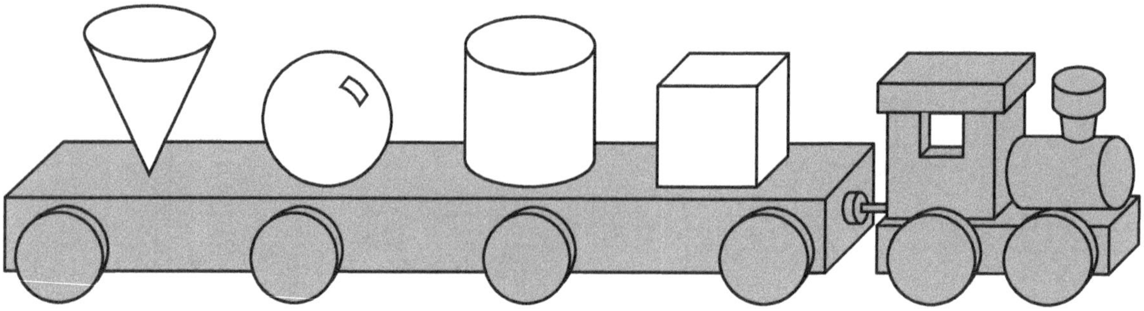

6.

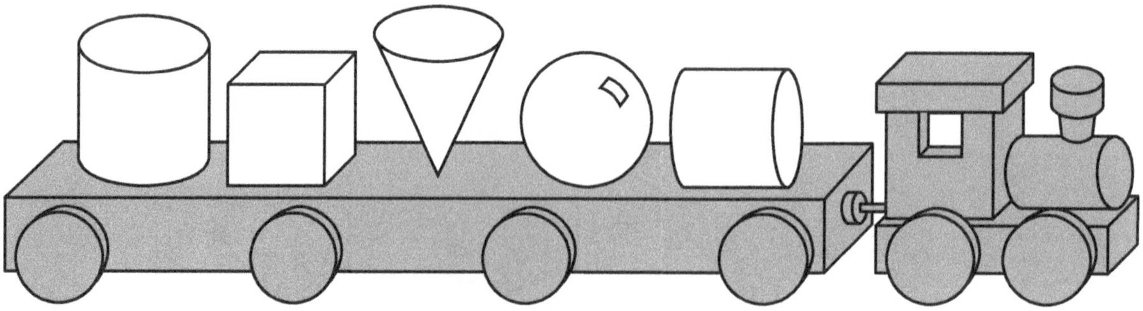

# GK-20 **Next To**

☐ Color the shape **next to** the .

1.

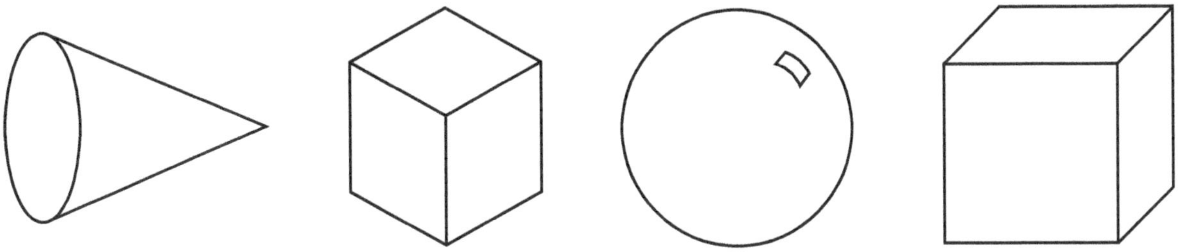

2.

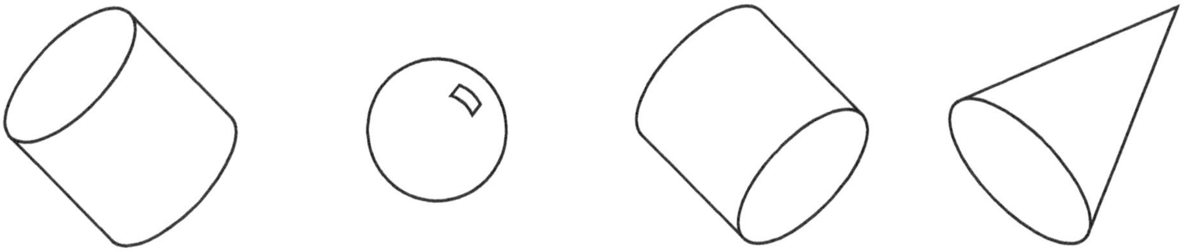

3.

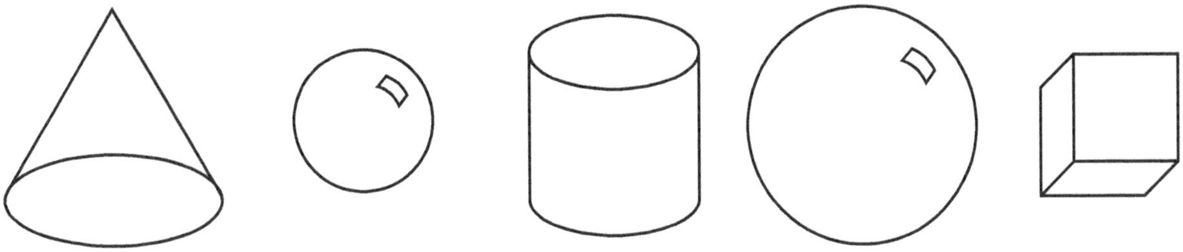

4.

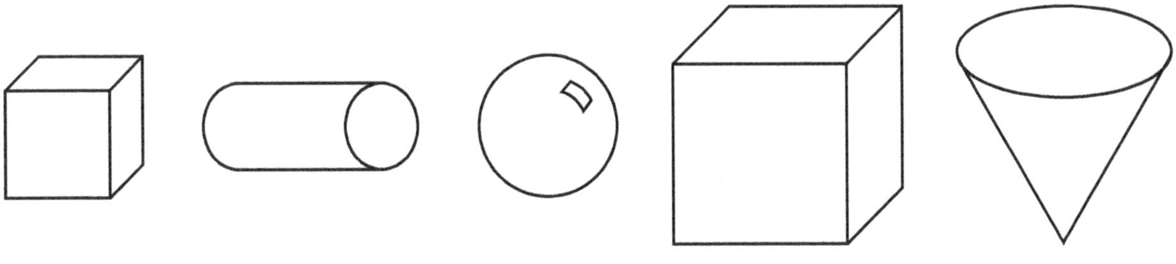

☐ Color the shapes next to the .

5.

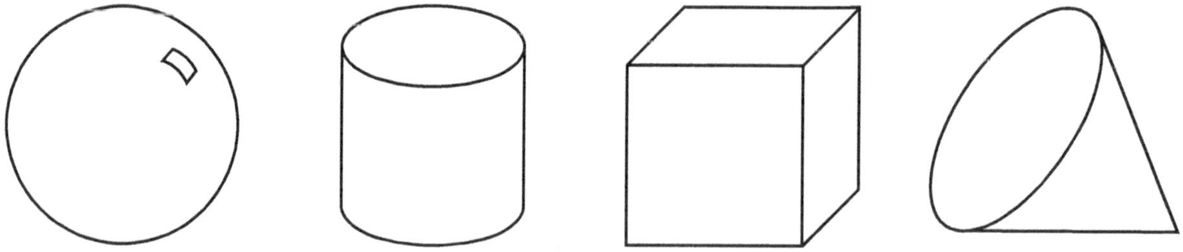

6.

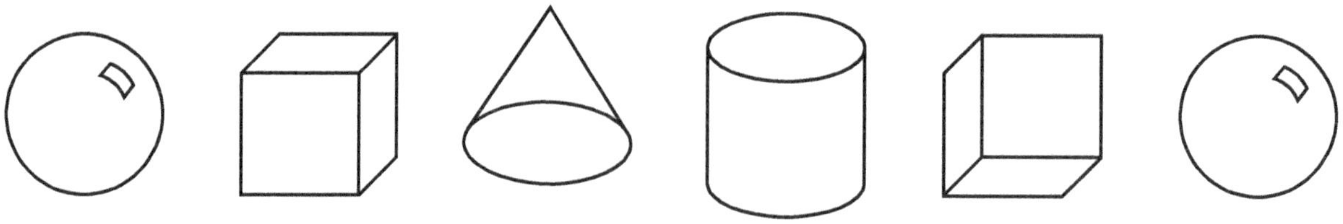

7.

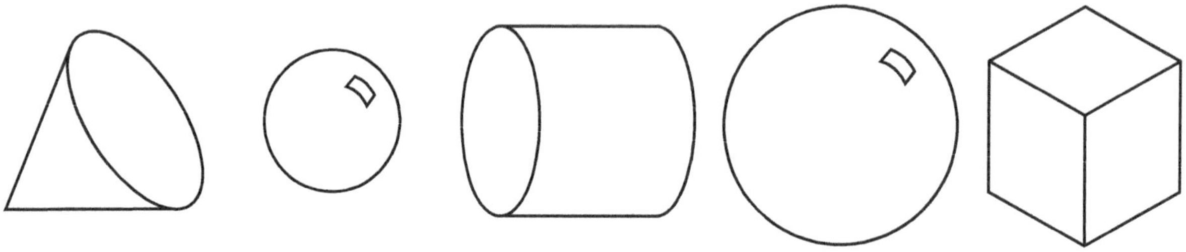

8.

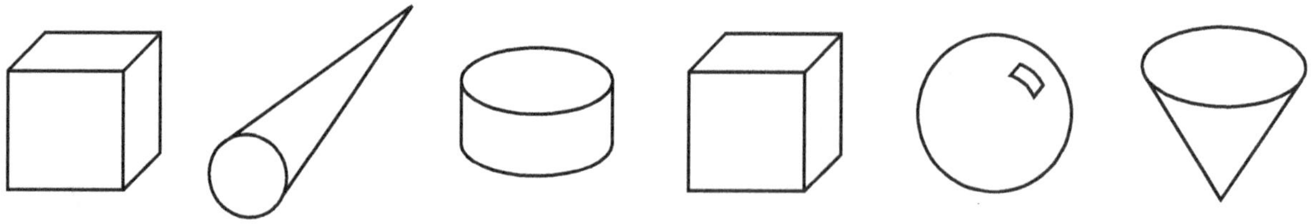

# GK-21 Building Solids

yellow | green | red | blue

☐ Color the solid shapes.

1.

Mona makes a building from blocks.

☐ Circle the shapes she uses.

2.

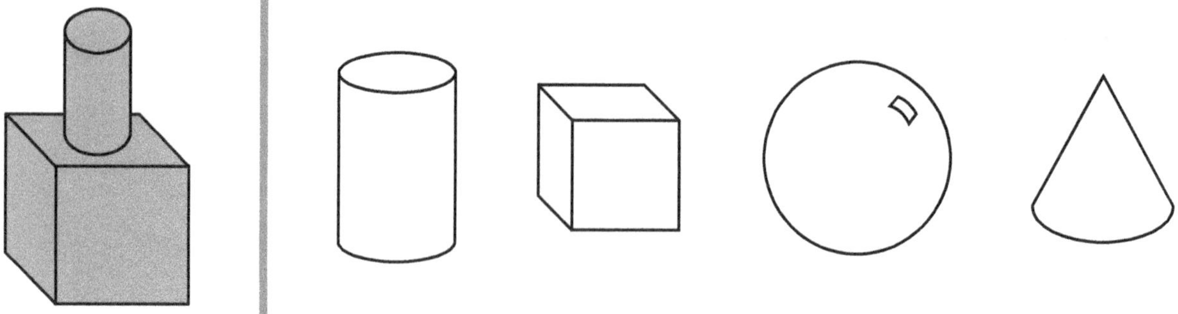

3.

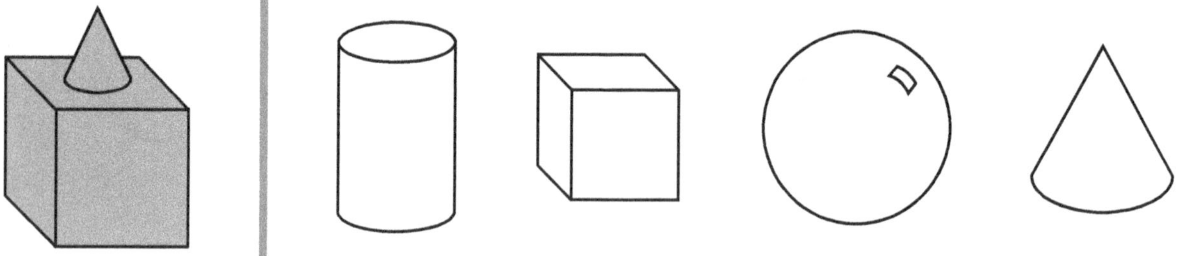

4.

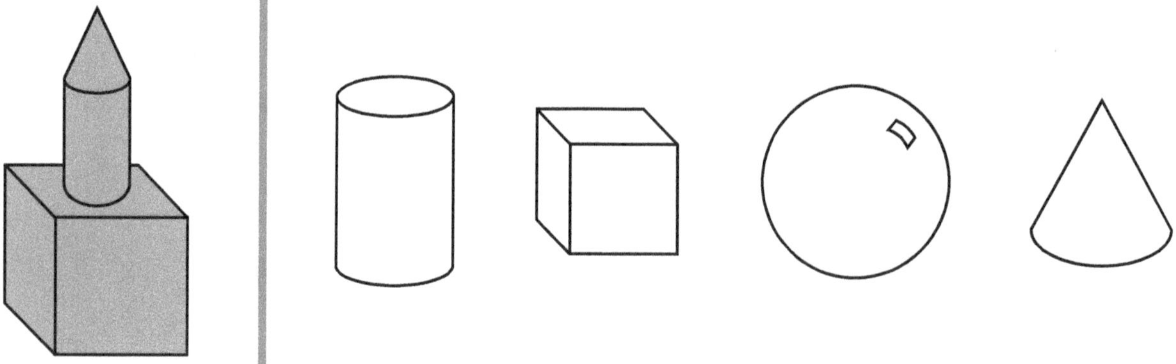

# NBTK-1 Counting to 100

☐ Trace.

1.

90 91 92

93 94 95

96 97 98

99 100

2.

9 9 9 9 9 9 9

☐ Write 9.

3.

# NBTK-2 The Numbers 11, 12, and 13

☐ How many shapes?

1.

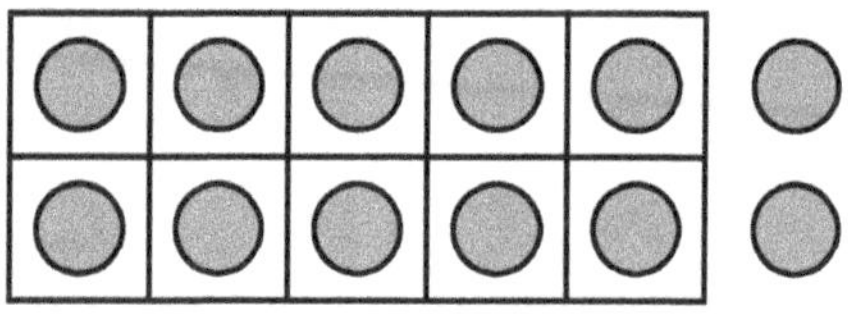

2.

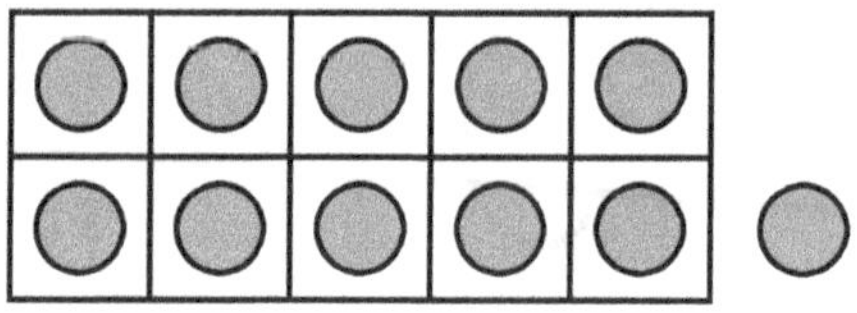

3.

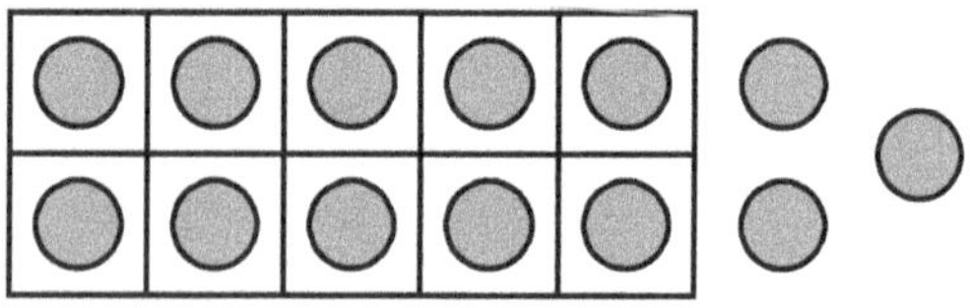

4.

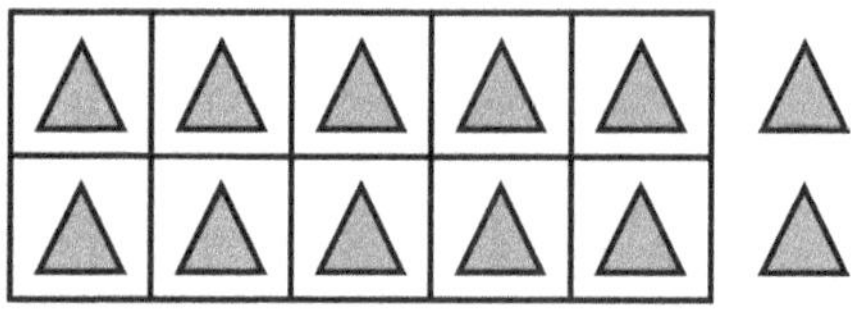

5.

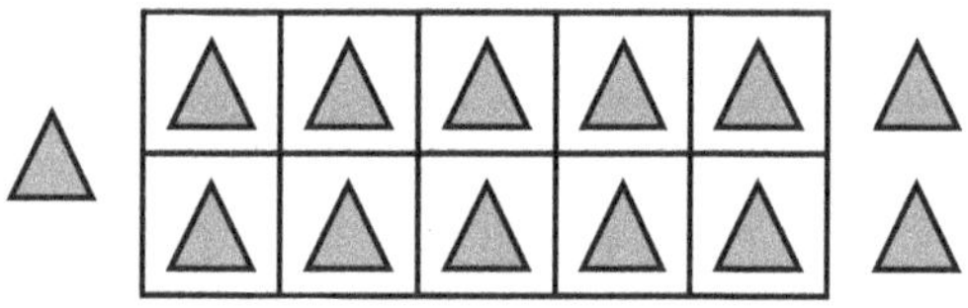

6.

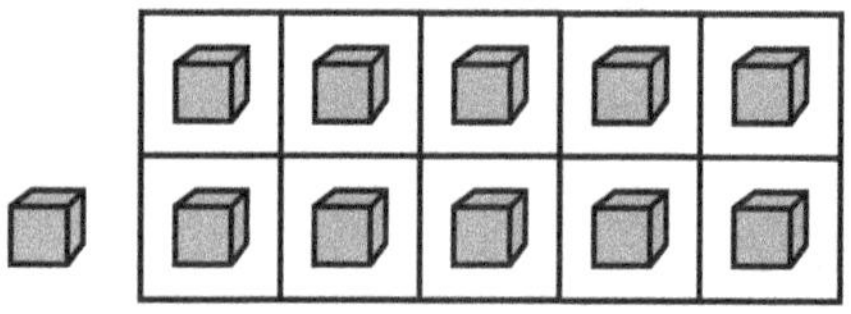

## How many shapes?

7.

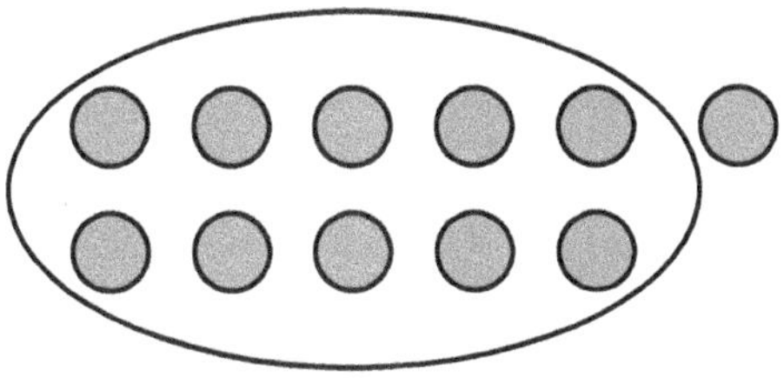

8.

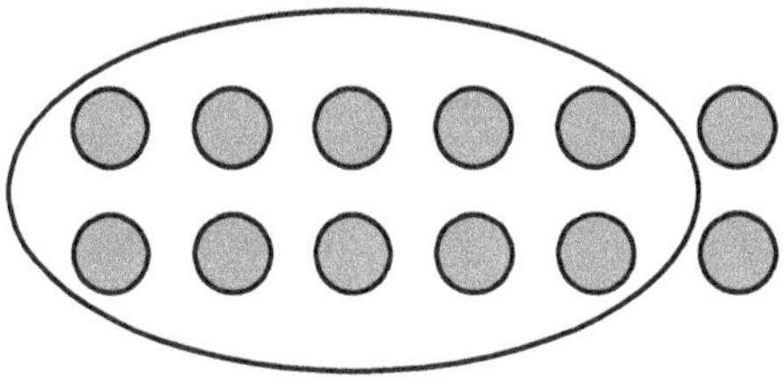

9.

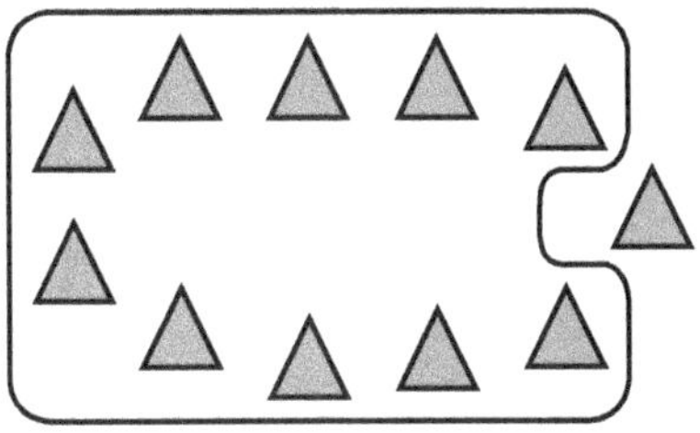

10.

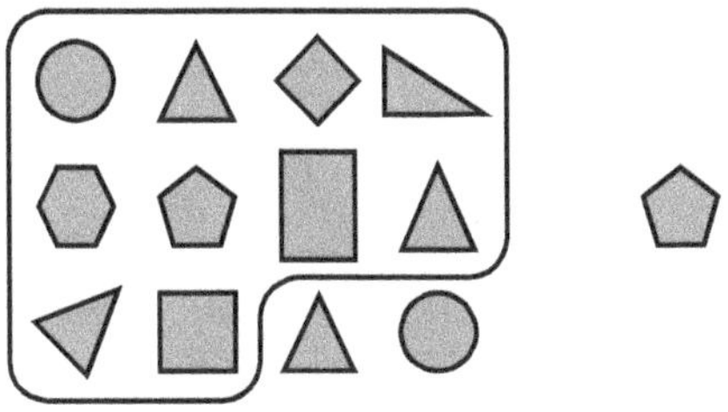

11.

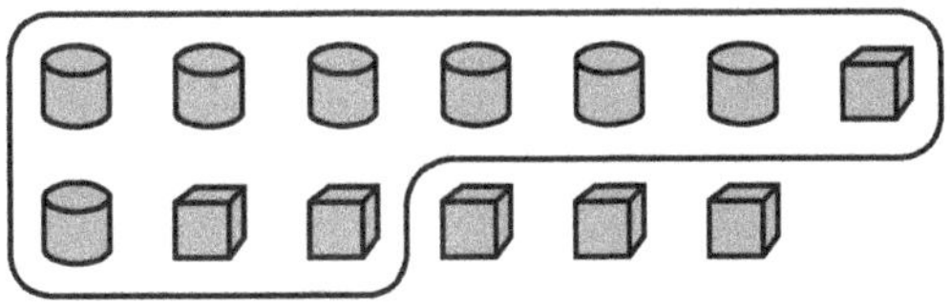

12.

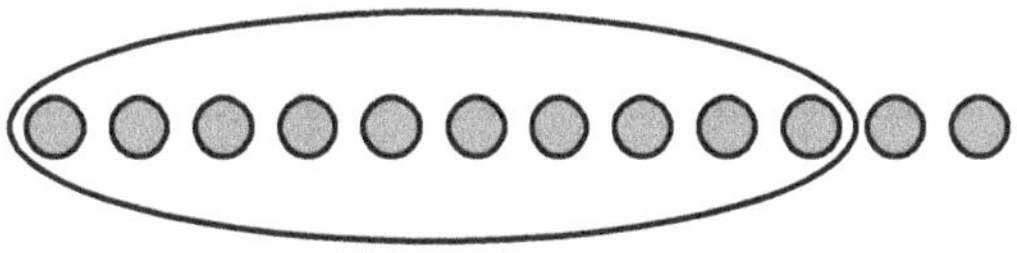

- [ ] Circle 10.
- [ ] How many shapes?

**13.**

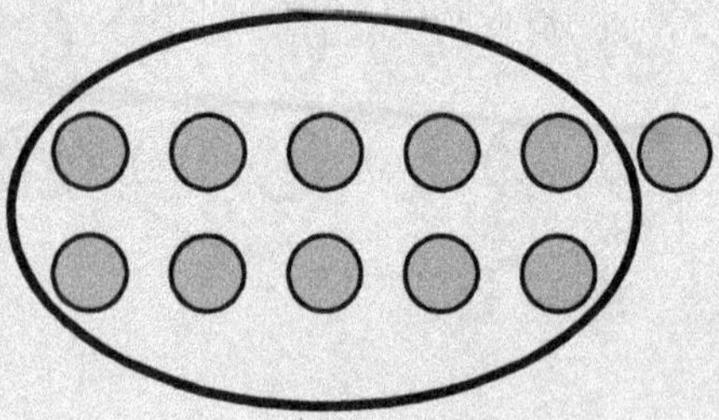

11

**14.**

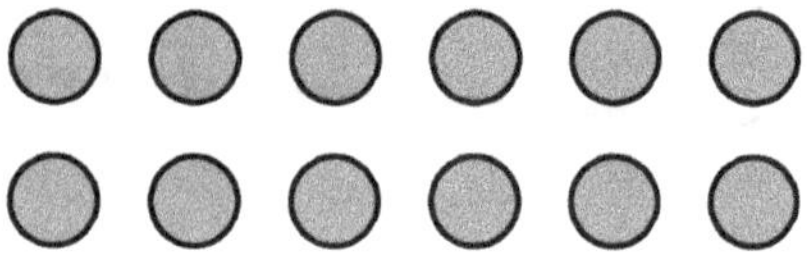

**15.**

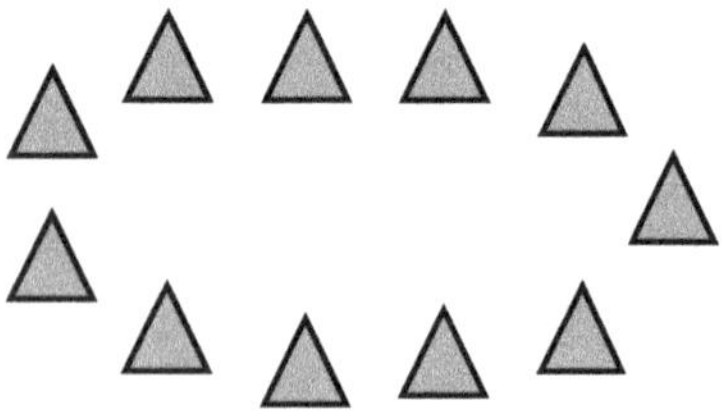

**16.**

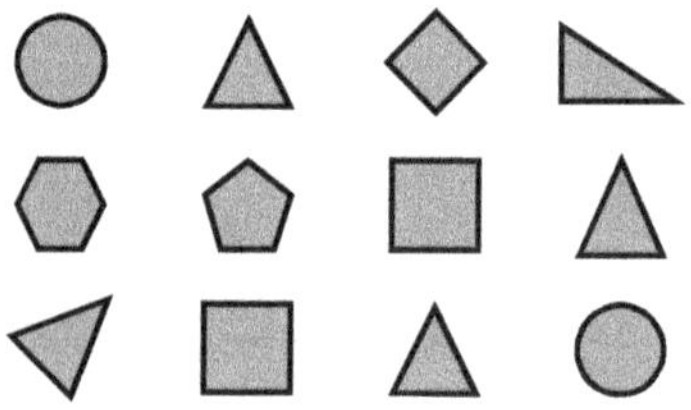

**17.**

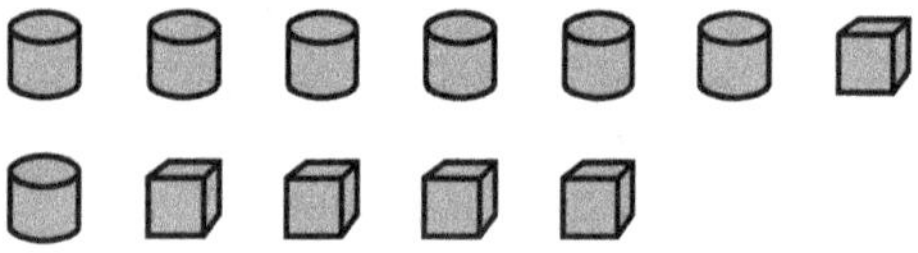

**18.**

☐ Color the number of shapes.

19.

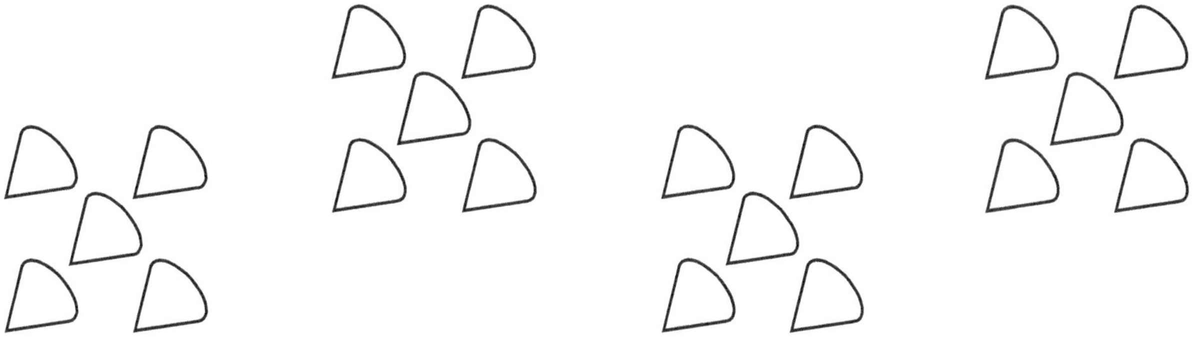

11

20.

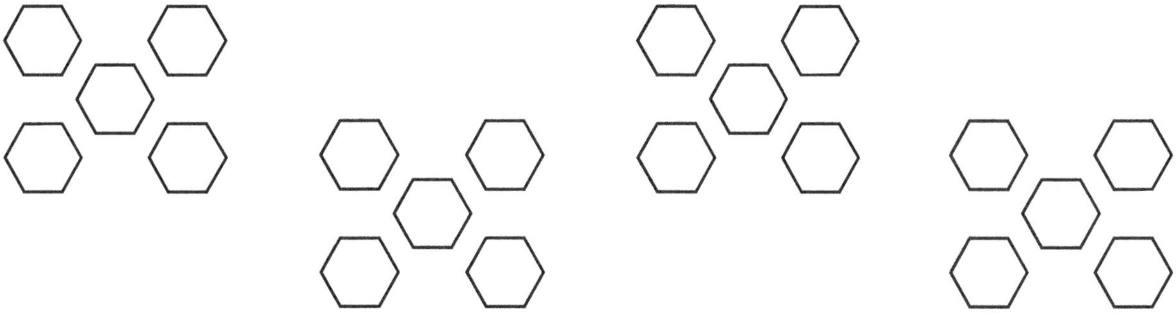

12

21.

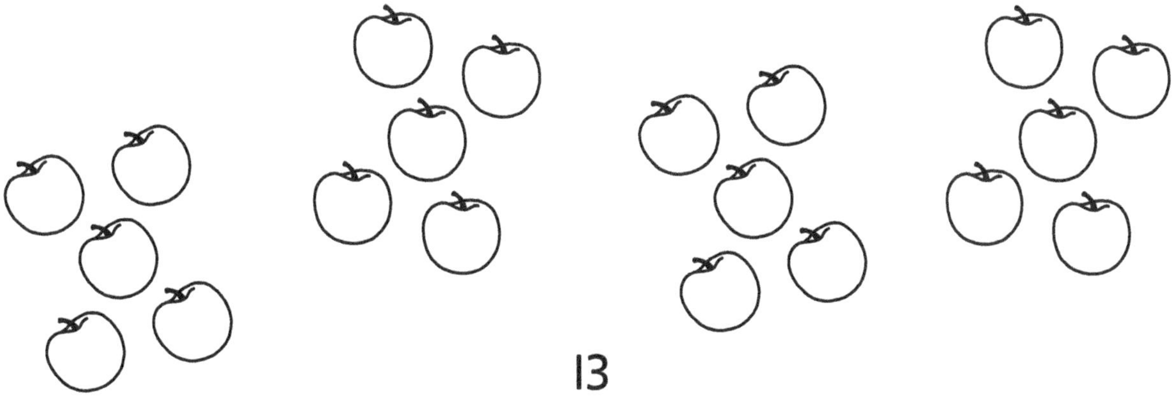

13

# NBTK-3 Taking Apart 11, 12, and 13

☐ Draw ◯ for the ones.

1.

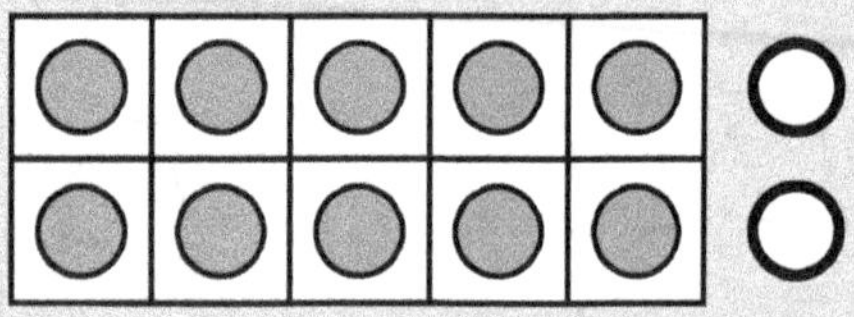

12

2.

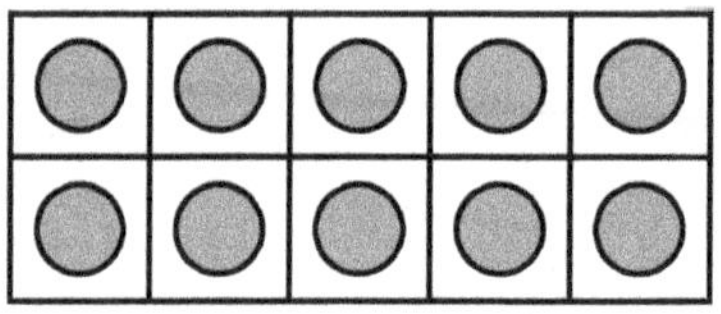

11

3.

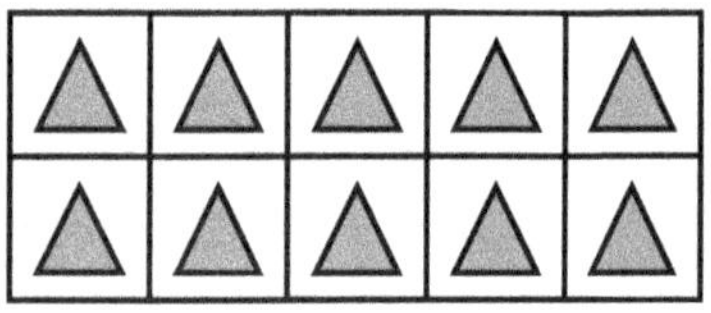

13

4.

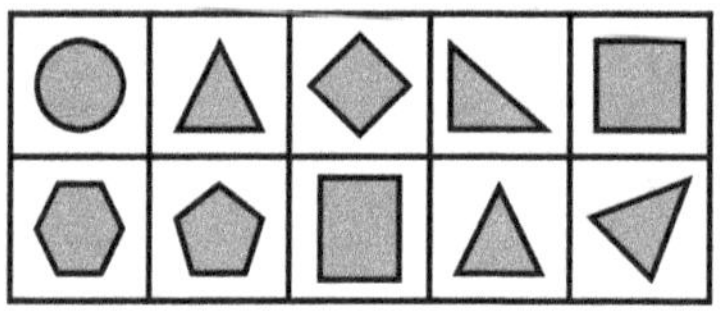

12

5.

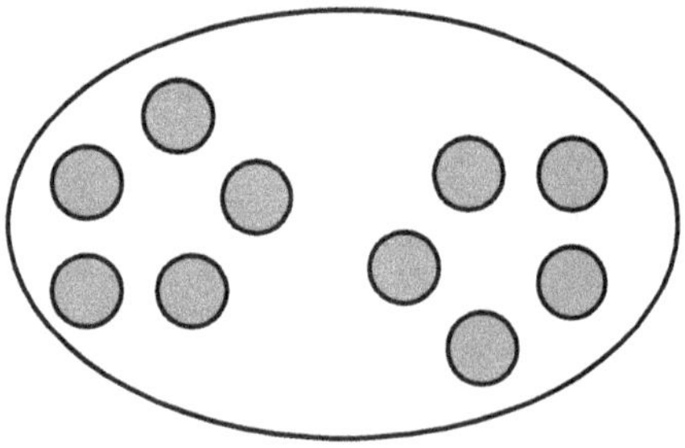

13

6.

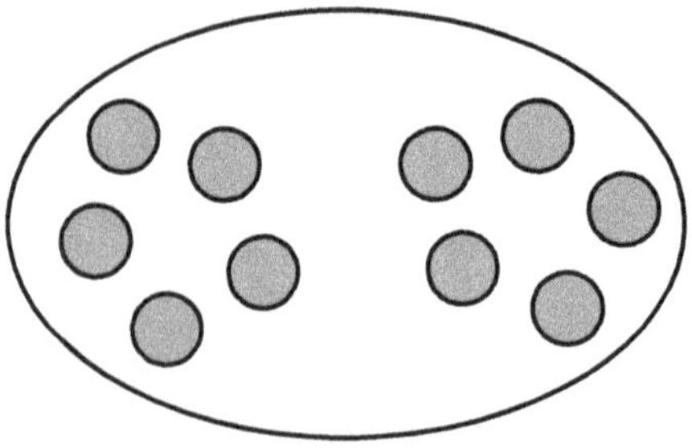

11

## ☐ How many ones?

**7.**

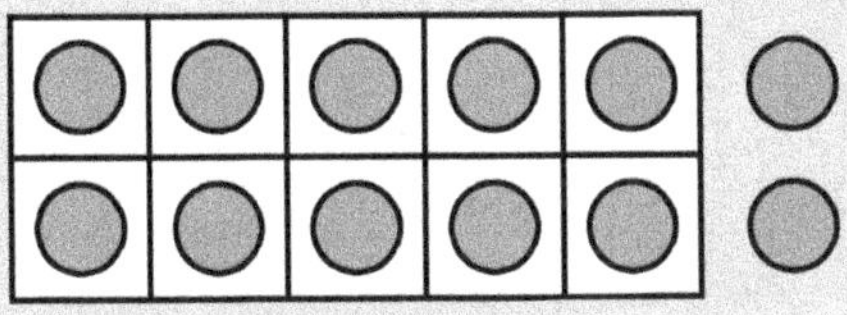

12

10 | 2

**8.**

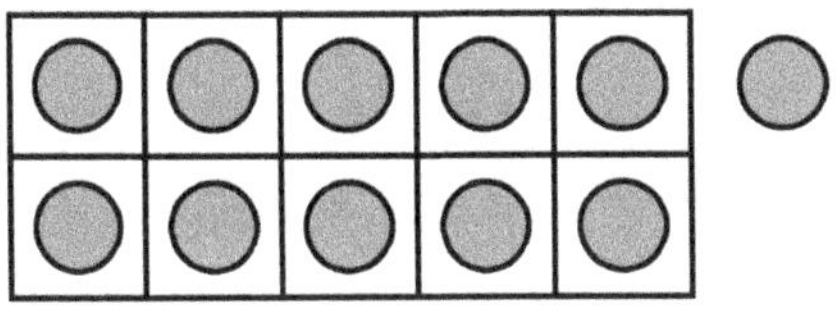

11

10 | ☐

**9.**

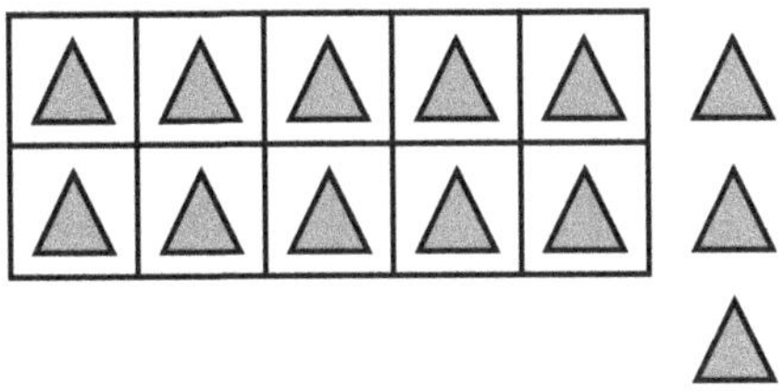

13

10 | ☐

**10.**

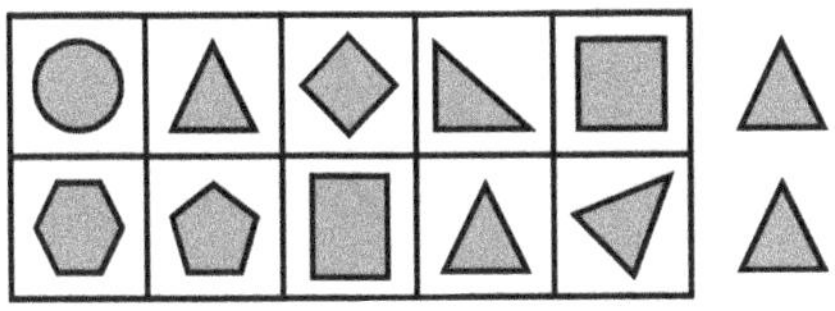

12

10 | ☐

**11.**

11

10 | ☐

**12.**

13

10 | ☐

☐ Write the ten.

**13.**

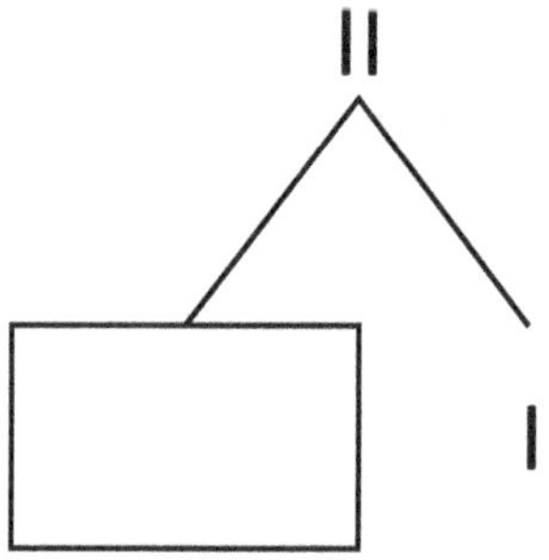


**14.**

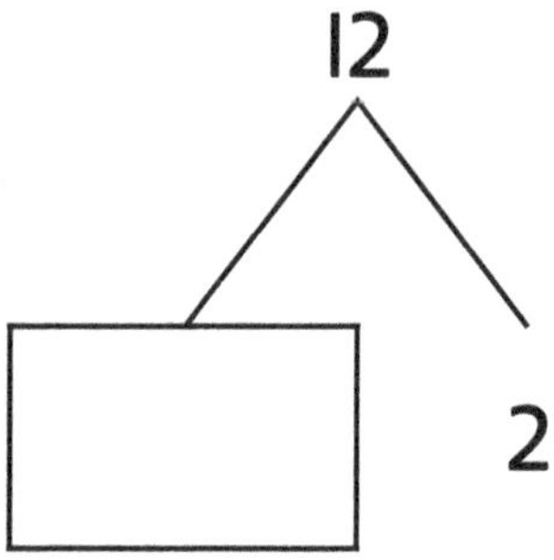


☐ Write the ten.

☐ How many ones?

**15.**

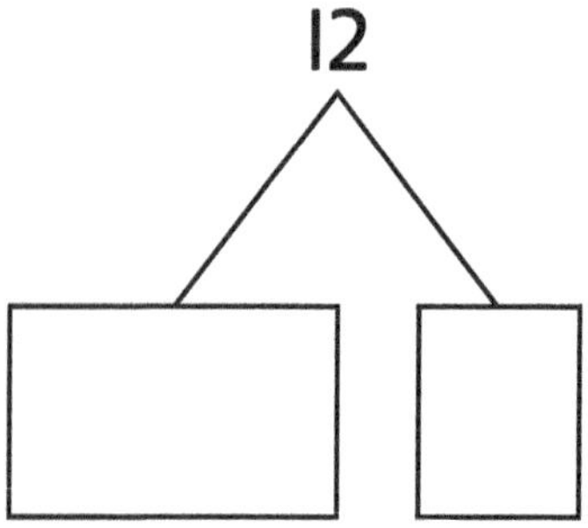


**16.**

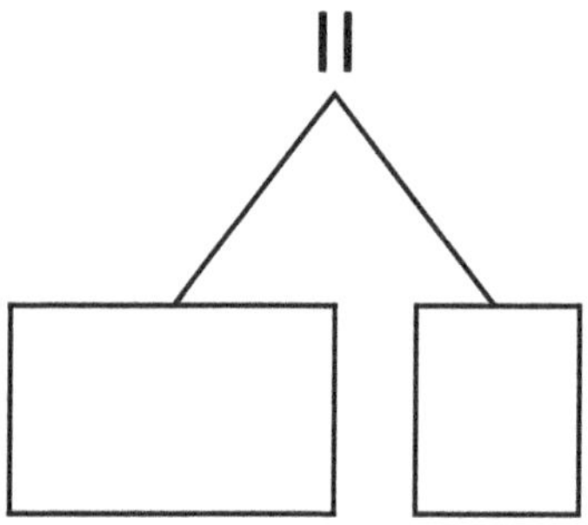


**17.**

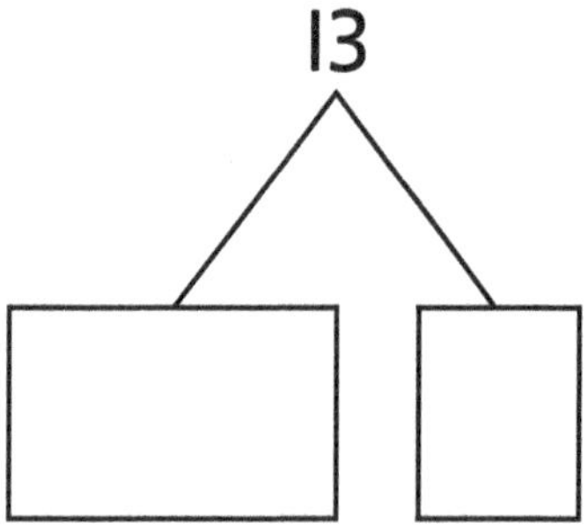


**18. BONUS**

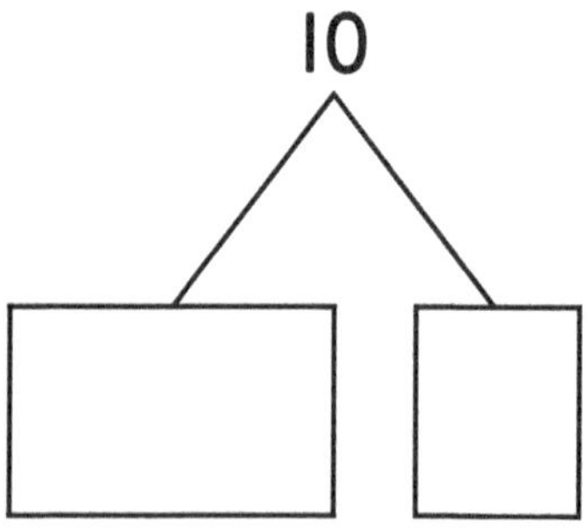

# NBTK-4 Making 11, 12, and 13

☐ Draw ◯ to show the addition.

1.

11 = 10 + 1

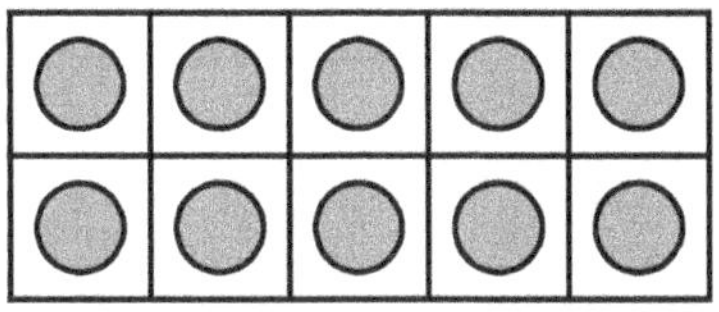

2.

12 = 10 + 2

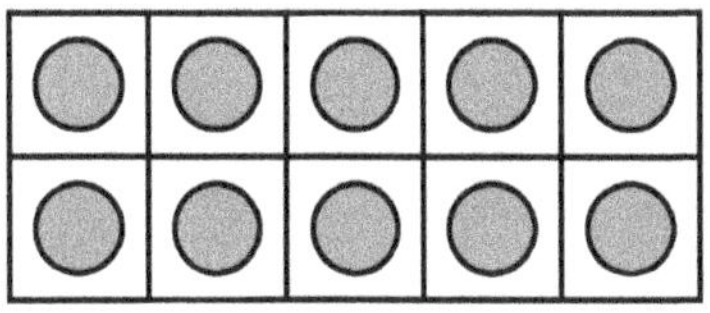

3.

13 = 10 + 3

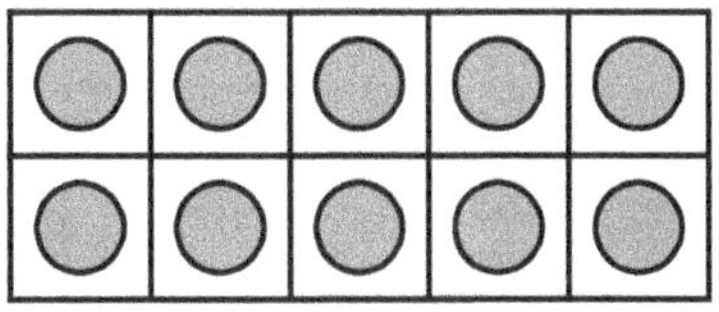

4.

11 = 10 + 1

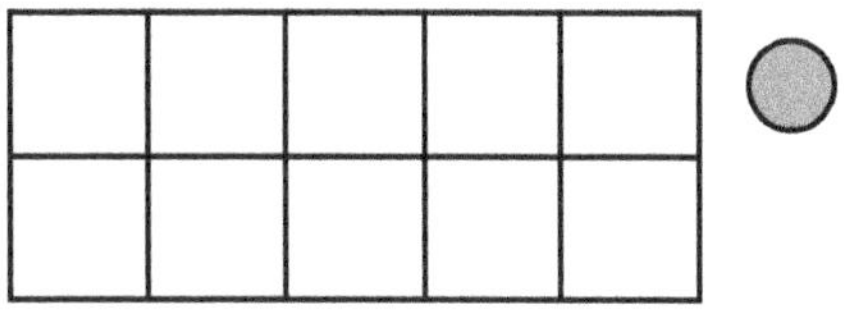

5.

13 = 10 + 3

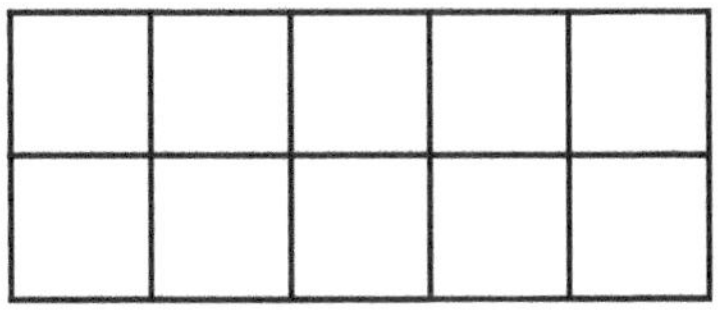

6.

12 = 10 + 2

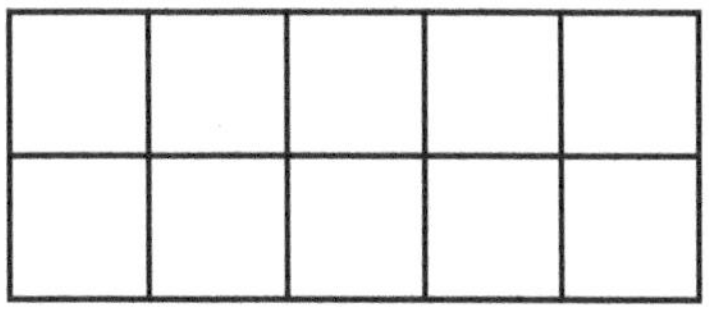

☐ Add.

7.

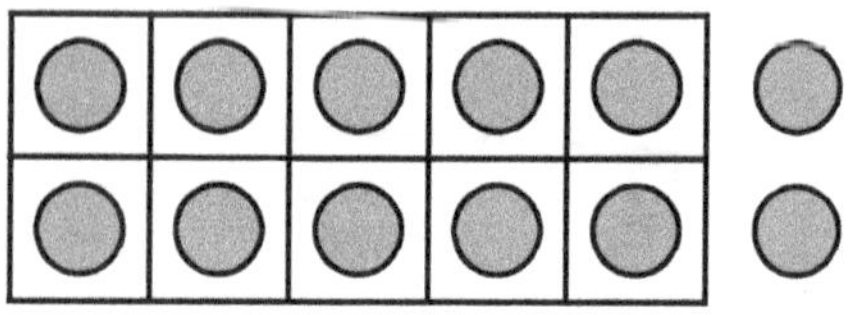

$10 + 2 =$ ☐

8.

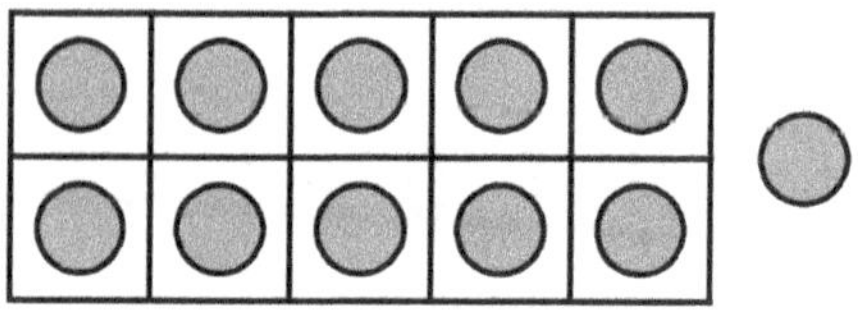

$10 + 1 =$ ☐

9.

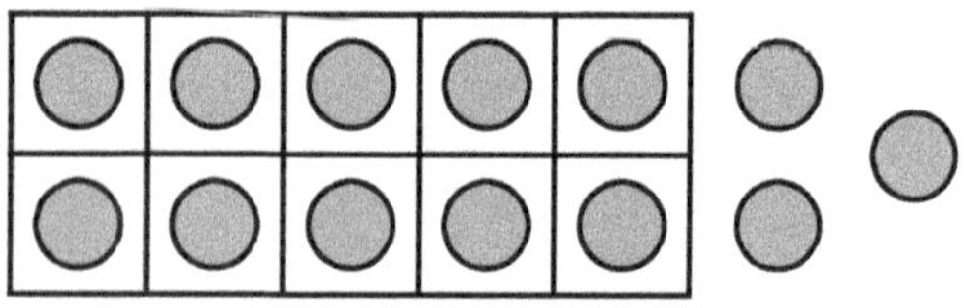

$10 + 3 =$ ☐

10.

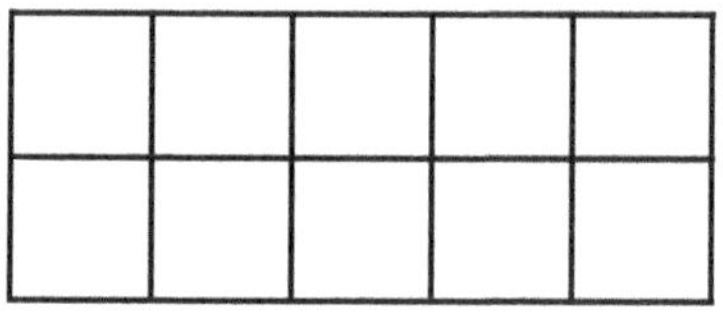

$10 + 2 =$ ☐

11.

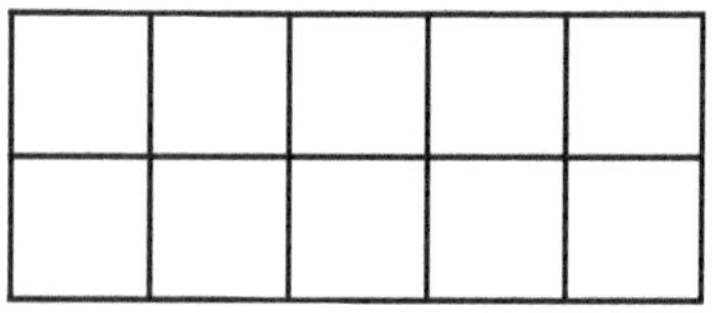

$10 + 3 =$ ☐

12. BONUS

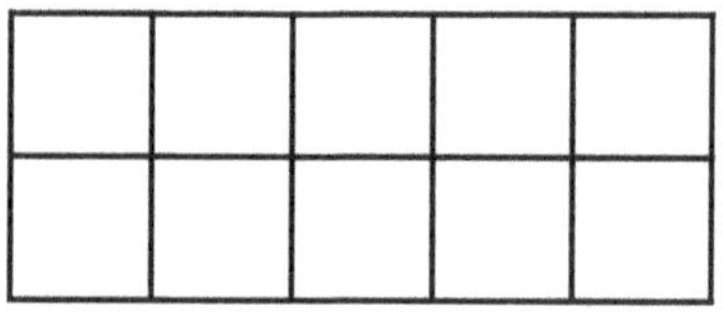

$1 + 10 =$ ☐

☐ What addition do you see?

**13.**

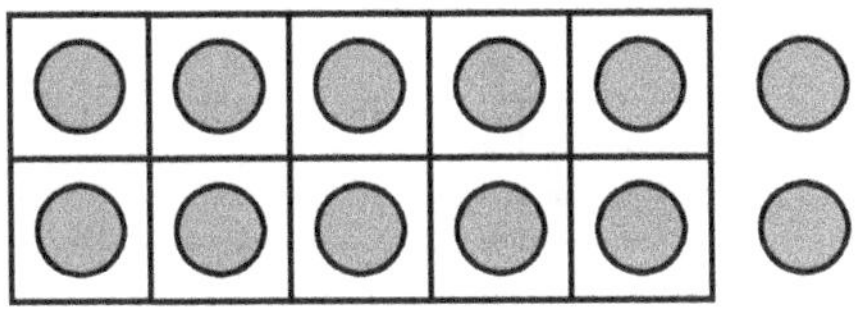

12 = ☐ + ☐

**14.**

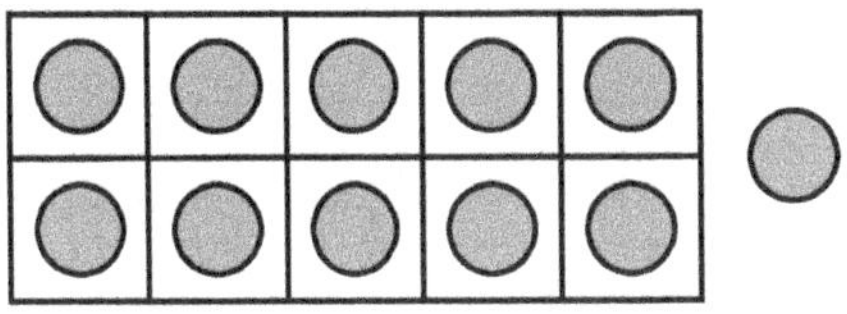

11 = ☐ + ☐

**15.**

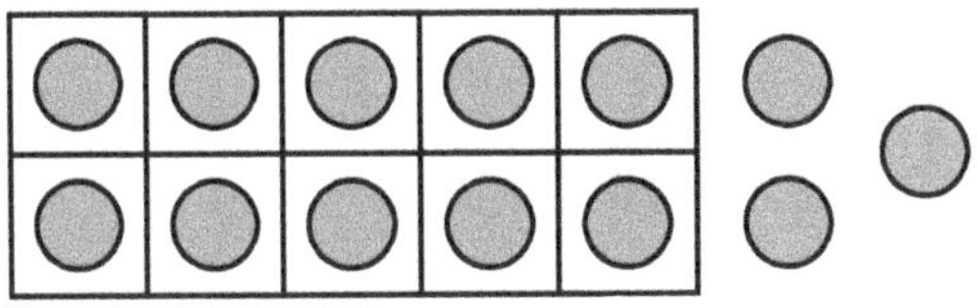

13 = ☐ + ☐

**16.**

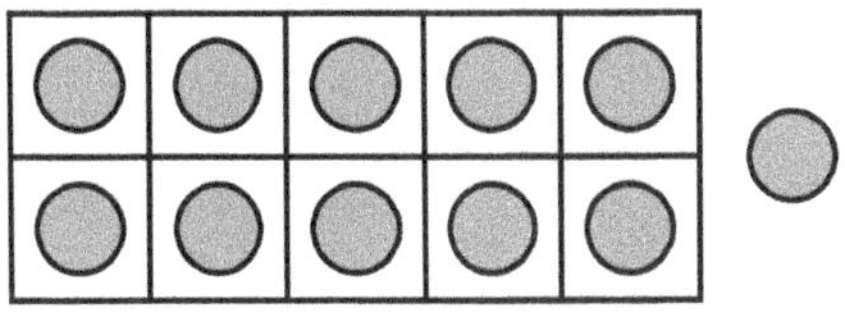

☐ = 10 + ☐

☐ Write the addition.

**17.**

12 = ☐ + ☐

**18.**

13 = ☐ + ☐

# The Numbers 14, 15, and 16

☐ How many ●?

1.

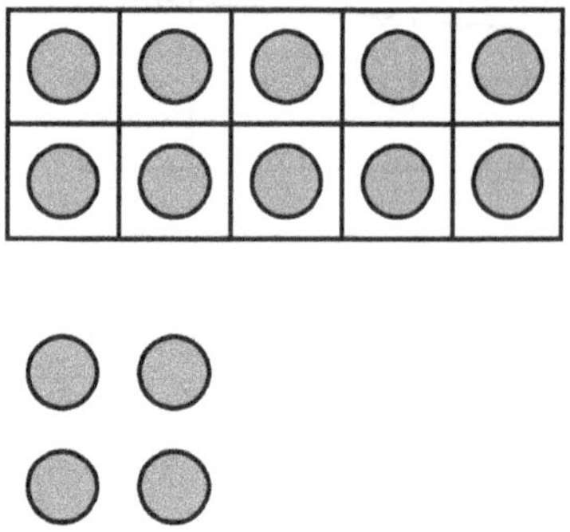

2.

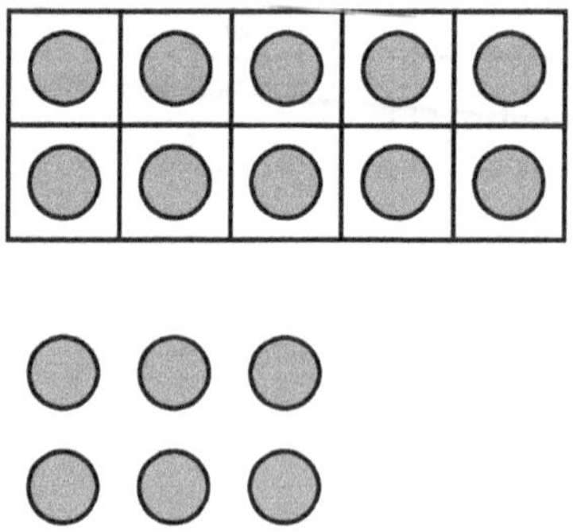

3.

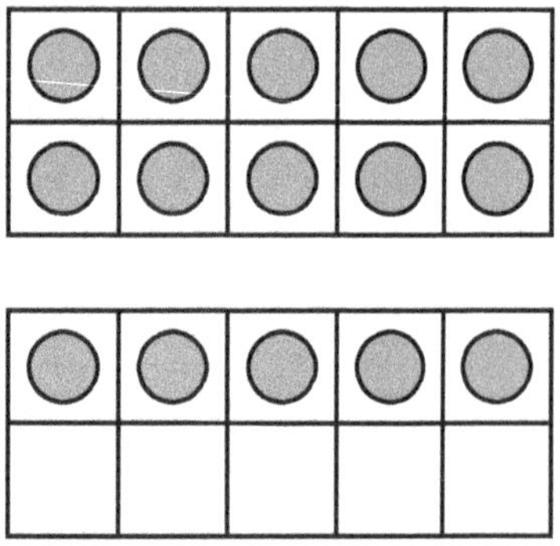

4.

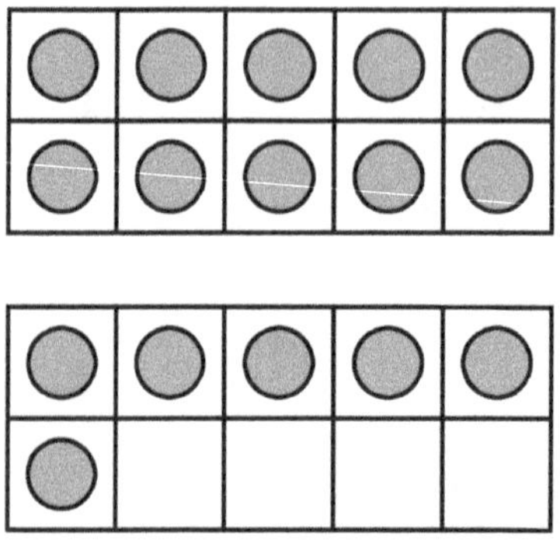

## ☐ How many shapes?

5.

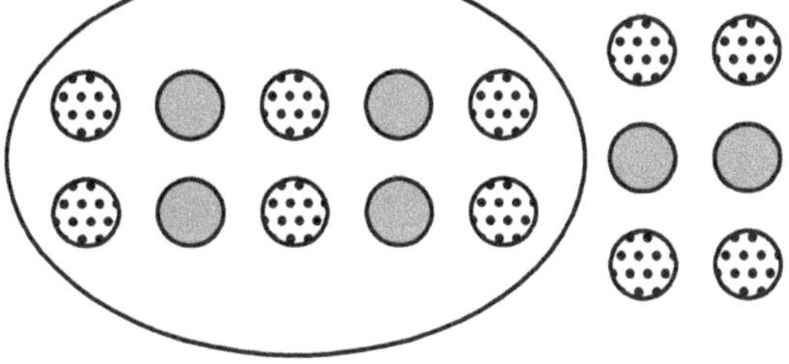

6.

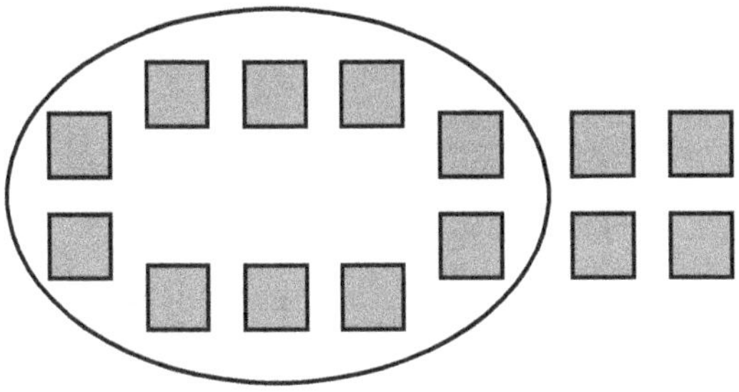

7.

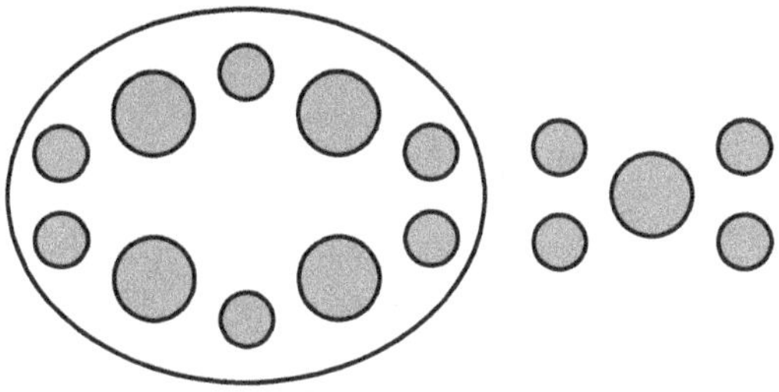

8.

9.

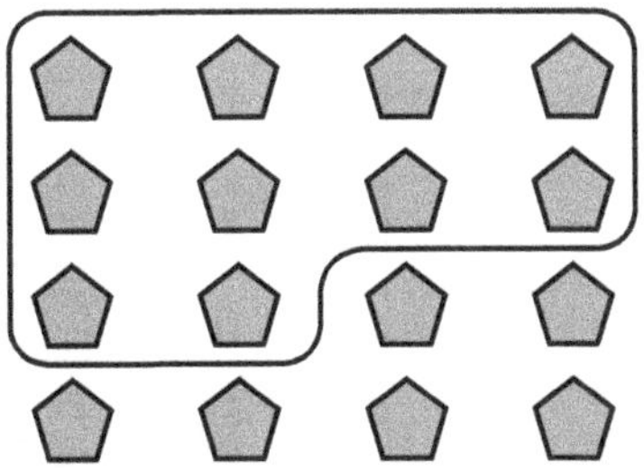

10.

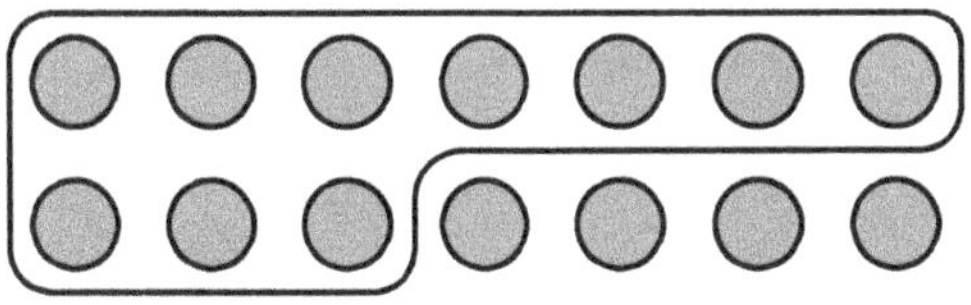

☐ Circle 10.

☐ How many shapes?

11.

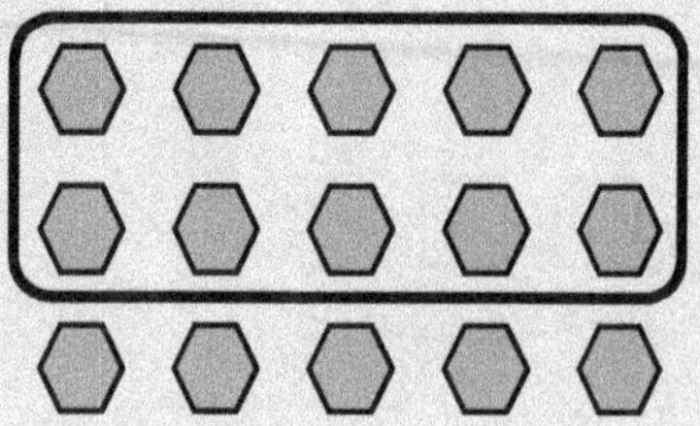

15

12.

13.

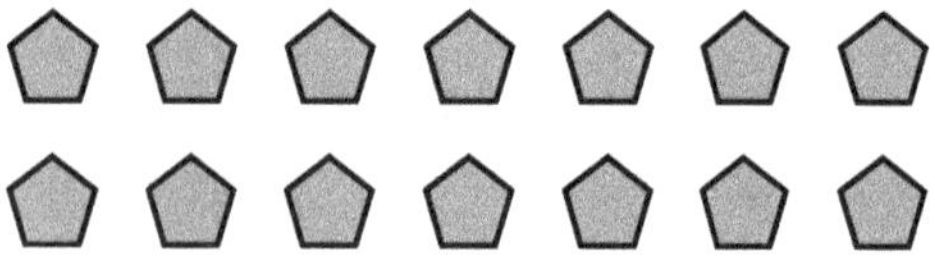

14.

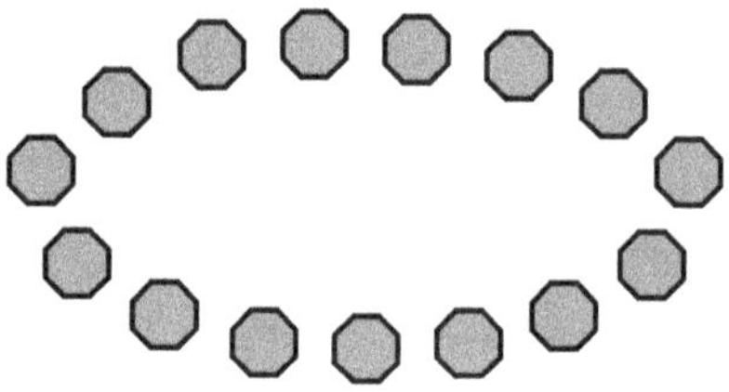

15.

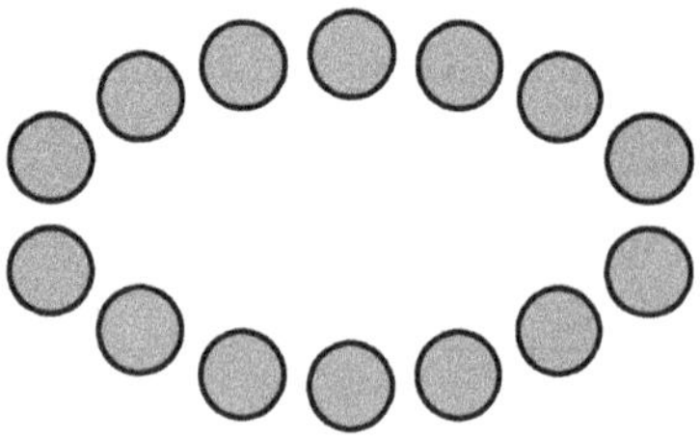

16.

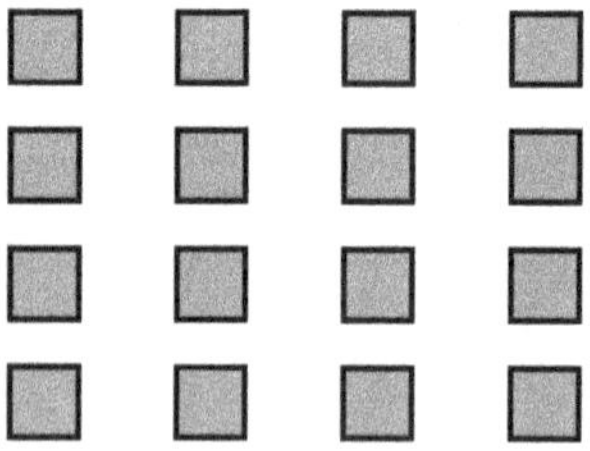

☐ Color the number of shapes.

17.

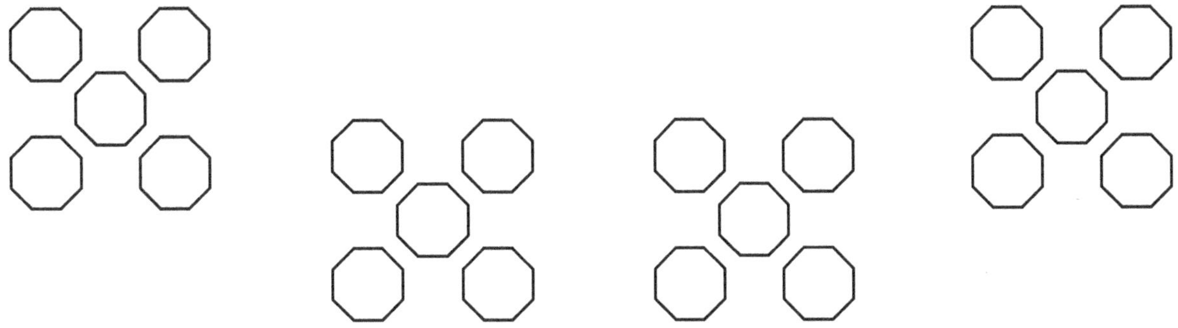

14

18.

15

19.

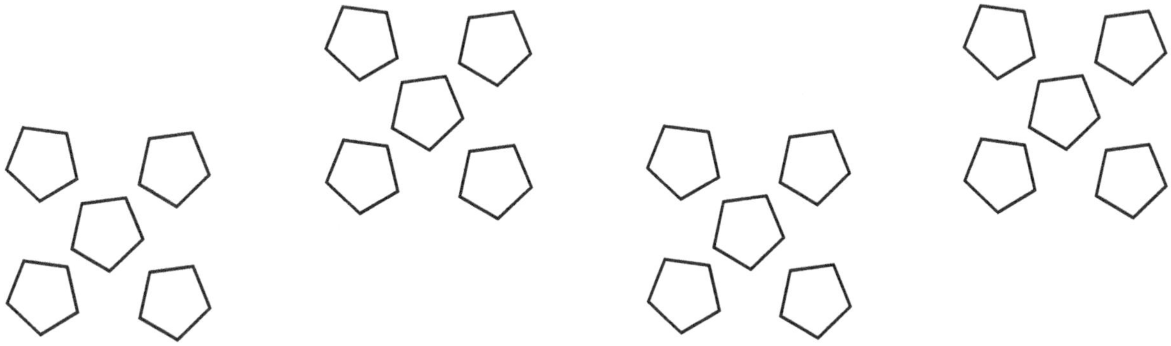

16

# NBTK-6 Taking Apart 14, 15, and 16

☐ Draw ○ for the ones.

1.

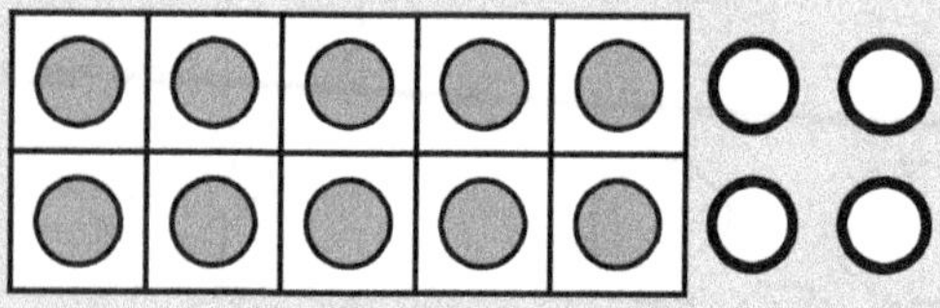

14

2.

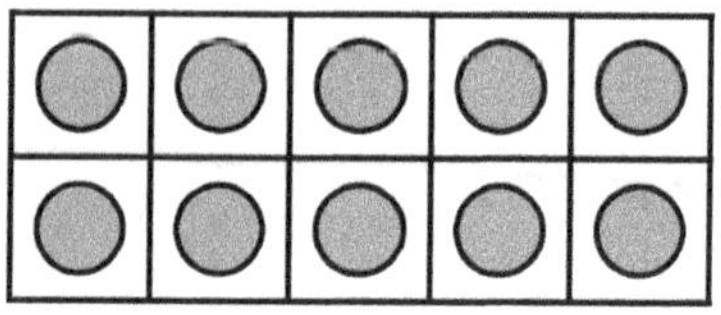

15

3.

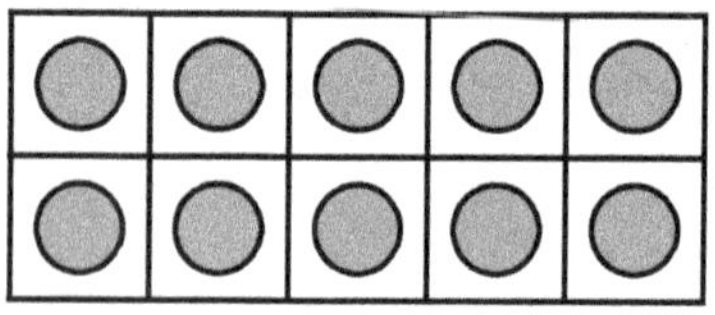

16

4.

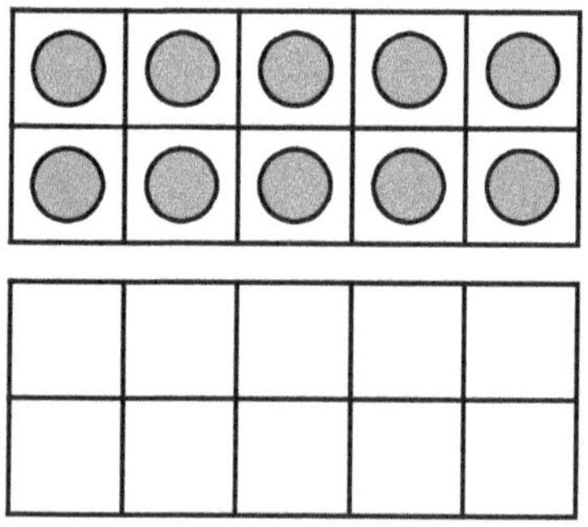

14

5.

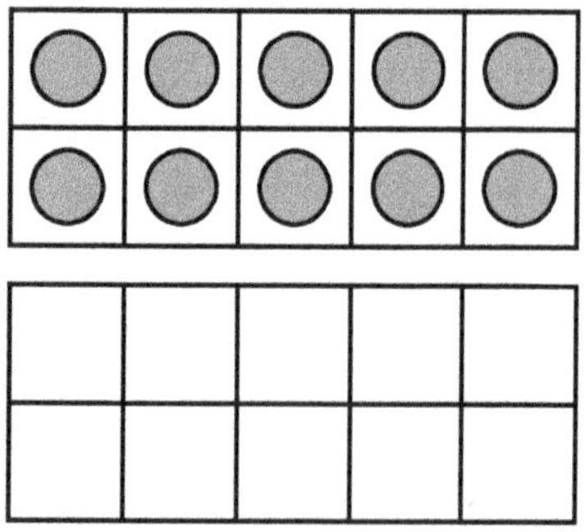

16

6.

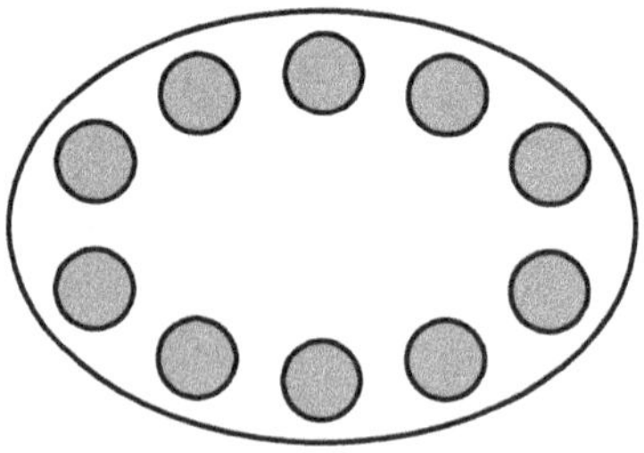

15

# ☐ How many ones?

**7.**

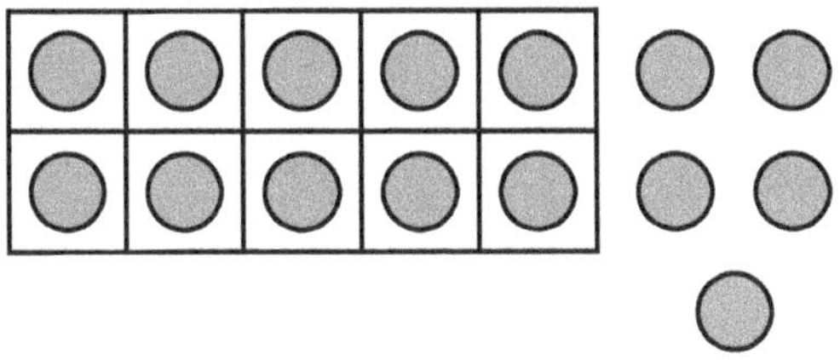

15

10 ☐

**8.**

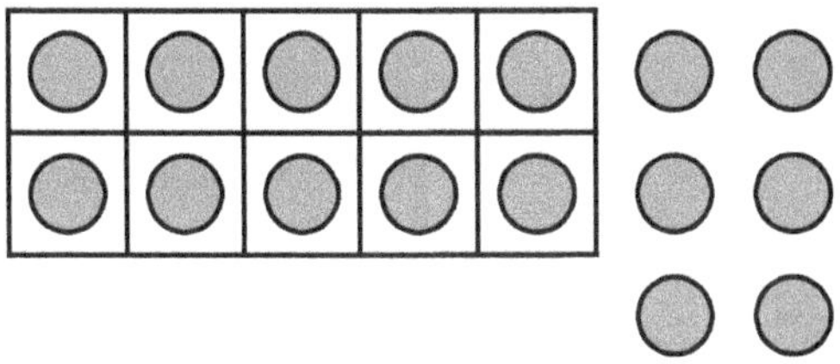

16

10 ☐

**9.**

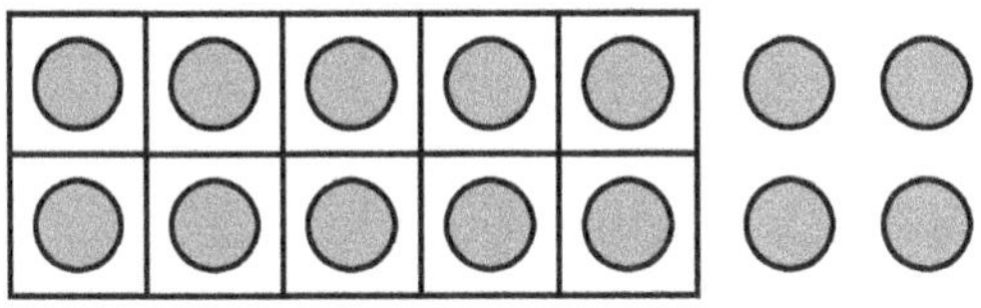

14

10 ☐

**10.**

15

10 ☐

**11.**

16

10 ☐

**12.**

14

10 ☐

☐ Write the ten.

13.

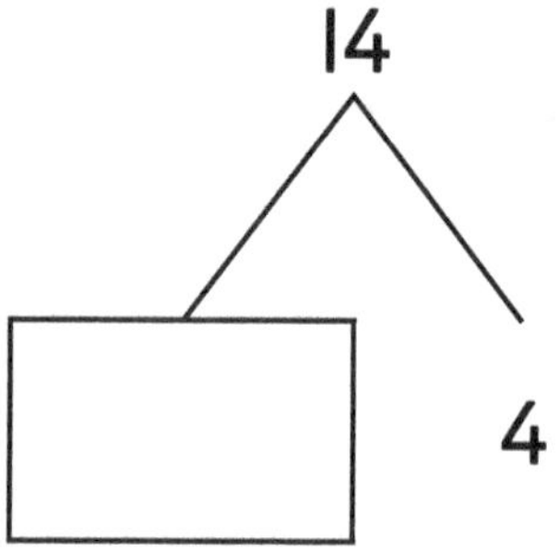


14.

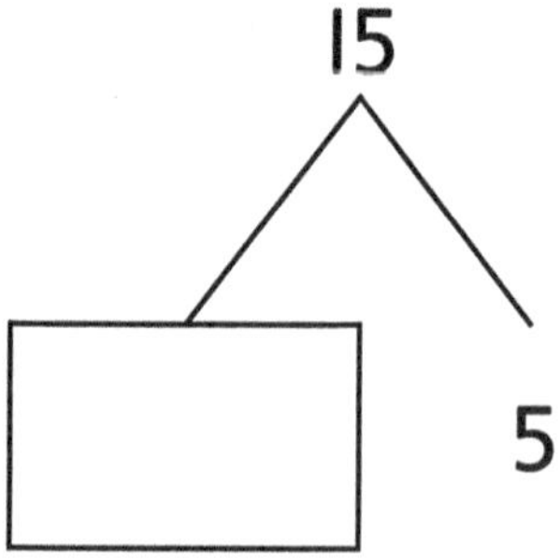


☐ Write the ten.

☐ How many ones?

15.

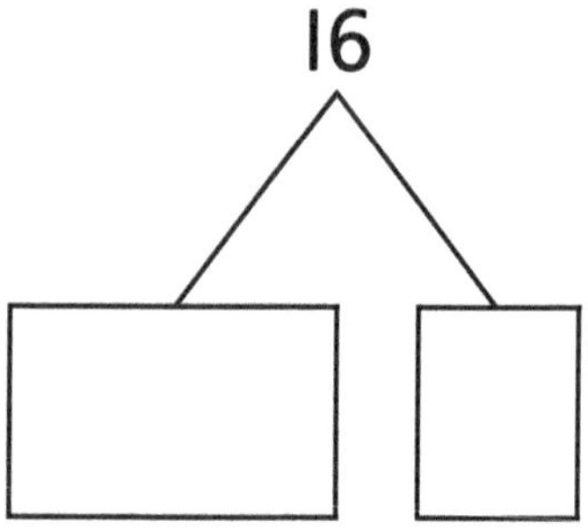


16.

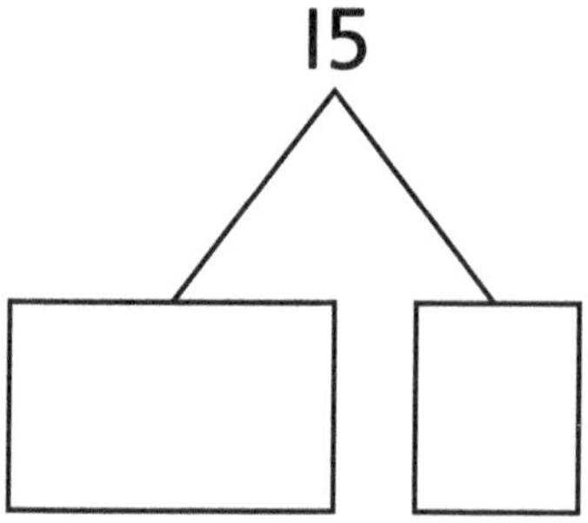


17.

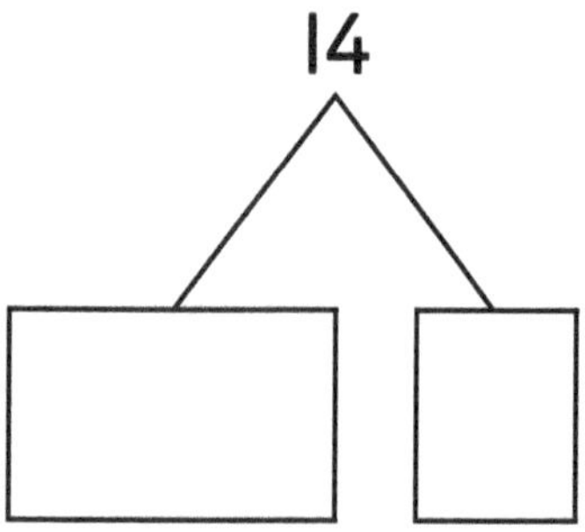


18.

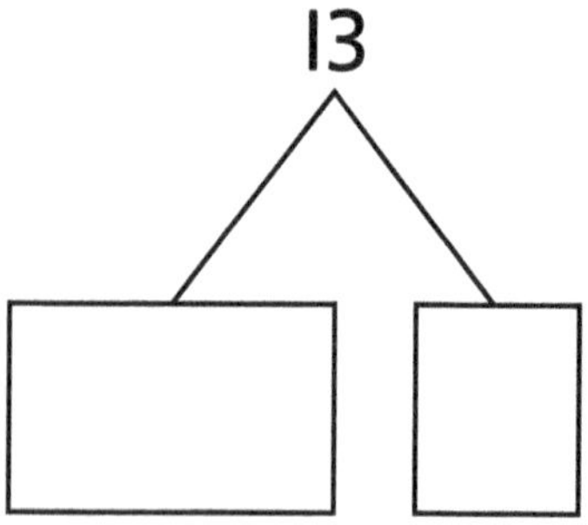

# NBTK-7 Making 14, 15, and 16

☐ Draw ◯ to show the addition.

1.

16 = 10 + 6

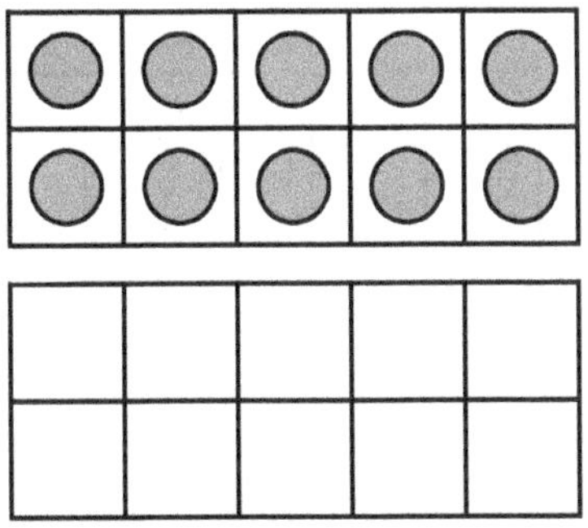

2.

14 = 10 + 4

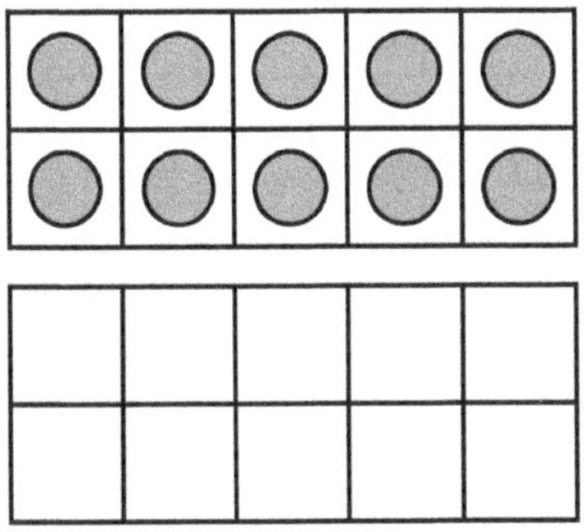

3.

15 = 10 + 5

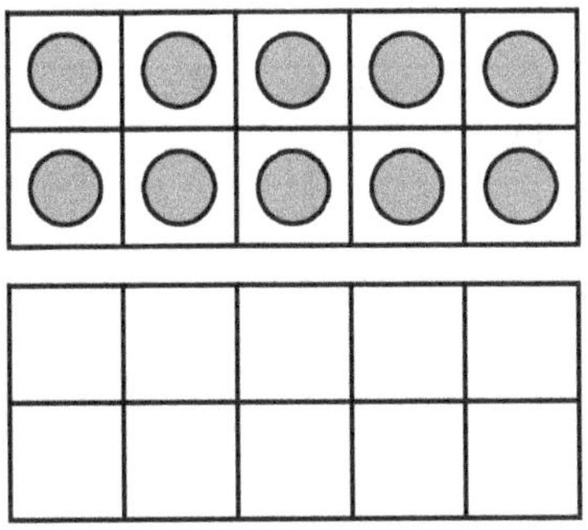

4.

14 = 10 + 4

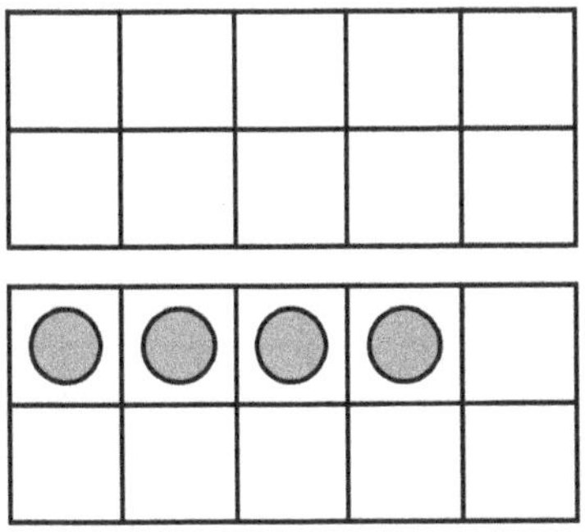

5.

16 = 10 + 6

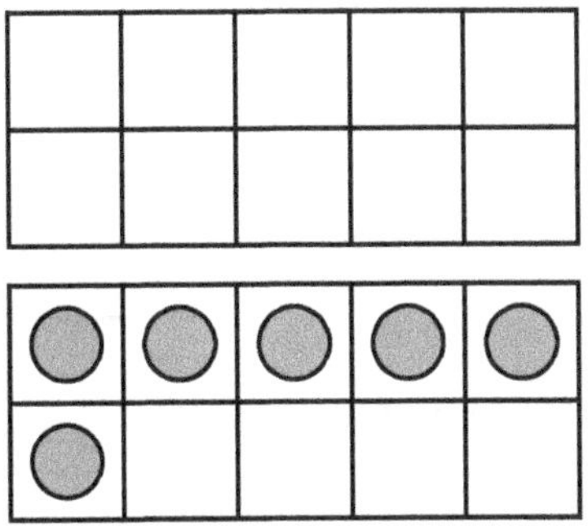

6.

15 = 10 + 5

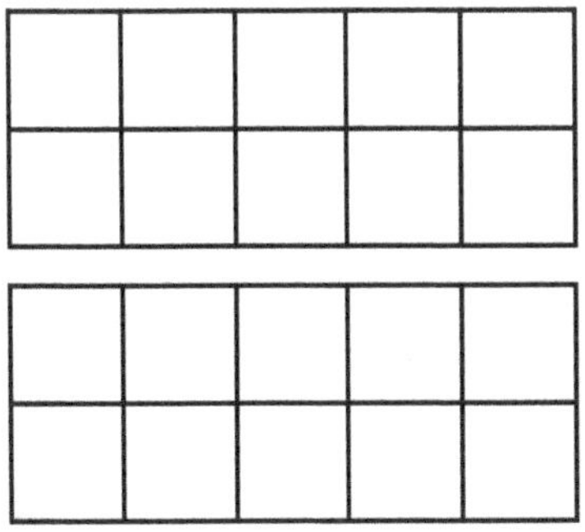

☐ Add.

7.

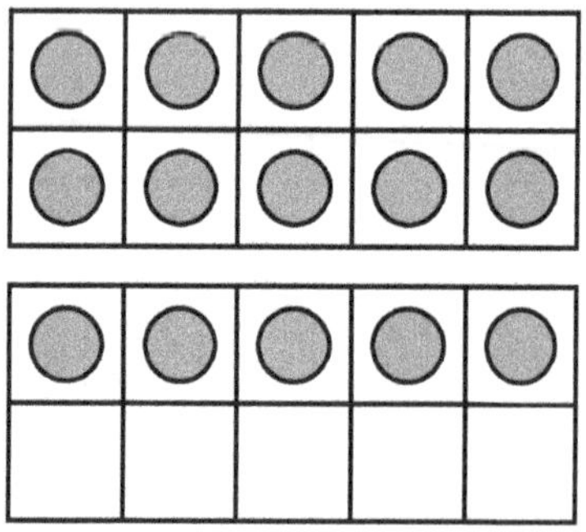

10 + 5 = ☐

8.

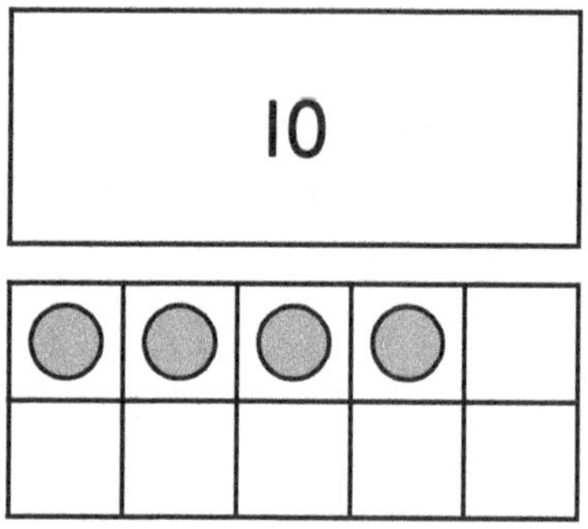

10 + 4 = ☐

9.

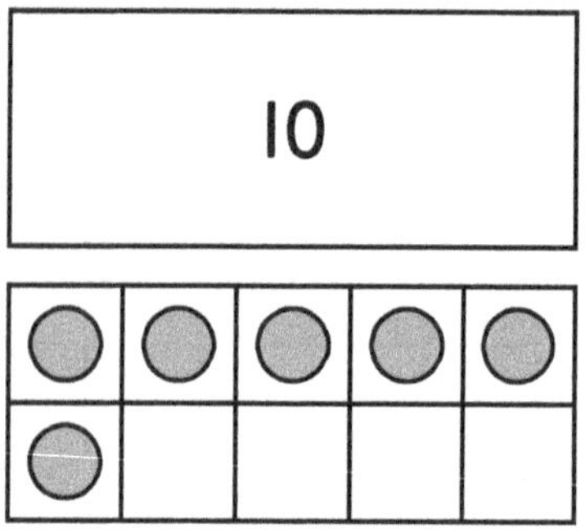

10 + 6 = ☐

10. BONUS

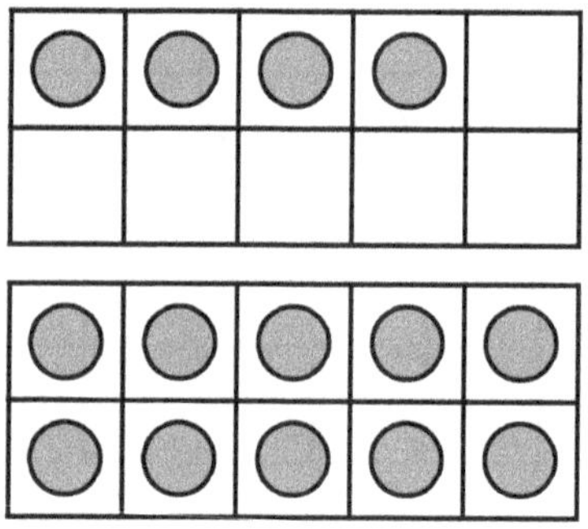

4 + 10 = ☐

11.

10 + 5 = ☐

12.

10 + 6 = ☐

## ☐ What addition do you see?

13.

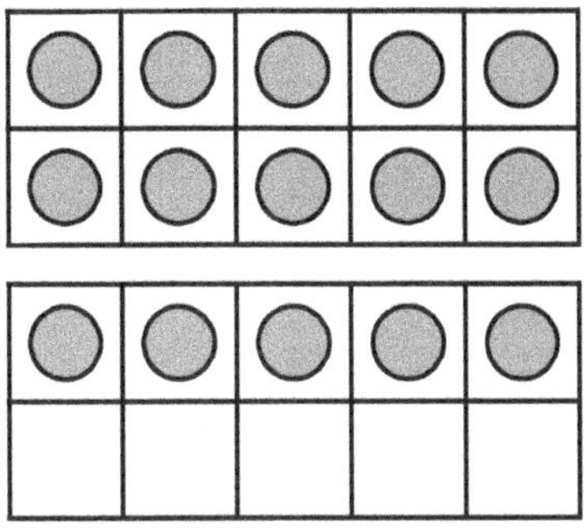

15 = ☐ + ☐

14.

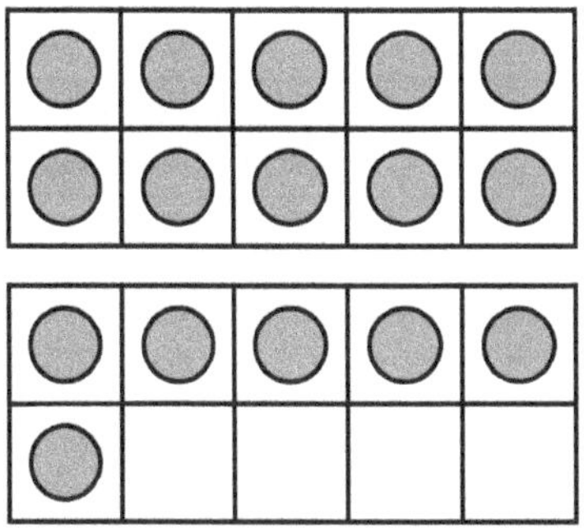

16 = ☐ + ☐

15.

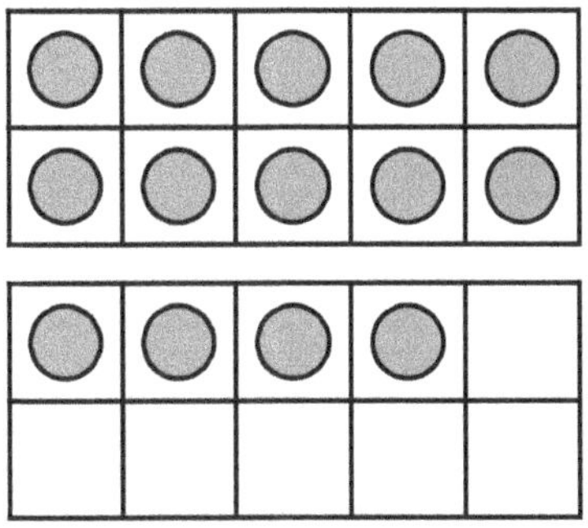

14 = ☐ + ☐

16.

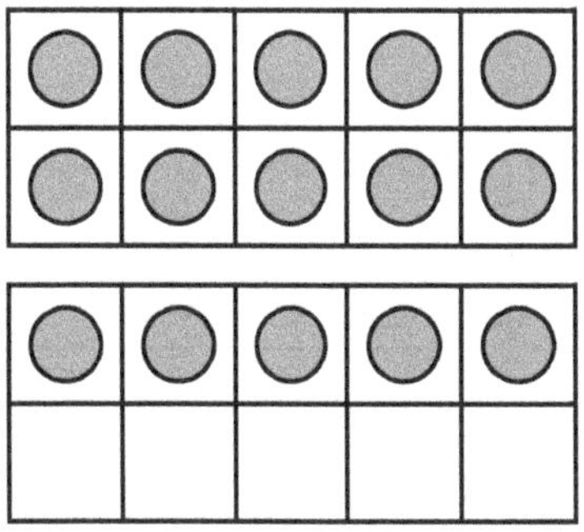

☐ = 10 + ☐

## ☐ Write the addition.

17.

15 = ☐ + ☐

18.

14 = ☐ + ☐

# NBTK-8 The Numbers 17, 18, and 19

☐ How many ●?

1.

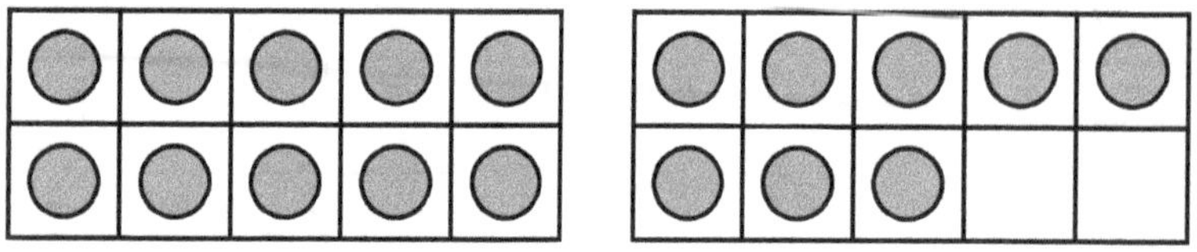

2.

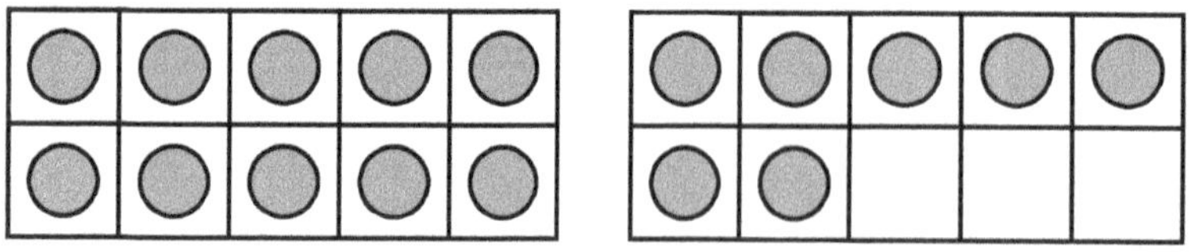

3.

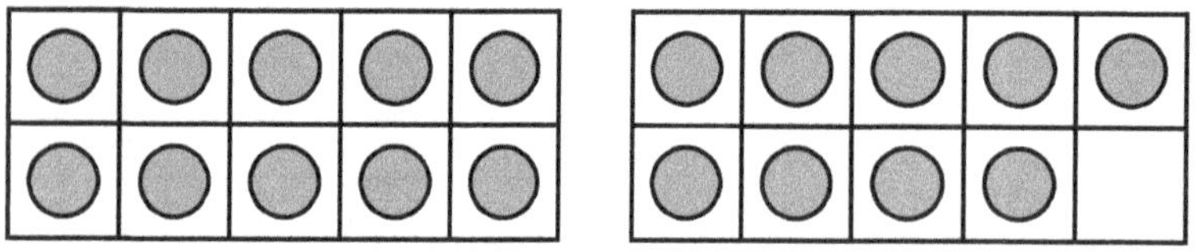

4.

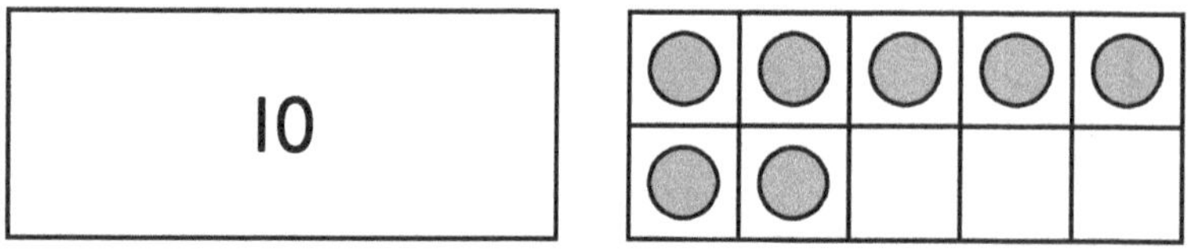


5.

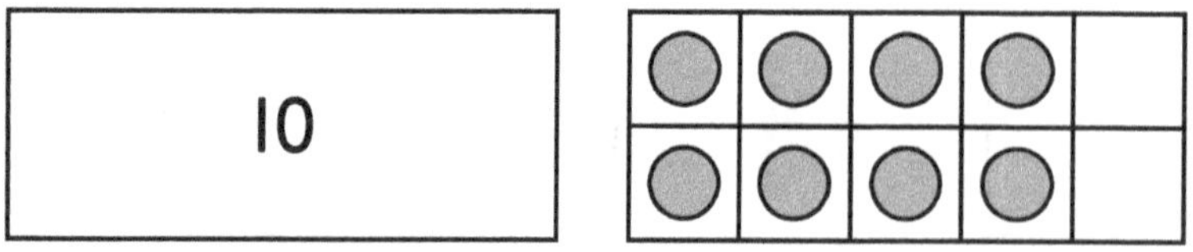

## How many shapes?

6.

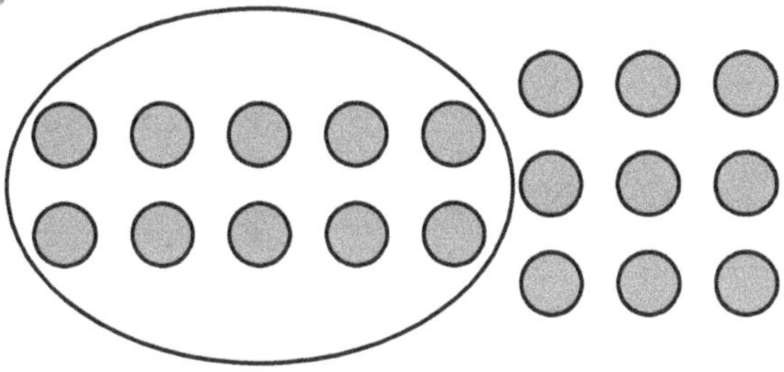

7.

8.

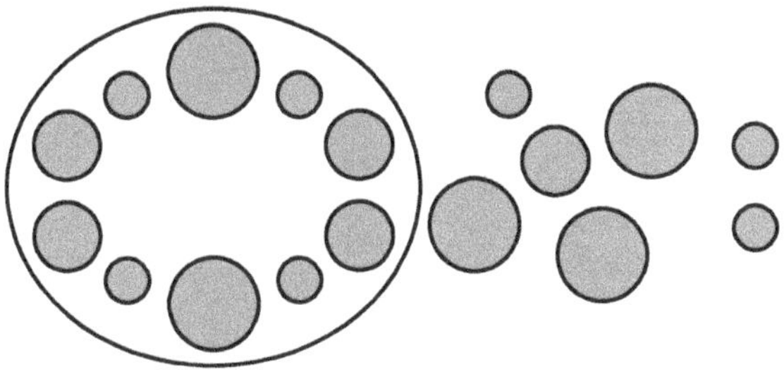

9.

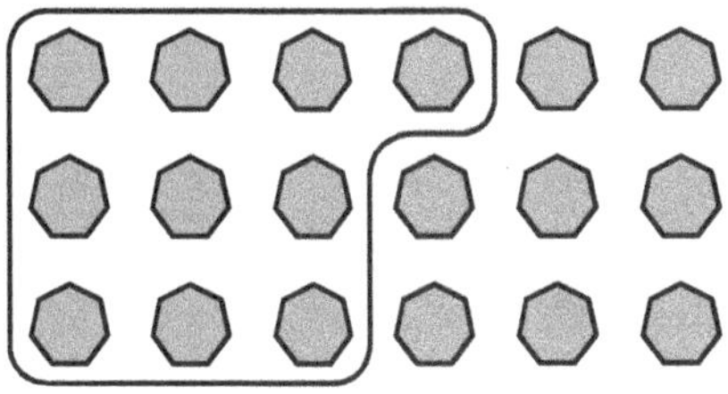

10.

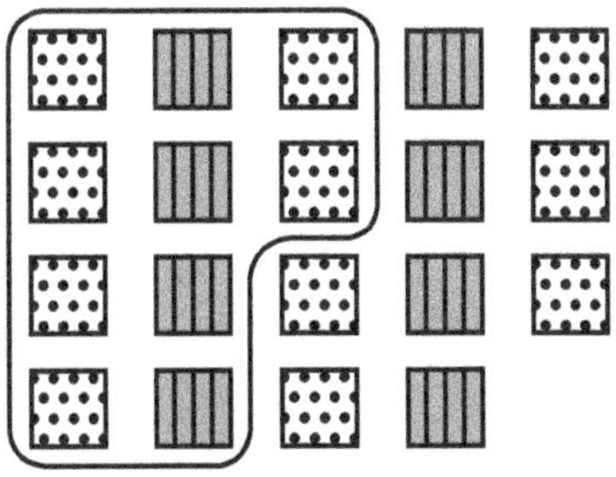

11.

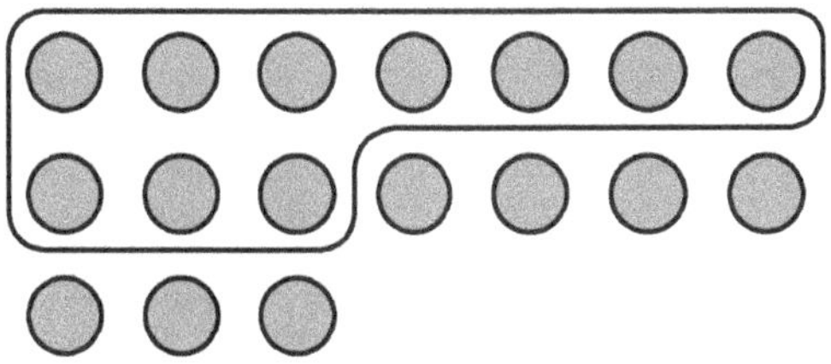

## ☐ How many shapes?

12.

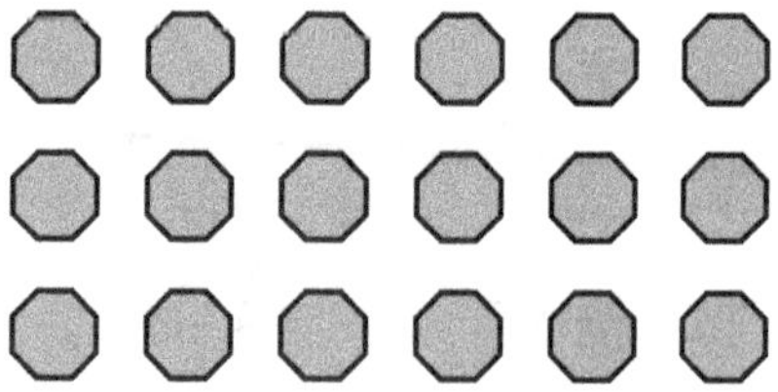

13.

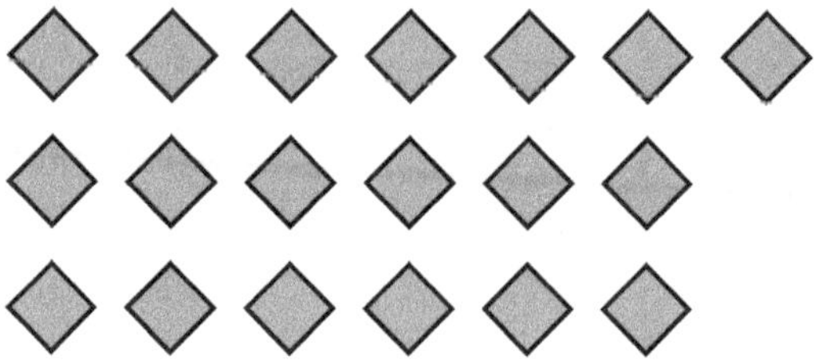

14.

15.

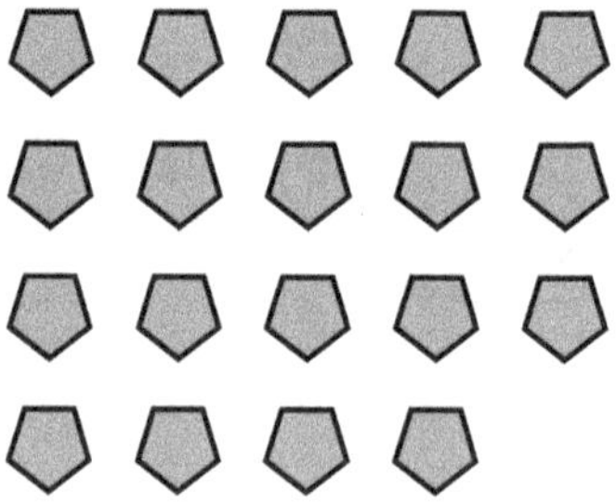

16.

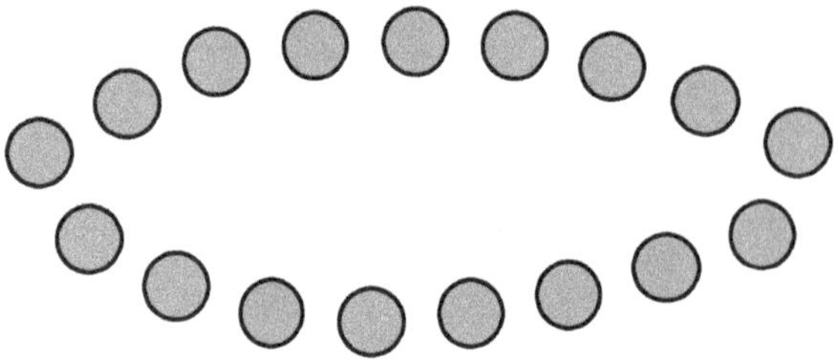

Color the number of shapes.

**17.**

17

**18.**

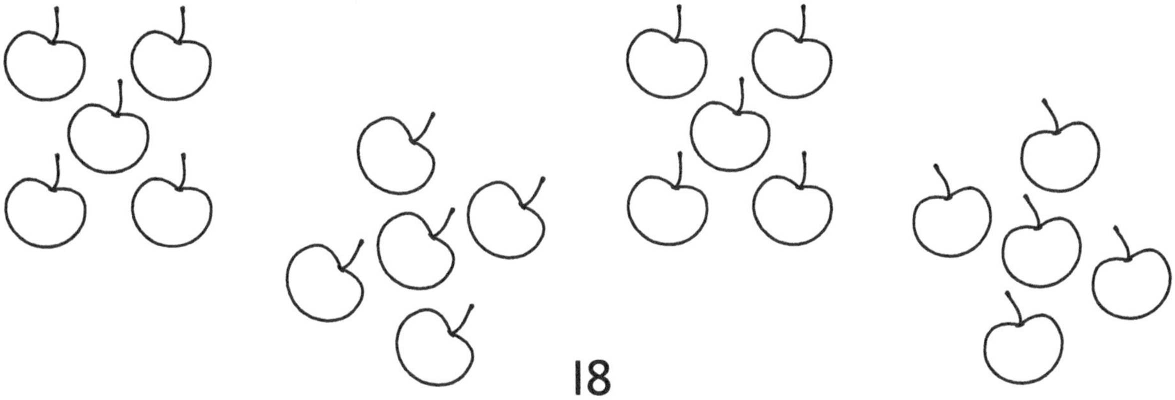

18

**19.**

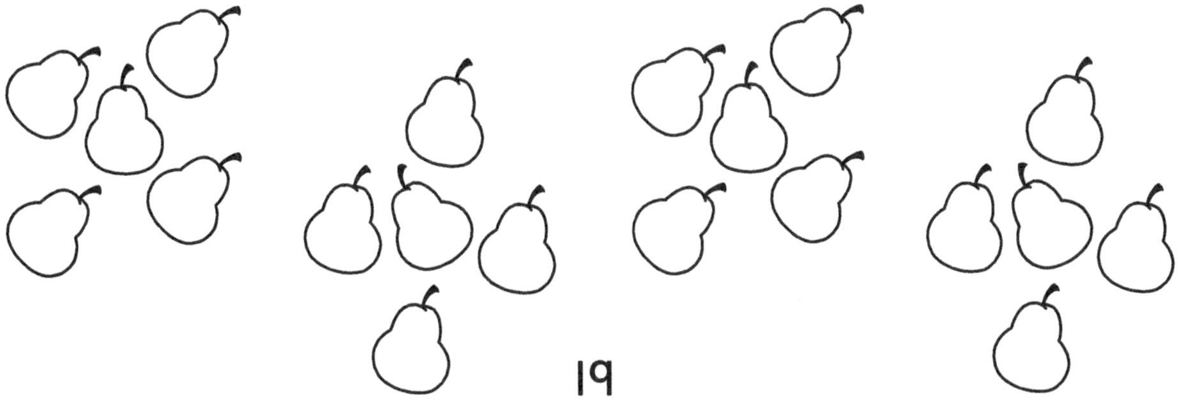

19

# NBTK-9 Taking Apart 17, 18, and 19

☐ Draw ◯ for the ones.

1.

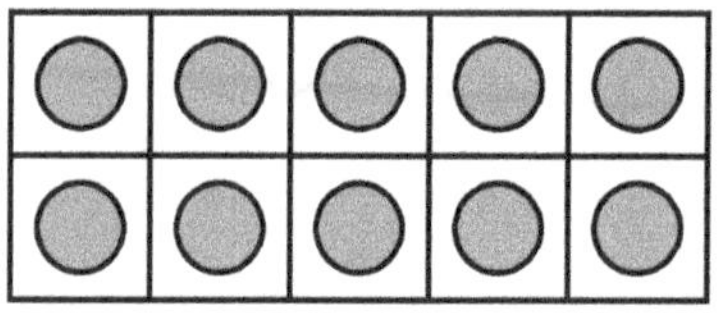

17

2.

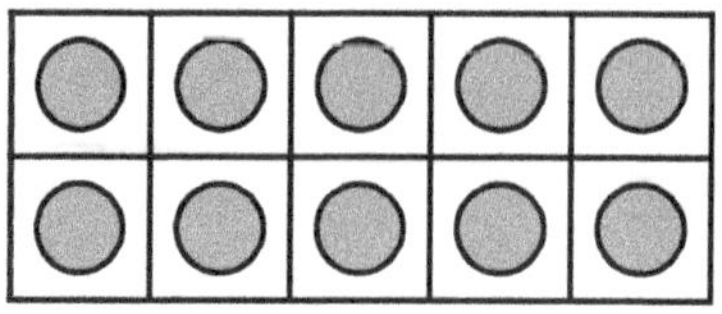

18

3.

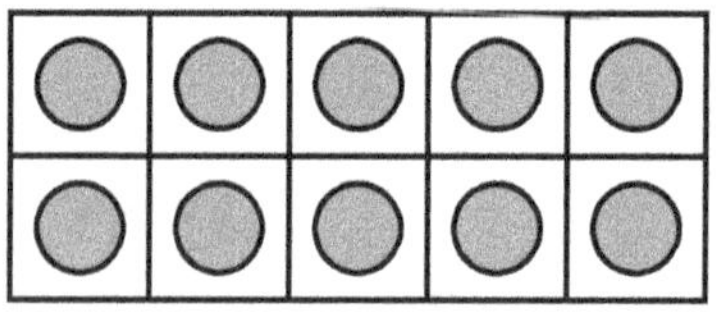

19

4.

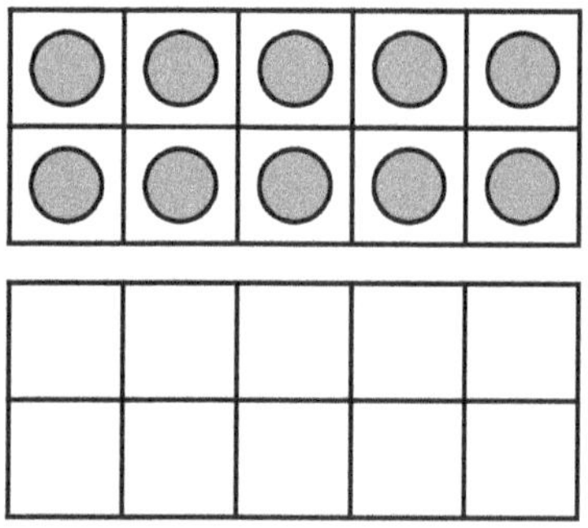

17

5.

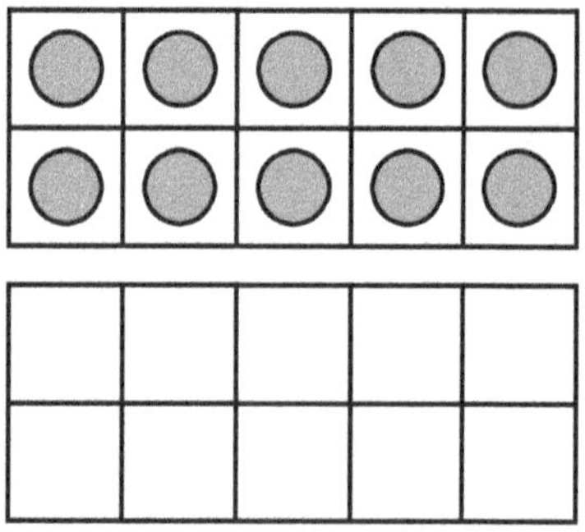

18

6.

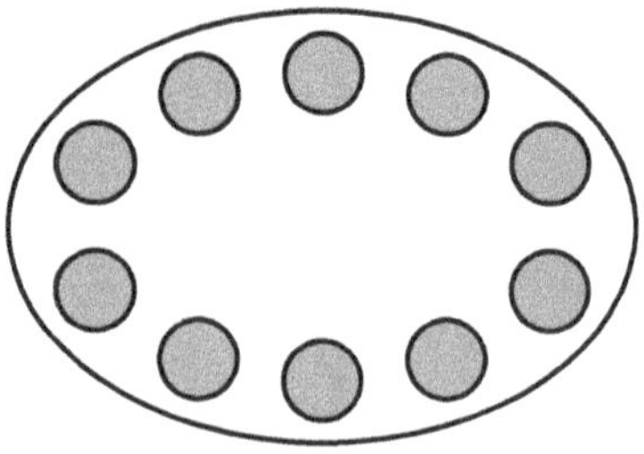

19

☐ How many ones?

7.

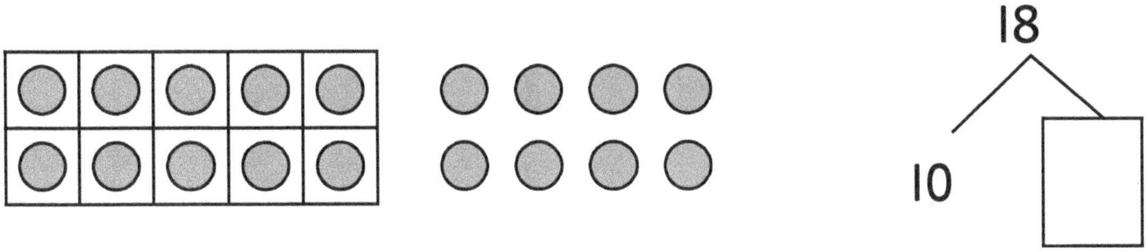


8.

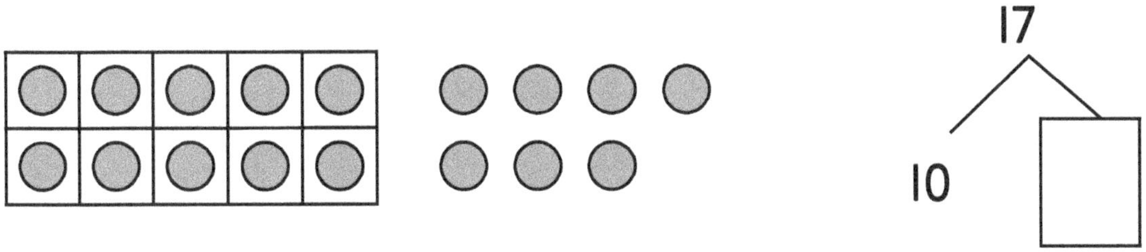


9.

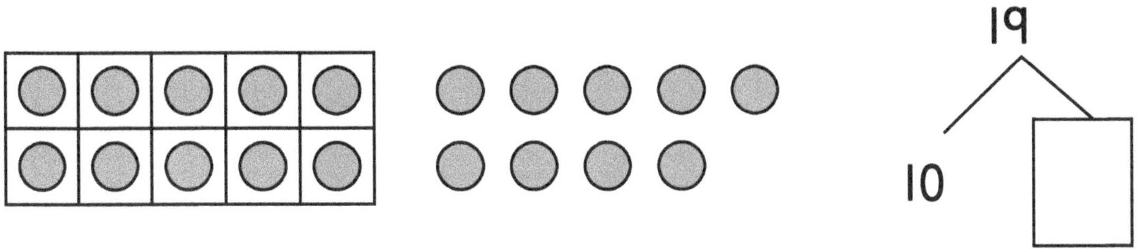


10.

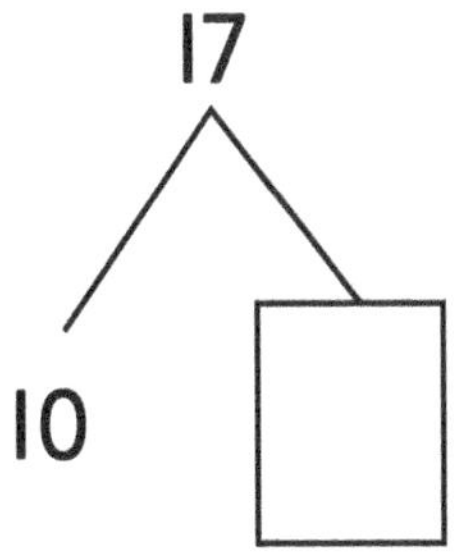


11.

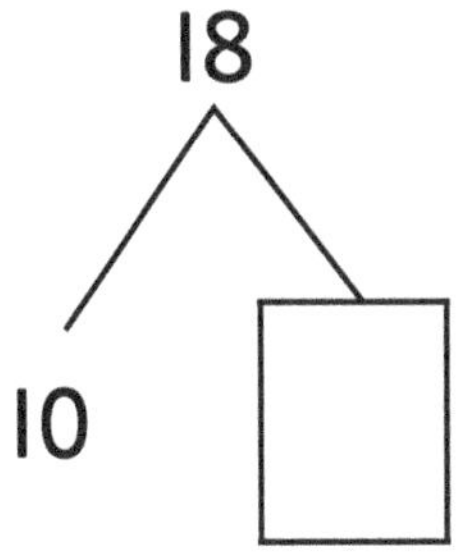


12.

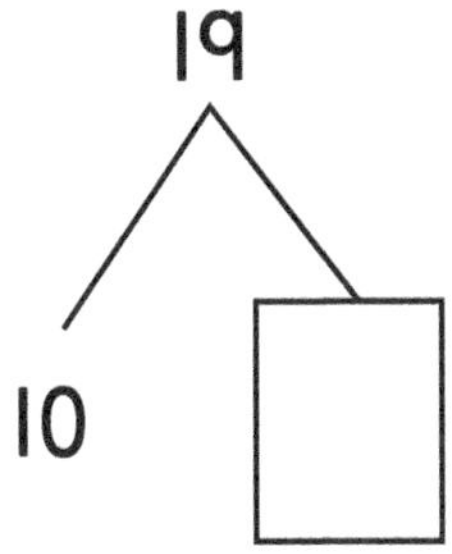

☐ Write the ten.

13.

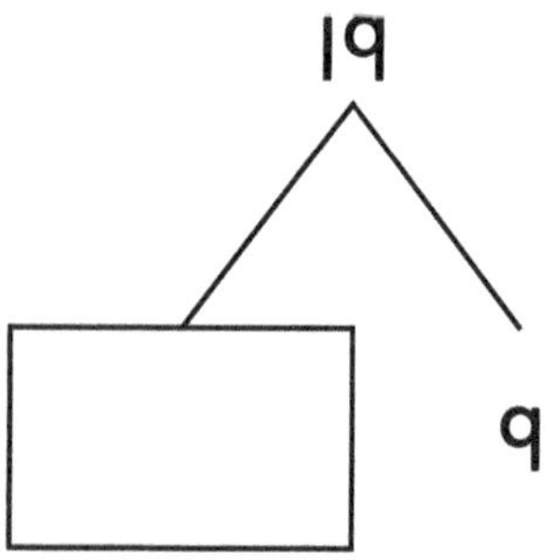


14.

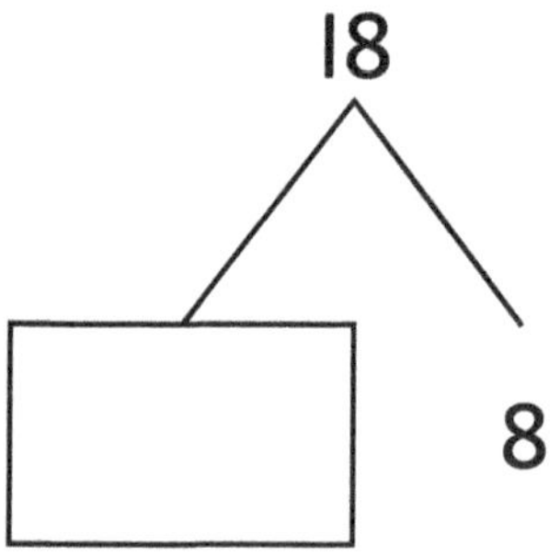


☐ Write the ten.

☐ Write the ones.

15.

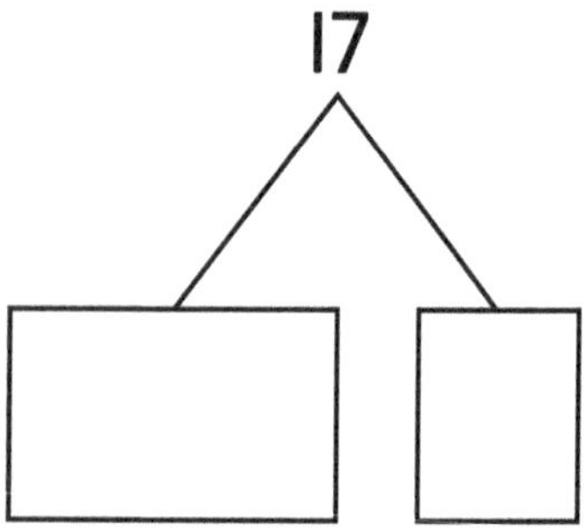


16.

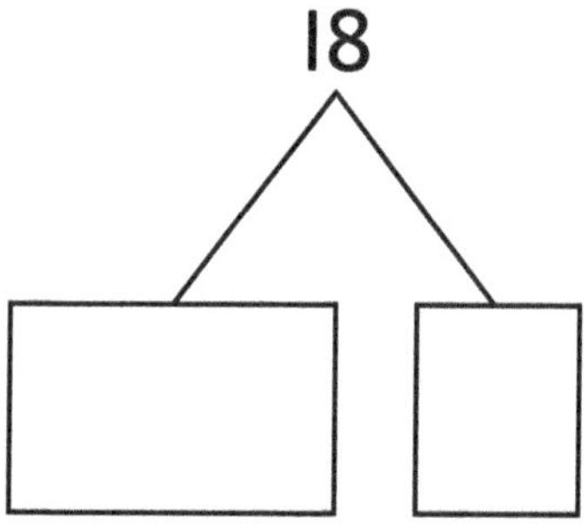


17.

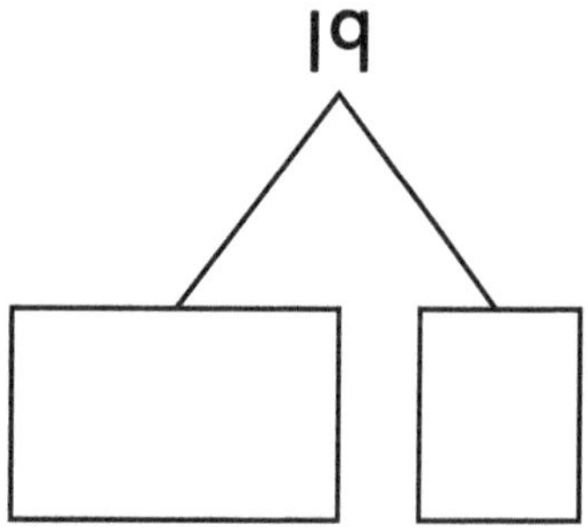


18.

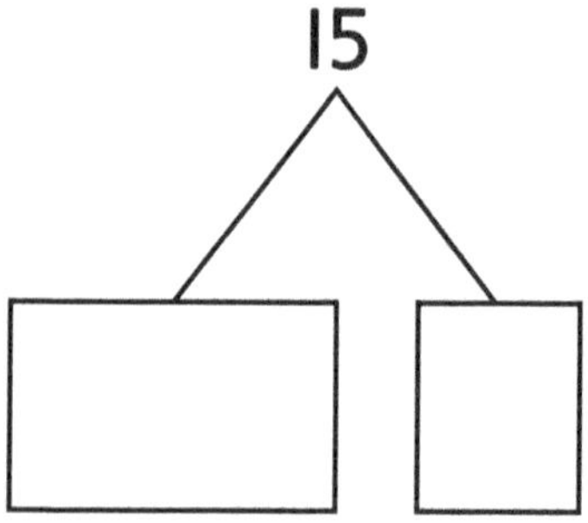

# NBTK-10 Making 17, 18, and 19

☐ Draw ◯ to show the addition.

1.

$17 = 10 + 7$

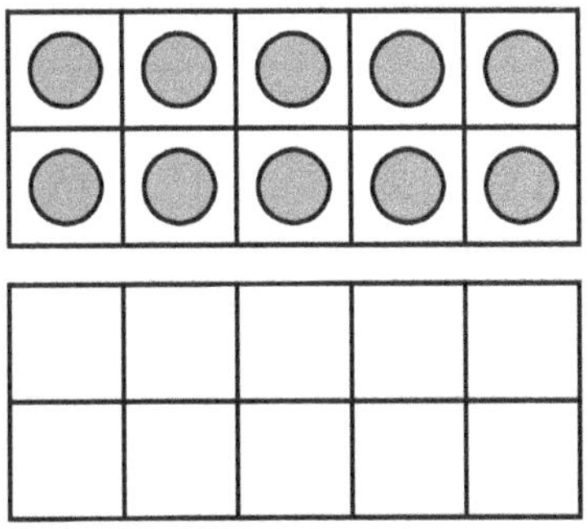

2.

$18 = 10 + 8$

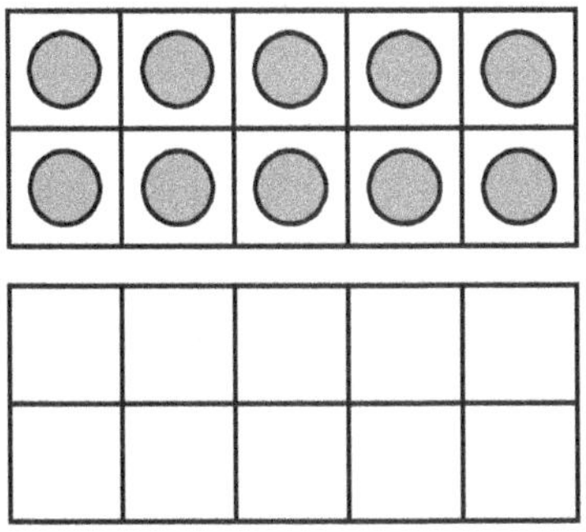

3.

$19 = 10 + 9$

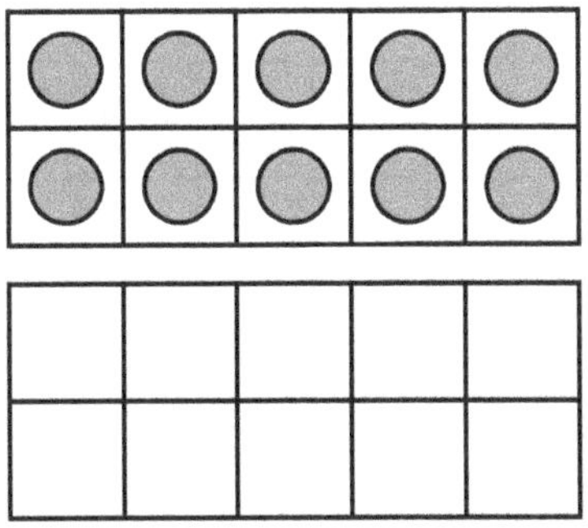

4.

$18 = 10 + 8$

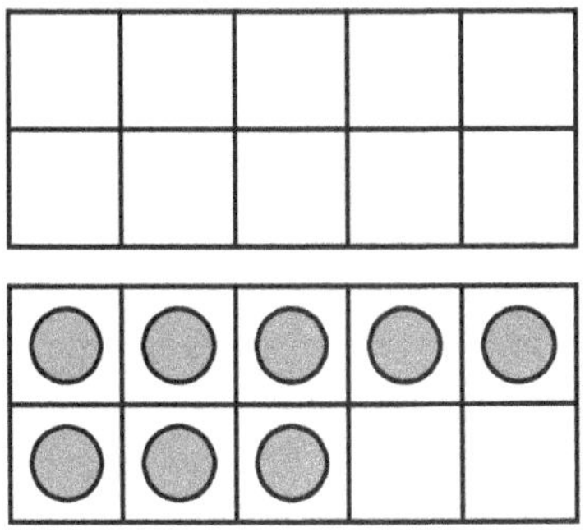

5.

$17 = 10 + 7$

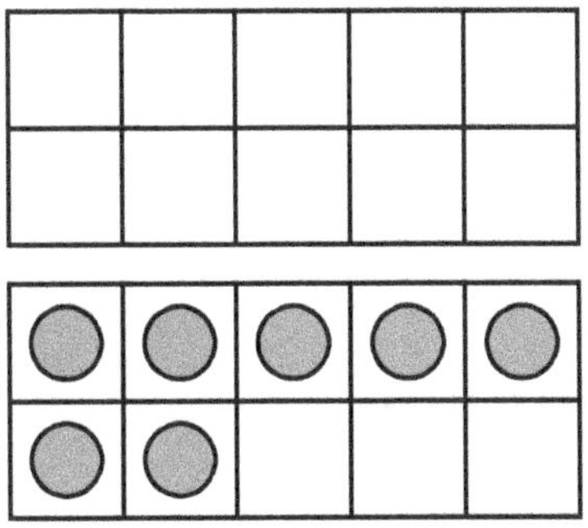

6.

$19 = 10 + 9$

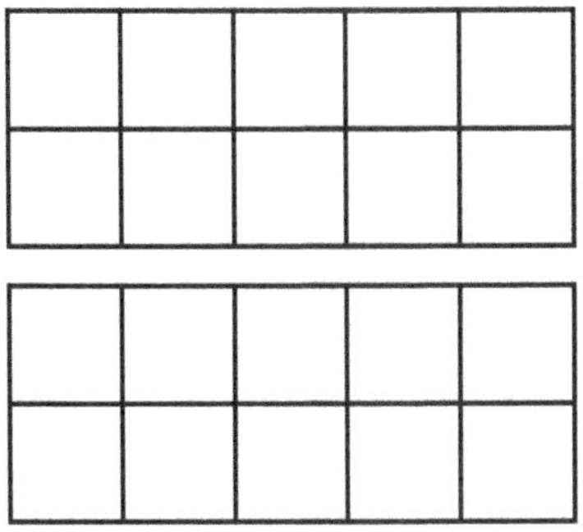

☐ Add.

**7.**

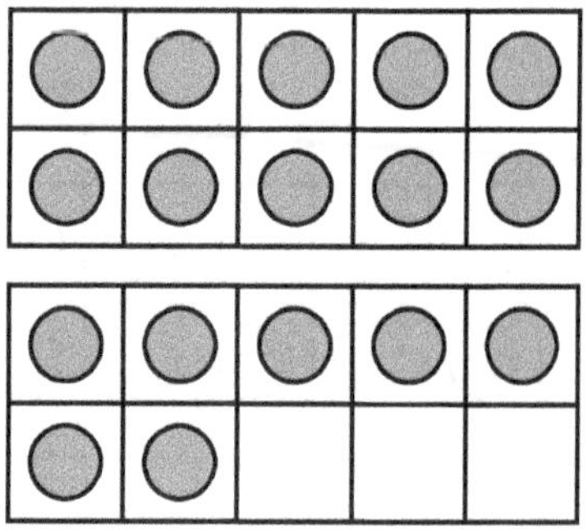

10 + 7 = ☐

**8.**

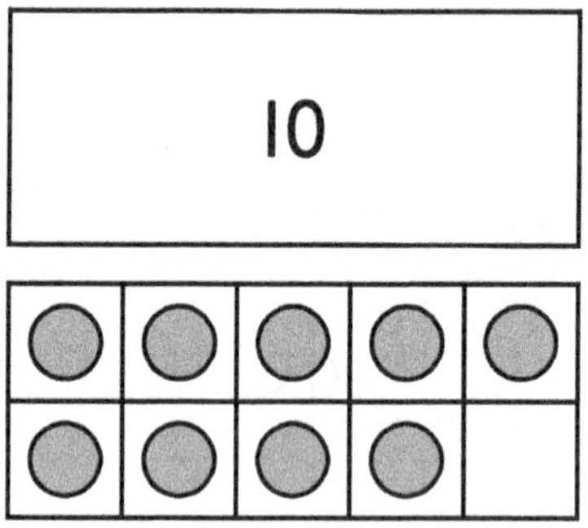


10 + 9 = ☐

**9.**

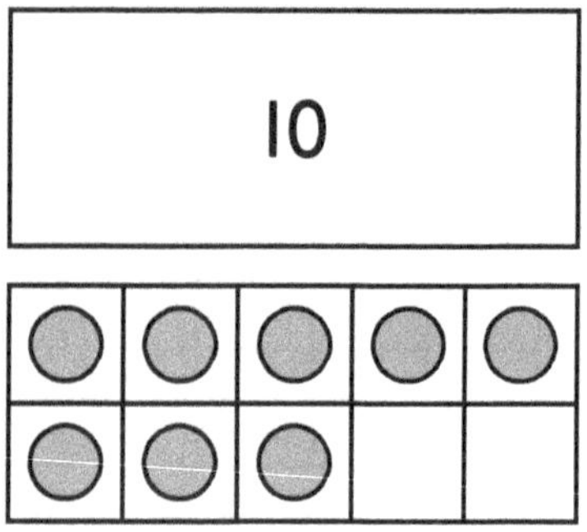


10 + 8 = ☐

**10. BONUS**

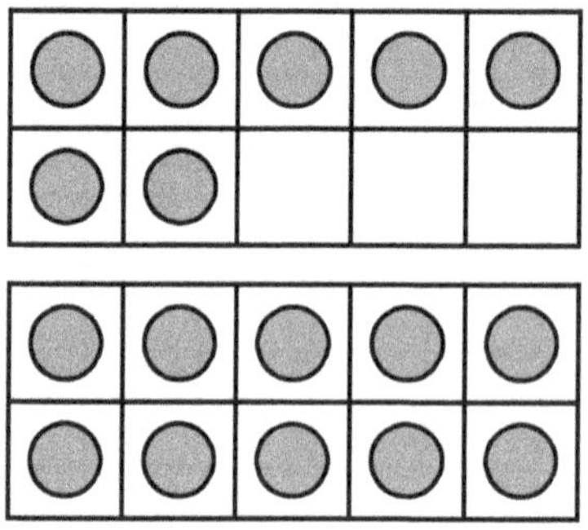

7 + 10 = ☐

**11.**

10 + 8 = ☐

**12.**

10 + 9 = ☐

## ☐ What addition do you see?

**13.**

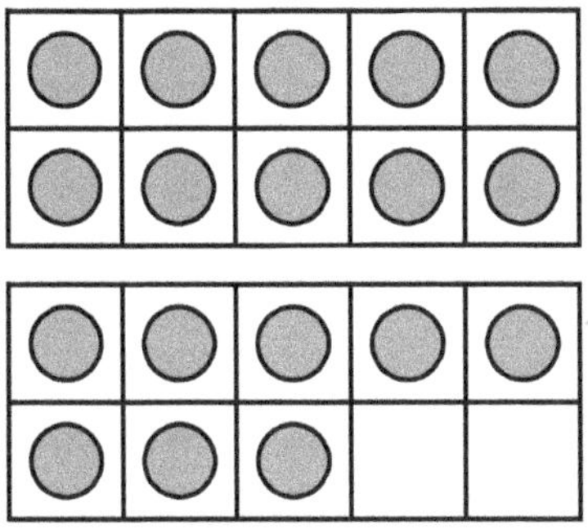

18 = ☐ + ☐

**14.**

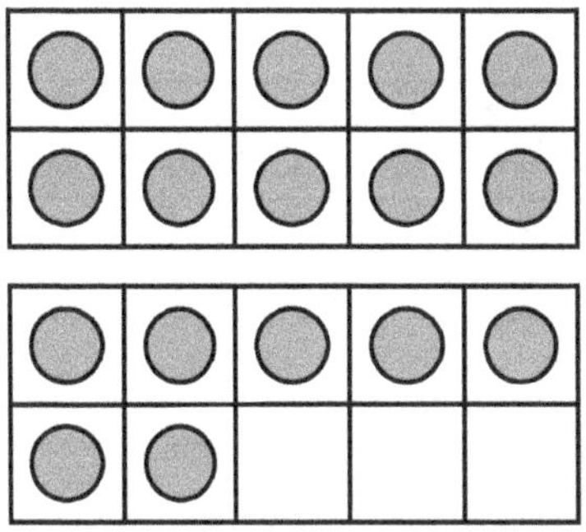

17 = ☐ + ☐

**15.**

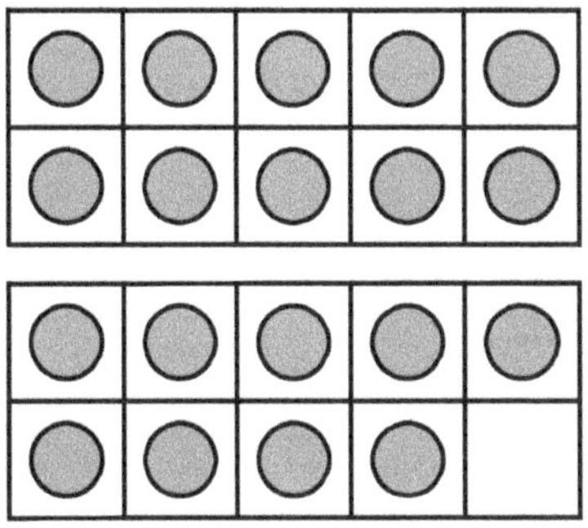

19 = ☐ + ☐

**16.**

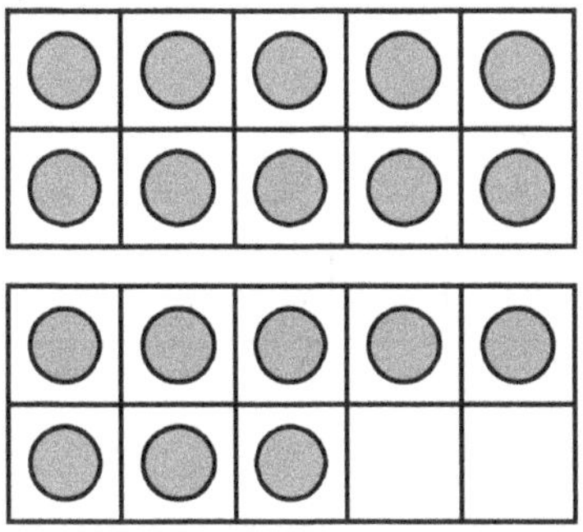

☐ = 10 + ☐

## ☐ Write the addition.

**17.**

17 = ☐ + ☐

**18.**

19 = ☐ + ☐

# The Number 20

How many ?

1.

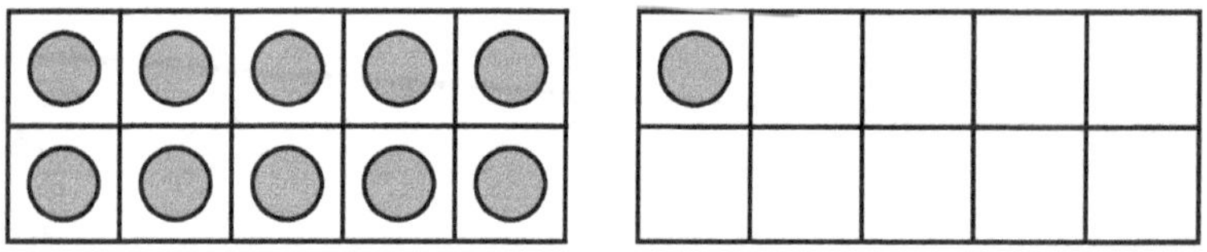

2.

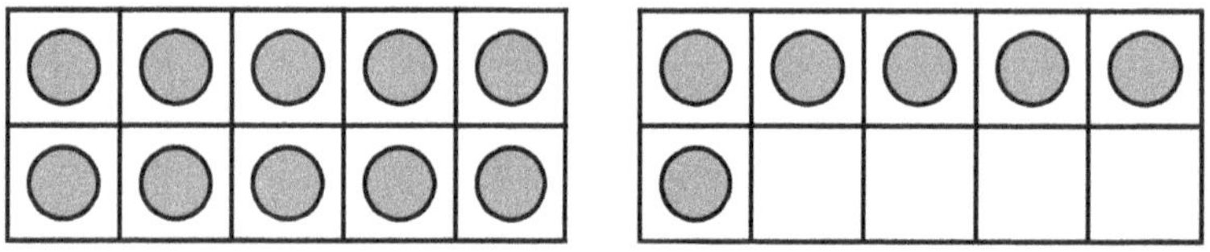

3.

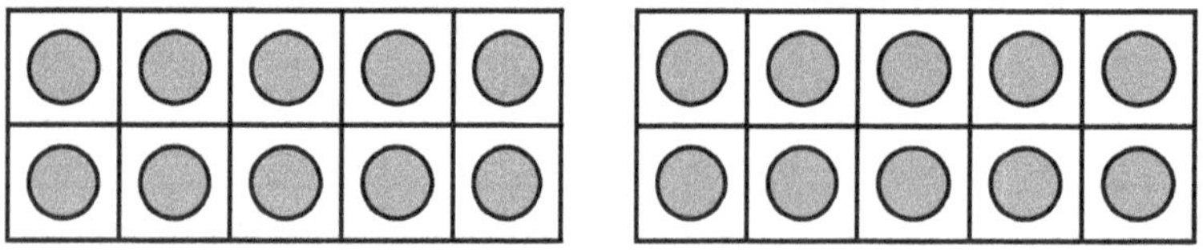

4.

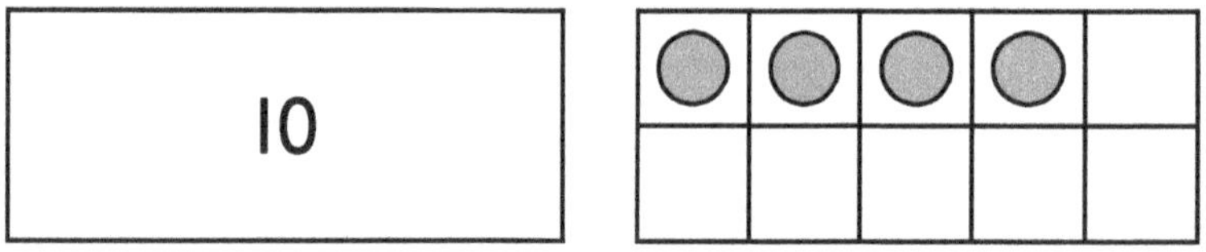


5.

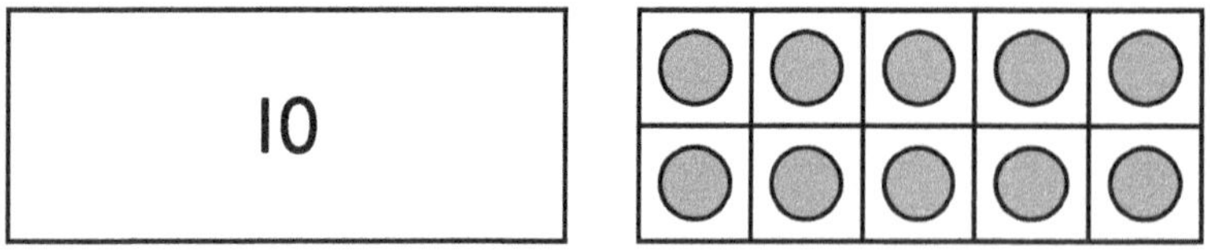

☐ Color the number of shapes.

6.

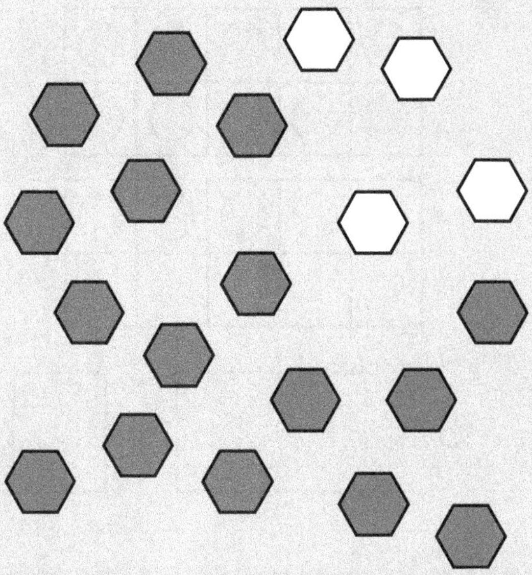

16

7.

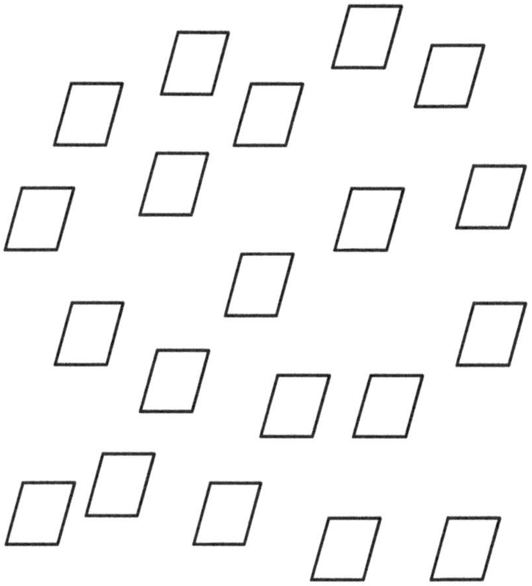

11

8.

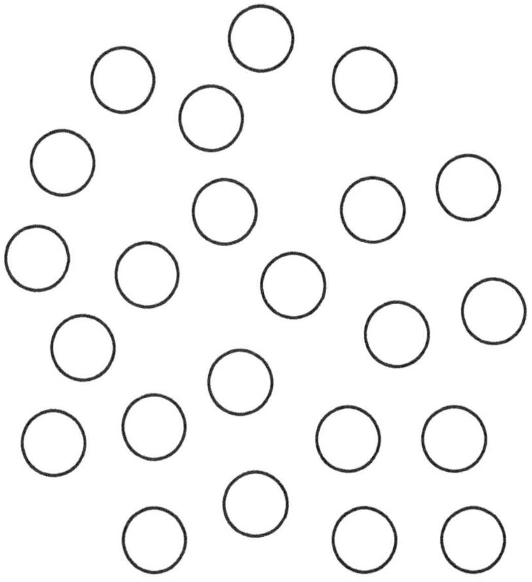

14

9.

20

## ☐ What addition do you see?

**10.**

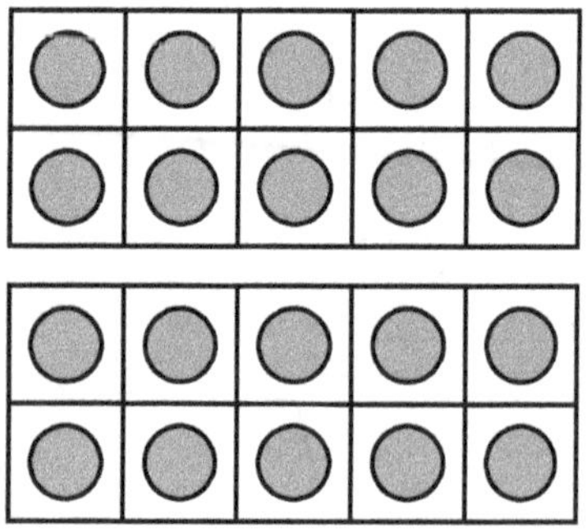

20 = 10 + ☐

**11.**

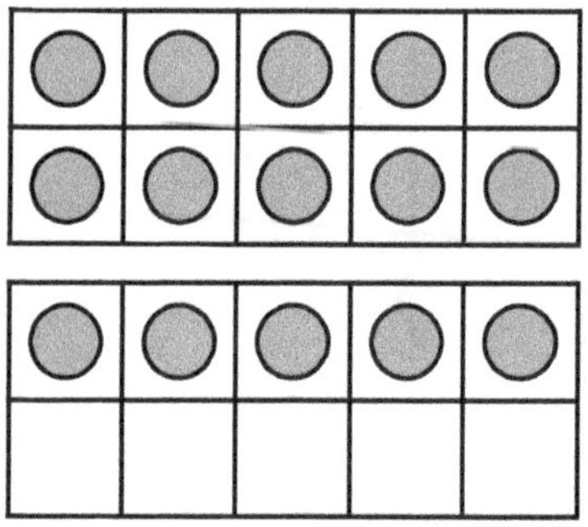

15 = ☐ + ☐

**12.**

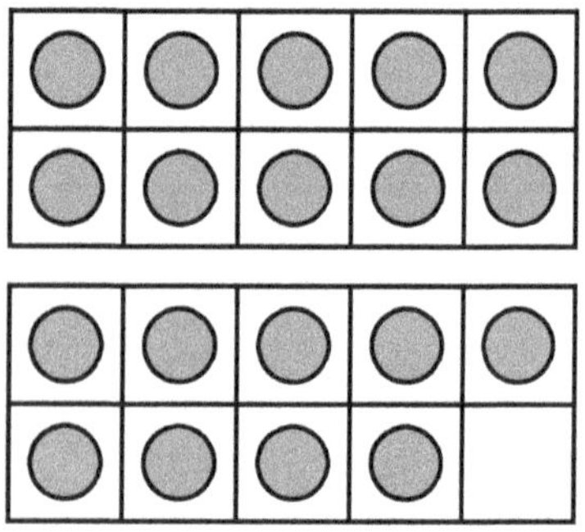

19 = ☐ + ☐

**13.**

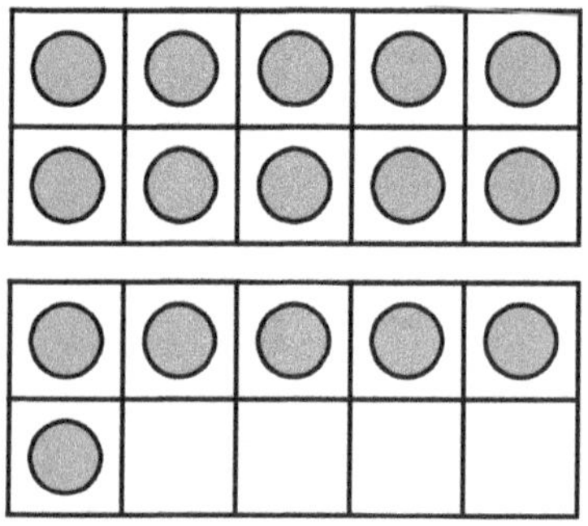

☐ = 10 + ☐

## ☐ Write the addition.

**14.**

20 = ☐ + 10

**15.**

18 = ☐ + ☐

# NBTK-12 Using a Chart to Count to 20

☐ How many ▢ do you see?

1.

| | | | | | | | | | |
|---|---|---|---|---|---|---|---|---|---|
| 1 | 2 | 3 | 4 | 5 | 6 | 7 | 8 | 9 | 10 |
| 11 | 12 | 13 | 14 | 15 | 16 | 17 | 18 | 19 | 20 |

______

2.

| | | | | | | | | | |
|---|---|---|---|---|---|---|---|---|---|
| 1 | 2 | 3 | 4 | 5 | 6 | 7 | 8 | 9 | 10 |
| 11 | 12 | 13 | 14 | 15 | 16 | 17 | 18 | 19 | 20 |

______

3.

| | | | | | | | | | |
|---|---|---|---|---|---|---|---|---|---|
| 1 | 2 | 3 | 4 | 5 | 6 | 7 | 8 | 9 | 10 |
| 11 | 12 | 13 | 14 | 15 | 16 | 17 | 18 | 19 | 20 |

______

☐ Color to show the number.

4.

| | | | | | | | | | |
|---|---|---|---|---|---|---|---|---|---|
| 1 | 2 | 3 | 4 | 5 | 6 | 7 | 8 | 9 | 10 |
| 11 | 12 | 13 | 14 | 15 | 16 | 17 | 18 | 19 | 20 |

5

5.

| | | | | | | | | | |
|---|---|---|---|---|---|---|---|---|---|
| 1 | 2 | 3 | 4 | 5 | 6 | 7 | 8 | 9 | 10 |
| 11 | 12 | 13 | 14 | 15 | 16 | 17 | 18 | 19 | 20 |

11

6.

| | | | | | | | | | |
|---|---|---|---|---|---|---|---|---|---|
| 1 | 2 | 3 | 4 | 5 | 6 | 7 | 8 | 9 | 10 |
| 11 | 12 | 13 | 14 | 15 | 16 | 17 | 18 | 19 | 20 |

20

# OAK-25 Counting by Tens

☐ Count by tens to 50.

1.

10 20 30 40 50

10 20 30 40 50

☐ Count by tens from 60 to 100.

2.

60 70 80 90 100

60 70 80 90 100

☐ Count by tens to 100.

3.

10 20 30 40 50

60 70 80 90 100

☐ How many legs?

4.

10

20

5.

10

# OAK-26 Acting Out Subtraction

☐ How many children stay?

1.

4 children

1 leaves

______ stay

2.

5 children

3 leave

______ stay

☐ How many 🍎 left?

**3.**

3 apples

1 eaten

______ apples left

**4.**

5 apples

2 eaten

______ apples left

☐ How many  left?

**5.**

4 bananas 2 eaten

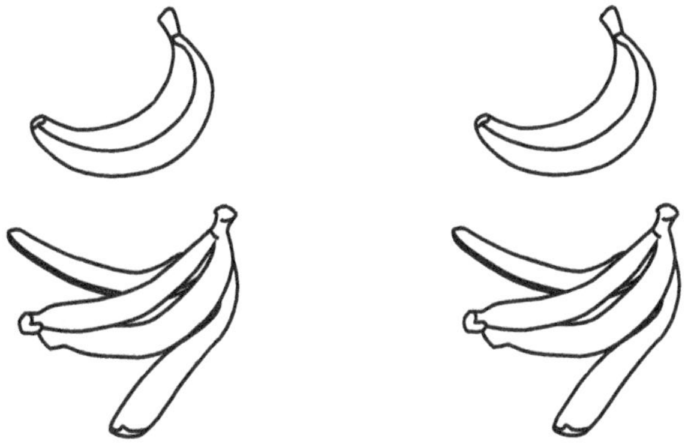

bananas left

**6.**

5 bananas 1 eaten

bananas left

# OAK-27 Subtracting with Objects (I)

Use blocks.

- ☐ Show on the log.
- ☐ Show how many hop off.
- ☐ How many stay?

**1.**

5 sit on a log. I hops off.

☐ stay.

**2.**

5 sit on a log. 2 hop off.

☐ stay.

Use blocks.

- ☐ Show on the log.
- ☐ Show how many hop off.
- ☐ How many stay?

**3.**

5 sit on a log. 4 hop off.

5 minus 4 = ☐

**4.**

5 sit on a log. 3 hop off.

5 minus 3 = ☐

Use blocks.

- ☐ Show on the log.
- ☐ Take away .
- ☐ How many stay?

**5.**

4 sit on a log. I hops off.

4 minus I = ☐

**6.**

3 sit on a log. 2 hop off.

3 minus 2 = ☐

Use blocks.

- [ ] Show on the log.
- [ ] Take away .
- [ ] How many stay?

**7.**

2 sit on a log. I leaves.

2 minus I = ☐

**8.**

4 sit on a log. 3 leave.

4 minus 3 = ☐

# OAK-28 Subtracting with Objects (2)

Use blocks.

- ☐ Show 🍎 in the bowl.
- ☐ Take away 🍎.
- ☐ How many are left?

**1.**

3 🍎 in a bowl

1 🍎 eaten

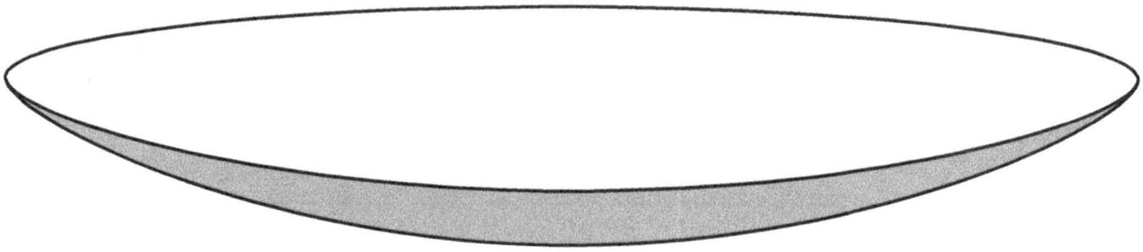

3 🍎 minus 1 🍎 = ☐ 🍎

**2.**

4 🍎 in a bowl

2 🍎 eaten

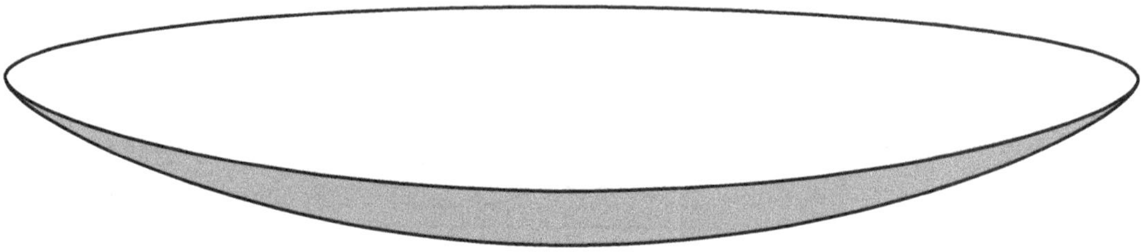

4 🍎 − 2 🍎 = ☐ 🍎

Use blocks.

- [ ] Show .
- [ ] Take away .
- [ ] How many stay?

**3.**

5  play.

1  hops away.

5  − 1  = ☐ 

**4.**

5  play.

3  hop away.

5  − 3  = ☐ 

☐ Use blocks to show .

☐ How many  stay?

**5.**

5  minus 2 

= ☐ 

**6.**

5  − 4 

= ☐ 

☐ Use blocks to show .

☐ How many  stay?

**7.**

4  – 1 

= □ 

**8.**

2  – 1 

= □ 

# OAK-29 Subtracting with Pictures

☐ How many  stay?

**1.**

5  play. 3  hop away.

5  − 3  = ☐ 

**2.**

4  play. 1  hops away.

4  − 1  = ☐ 

☐ Cross out ○.

☐ How many stay?

**3.**

5 play.

2 hop away.

5 − 2 =

**4.**

3 play.

1 hops away.

3 − 1 =

☐ Cross out ○.

☐ How many stay?

**5.**

4 play. 3 hop away.

4 − 3 = ☐

**6.**

5 play. 1 hops away.

5 − 1 = ☐

☐ Draw ◯.

☐ Cross out ◯.

☐ How many stay?

**7.**

3 play. 2 hop away.

3 − 2 = ☐

**8.**

5 play. 4 hop away.

5 − 4 = ☐

# OAK-30 Subtraction Expressions

☐ Write the subtraction.

**1.**

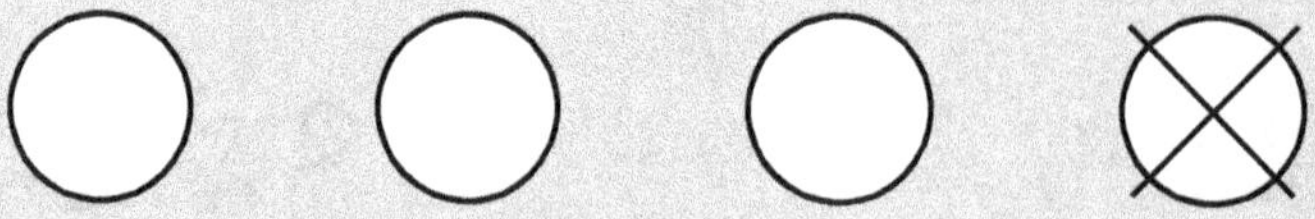

4 – 1

**2.**

5 – ______

**3.**

3 – ______

☐ Cross out ○ to show the subtraction.

4.

4 – 3

5.

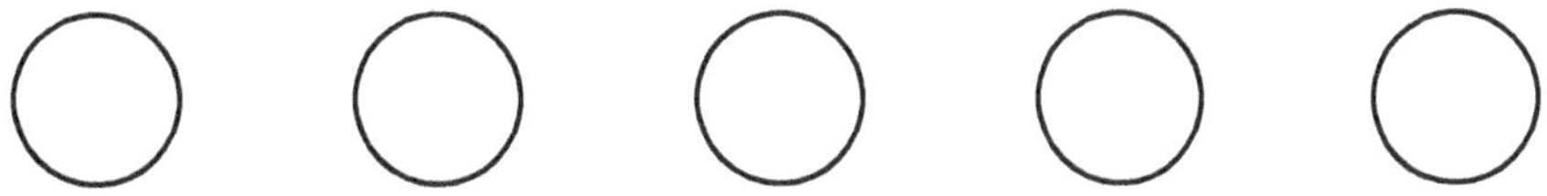

5 – 2

6.

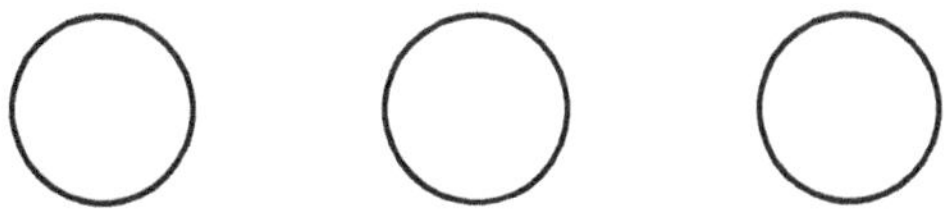

3 – 1

☐ Show the subtraction.

7.

2 − 1

8.

4 − 2

9.

5 − 4

# OAK-31 Subtracting

☐ Draw a picture to subtract.

1.

4 − 1 = ______

2.

5 − 2 = ______

3.

2 − 1 = ______

☐ Subtract.

4.

$5 - 3 =$ ______

5.

$3 - 2 =$ ______

6.

$4 - 3 =$ ______

☐ Subtract.

7.

$3 - 1 =$ ______

8.

$5 - 4 =$ ______

9.

$4 - 2 =$ ______

# OAK-32 Writing Subtractions

☐ Write the subtraction.

**1.**

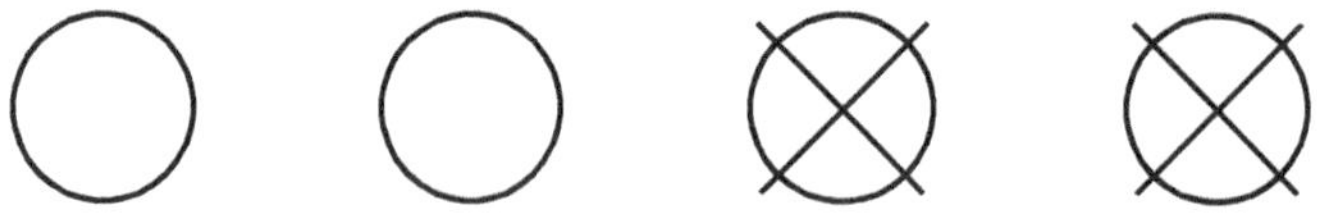

4 − __2__ = ____

**2.**

5 − ____ = ____

**3.**

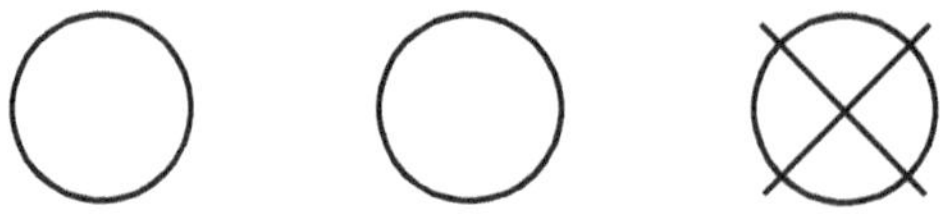

3 − ____ = ____

☐ Write the subtraction.

4.

4 – ____ = ____

5.

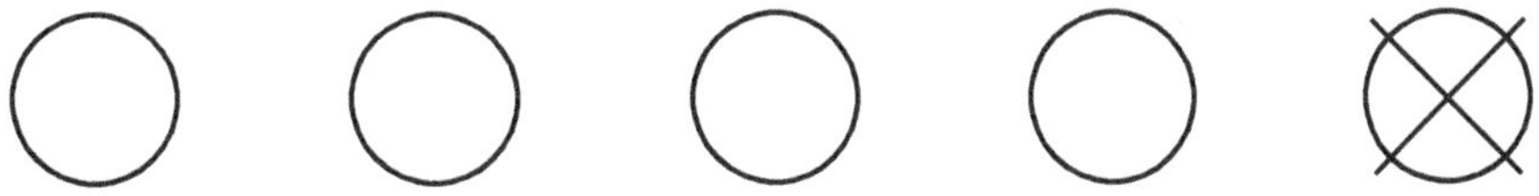

____ – ____ = ____

6.

____ – ____ = ____

# OAK-33 Composing 5

☐ How many more make 5?

1.

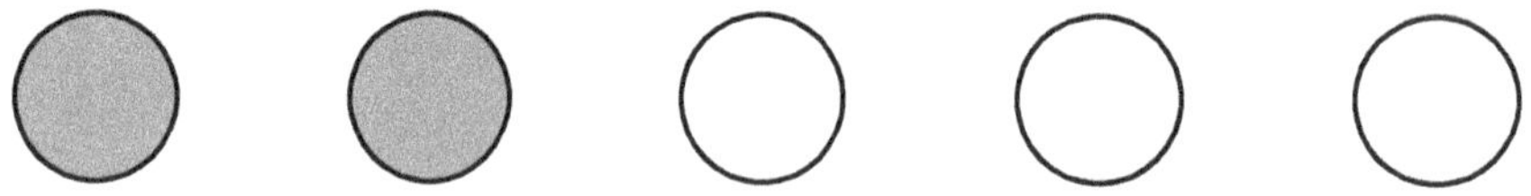

2 + _____ = 5

2.

3 + _____ = 5

3.

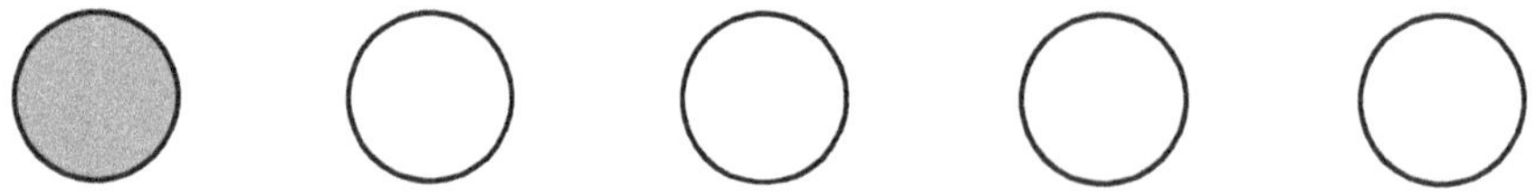

1 + _____ = 5

How many more make 5?

□ Color ○ to find out.

**4.**

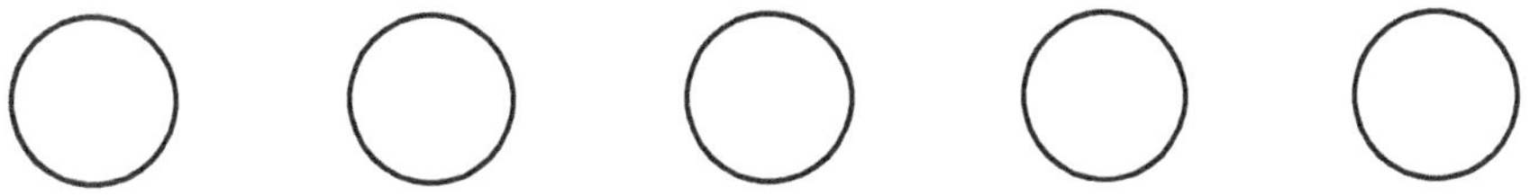

4 + ______ = 5

**5.**

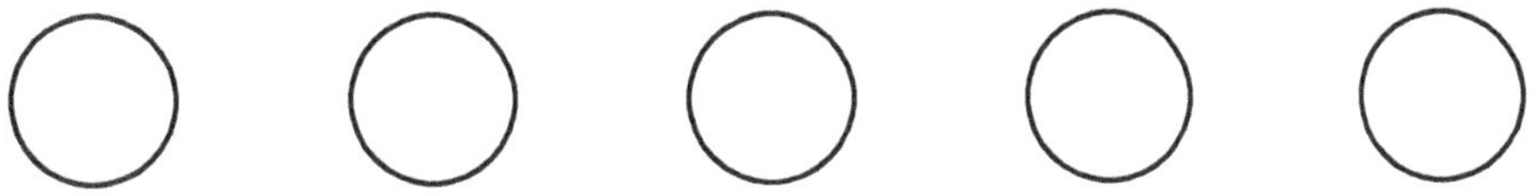

1 + ______ = 5

**6.**

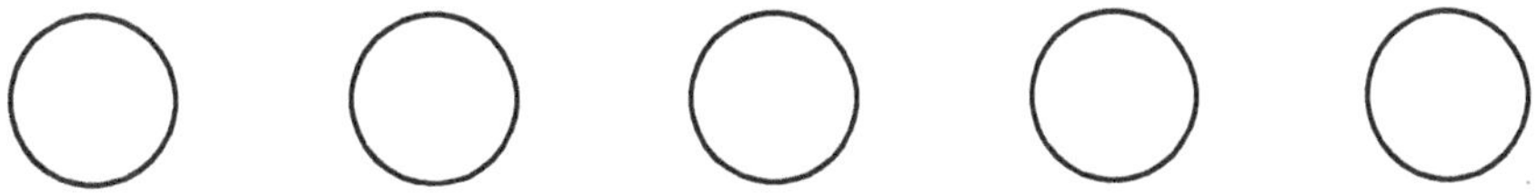

3 + ______ = 5

# OAK-34 Counting On to 50

☐ Count on to 25.

**1.**

1 2 3 4 5

6 7 8 9 10

11 12 13 14 15

16 17 18 19 20

21 22 23 24 25

Count on to 50.

2.

26 27 28 29 30

31 32 33 34 35

36 37 38 39 40

41 42 43 44 45

46 47 48 49 50

# OAK-35 Acting Out Subtraction within 10

☐ How many  left?

**1.**

9 apples

2 eaten

________ apples left

**2.**

10 apples

4 eaten

________ apples left

☐ How many  left?

3.

8 bananas

1 eaten

_____ bananas left

4.

7 bananas

2 eaten

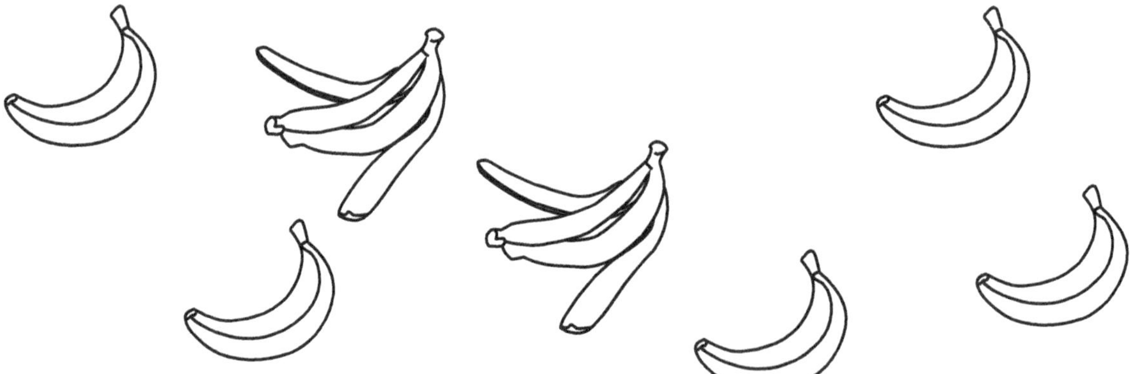

_____ bananas left

# OAK-36 Subtracting from 10 with Objects

Use blocks.

- ☐ Show  in the frame.
- ☐ Show how many  hop off.
- ☐ How many stay?

**1.**

10  sit on a log.

3  hop off.

| | | | | |
|---|---|---|---|---|
| | | | | |
| | | | | |

______  stay.

**2.**

10  sit on a log.

2  hop off.

| | | | | |
|---|---|---|---|---|
| | | | | |
| | | | | |

______  stay.

Use blocks.

- [ ] Show  in the frame.
- [ ] Show how many  hop off.
- [ ] How many stay?

**3.**

| | | | | |
|---|---|---|---|---|
| | | | | |

10  − 4  = ______ 

**4.**

| | | | | |
|---|---|---|---|---|
| | | | | |

10  − 6  = ______ 

Use blocks.

- ☐ Show  in the frame.
- ☐ Show how many  hop off.
- ☐ How many stay?

**5.**

| | | | | |
|---|---|---|---|---|
| | | | | |

10  − 7  = ______ 

**6.**

| | | | | |
|---|---|---|---|---|
| | | | | |

10  − 5  = ______ 

# OAK-37 Subtracting within 10 with Objects

Use blocks.

- ☐ Show 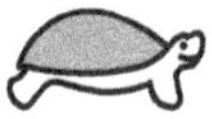 in the frame.
- ☐ Show how many 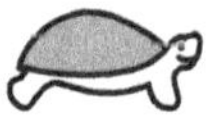 swim away.
- ☐ How many are left?

**1.**

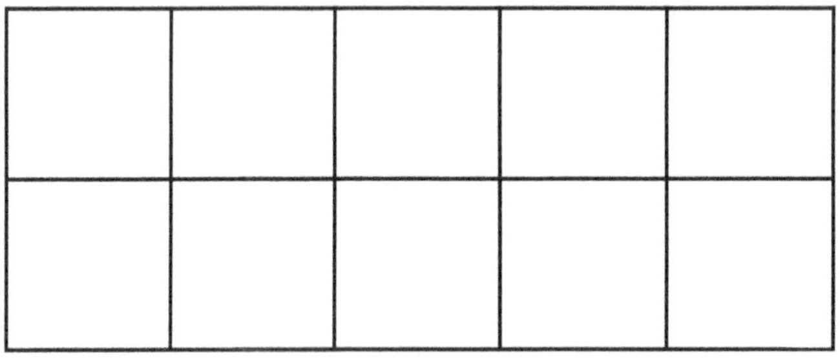

9  – 1  = _____ 

**2.**

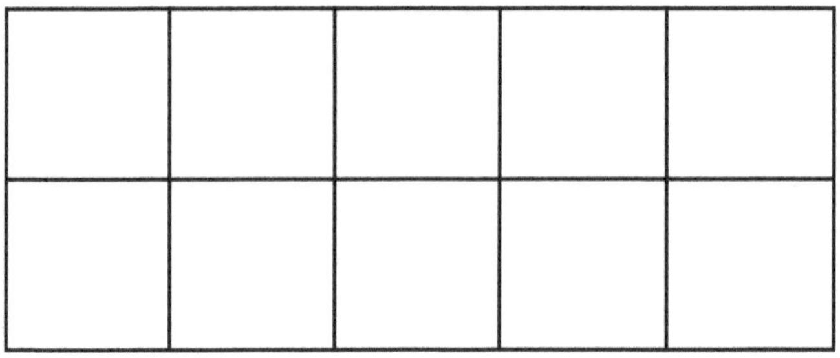

7  – 2  = _____ 

☐ Use blocks to show .

☐ How many  stay?

**3.**

| | | | | |
|---|---|---|---|---|
| | | | | |

8  – 2  = ______ 

**4.**

| | | | | |
|---|---|---|---|---|
| | | | | |

7  – 3  = ______ 

☐ Use blocks to show  .

☐ How many are left?

**5.**

8  − 5  = _____ 

**6.**

6  − 2 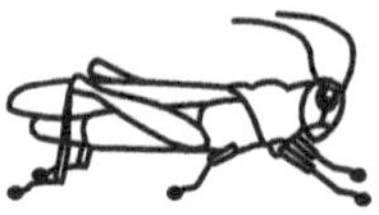 = _____ 

# OAK-38 Subtracting within 10 with Pictures

- [ ] Draw ○ to show  .
- [ ] Cross out ○ to show  eaten.
- [ ] How many  are left?

**1.**

| | | | | |
|---|---|---|---|---|
| | | | | |

10  − 4  = _____ 

**2.**

| | | | | |
|---|---|---|---|---|
| | | | | |

8  − 2  = _____ 

☐ Draw ◯ to show snails.
☐ Cross out ◯ to show snails that go away.
☐ How many snails stay?

**3.**

| | | | | |
|---|---|---|---|---|
| | | | | |
| | | | | |

7  − 5 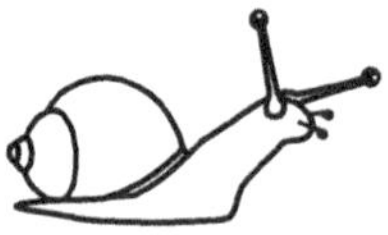 = ____ 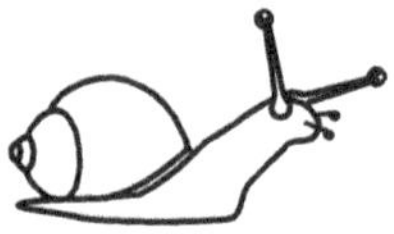

**4.**

| | | | | |
|---|---|---|---|---|
| | | | | |
| | | | | |

9 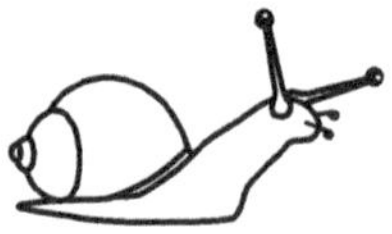 − 6 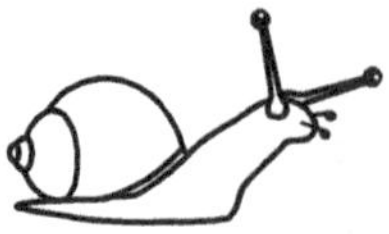 = ____ 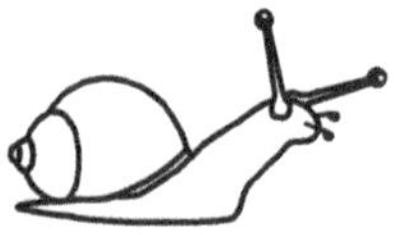

☐ Draw ○ to show .

☐ Cross out ○ to show  that hop away.

☐ How many  stay?

**5.**

6  − 3  = ______ 

**6.**

8  − 4  = ______ 

# Subtracting within 10

- [ ] Subtract.
- [ ] Draw ◯ or use blocks.

**1.**

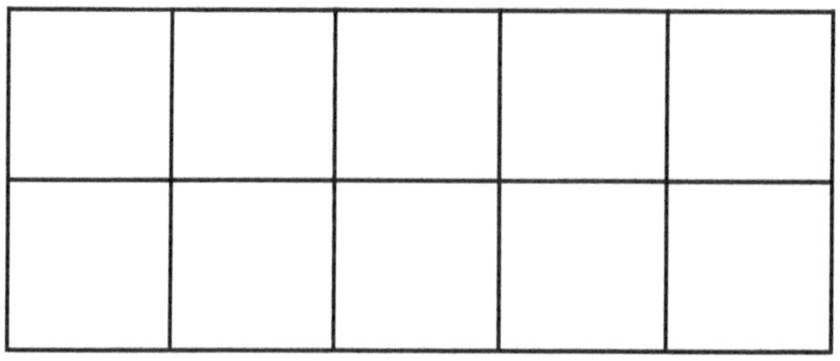

10 − 3 = ______

**2.**

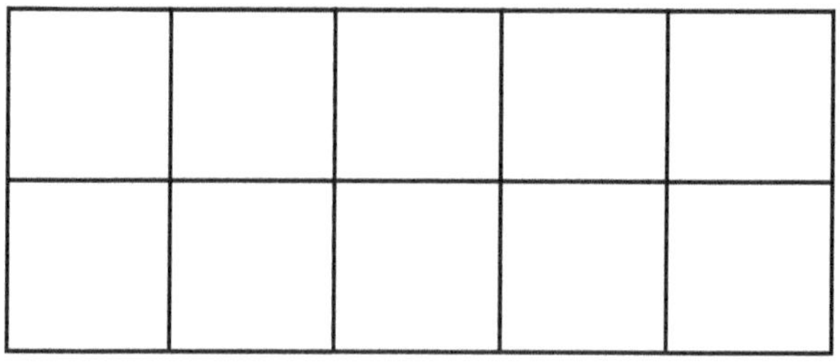

9 − 5 = ______

**3.**

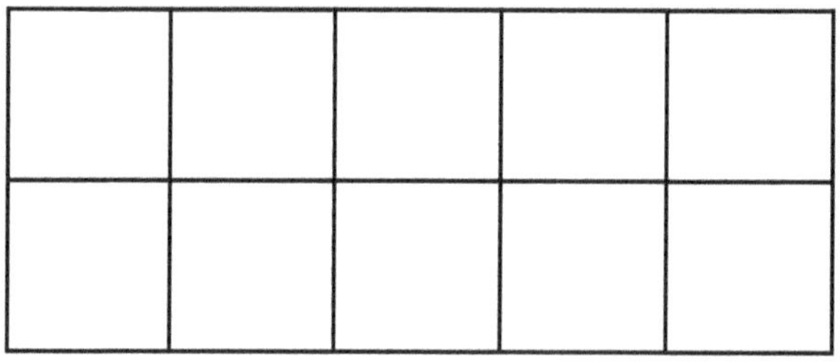

7 − 6 = ______

☐ Subtract.

4.

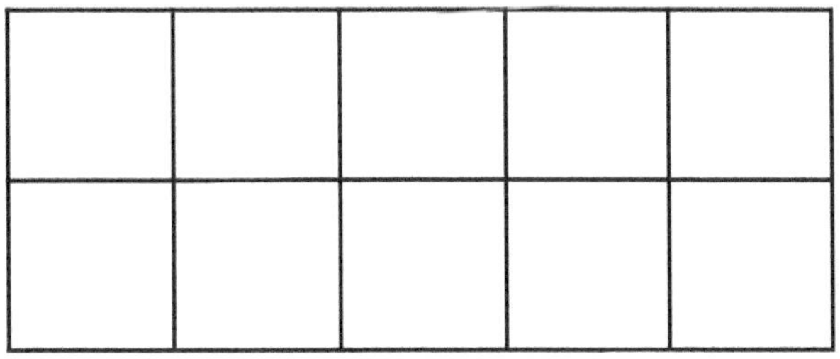

8 − 3 = ______

5.

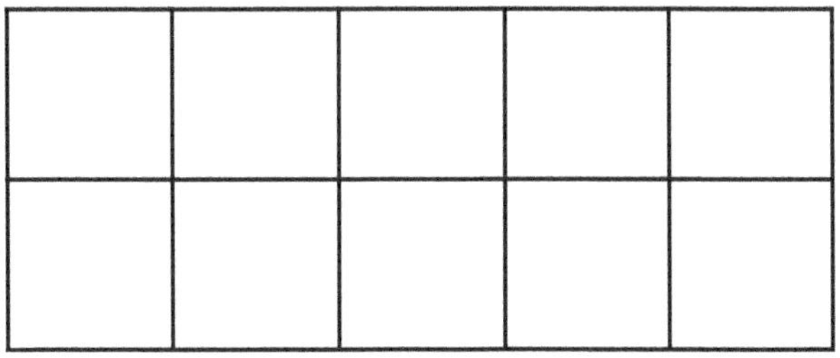

6 − 5 = ______

6.

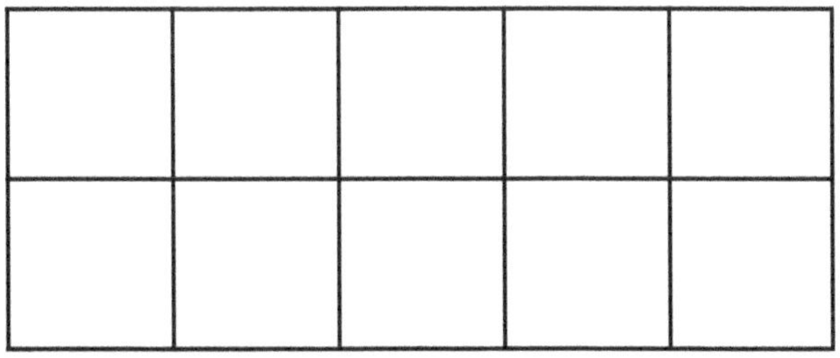

10 − 7 = ______

☐ Subtract.

7.

$6 - 4 =$ ______

8.

$10 - 6 =$ ______

9.

$8 - 5 =$ ______

# OAK-40 Writing Subtractions within 10

☐ Write the subtraction.

1.

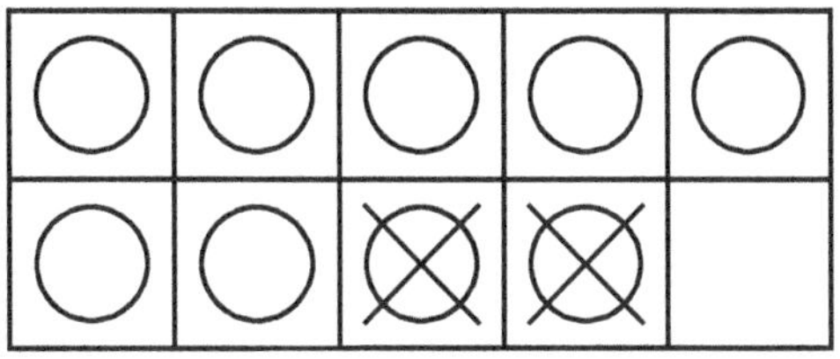

9 − __2__ = ____

2.

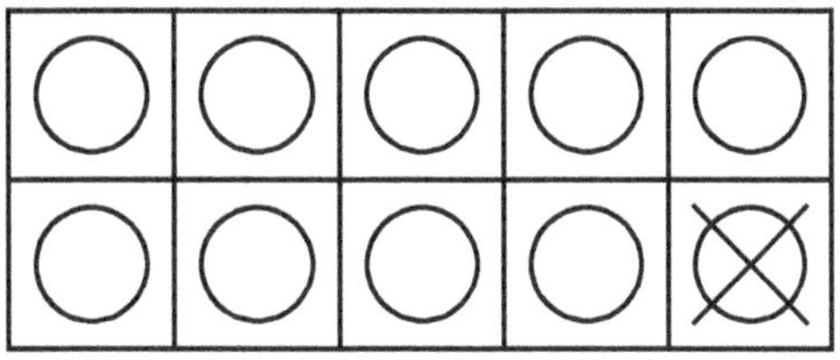

10 − ____ = ____

3.

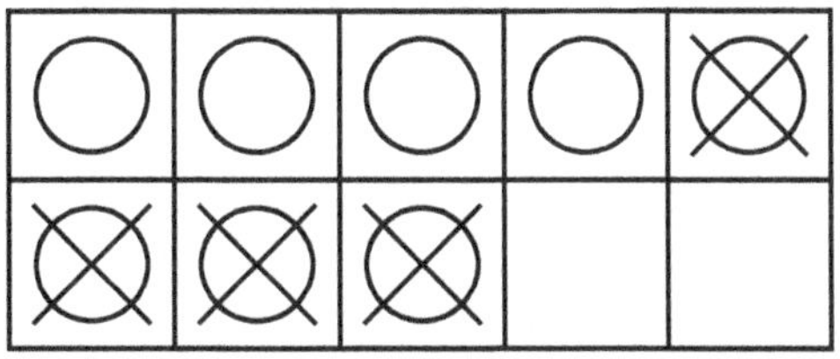

8 − ____ = ____

☐ Write the subtraction.

4.

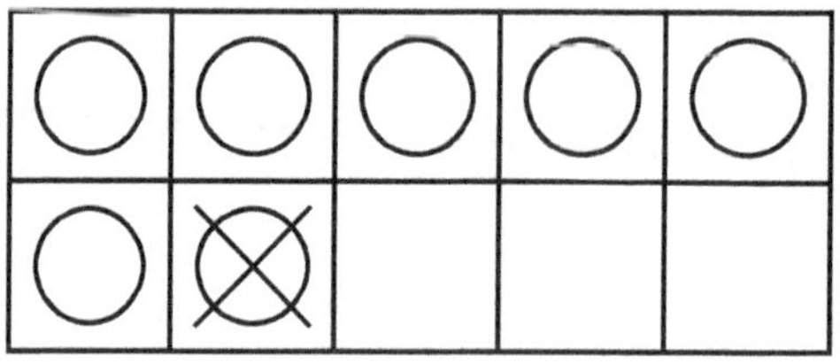

7 – ____ = ____

5.

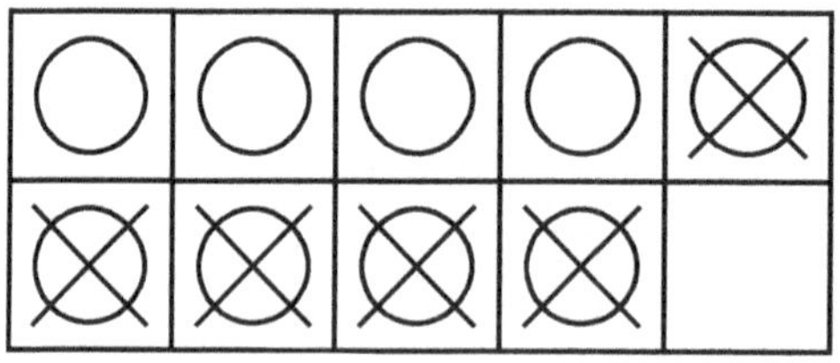

____ – ____ = ____

6.

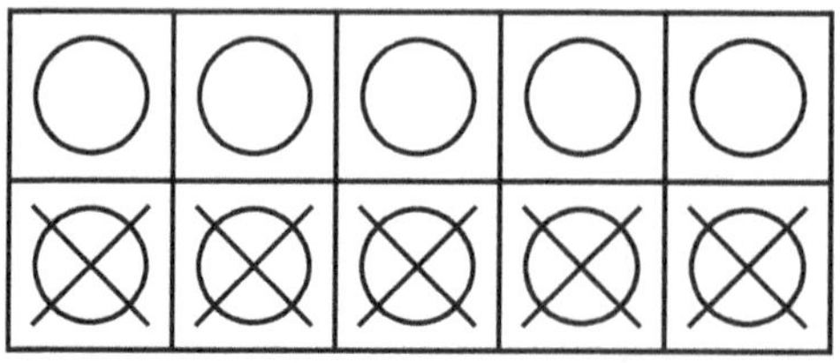

____ – ____ = ____

Write the subtraction.

7.

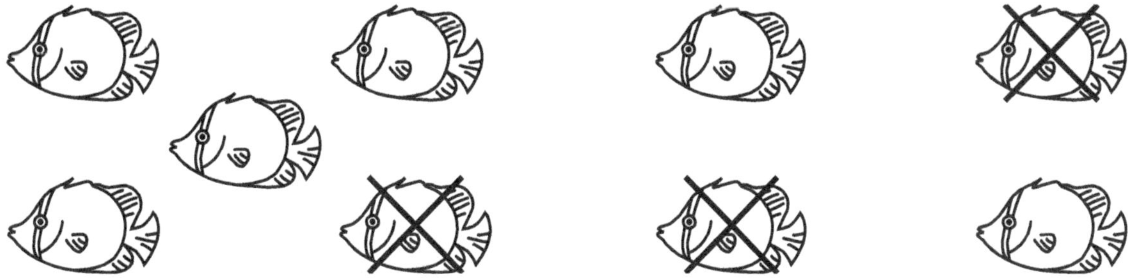

9 − ____ = ____

8.

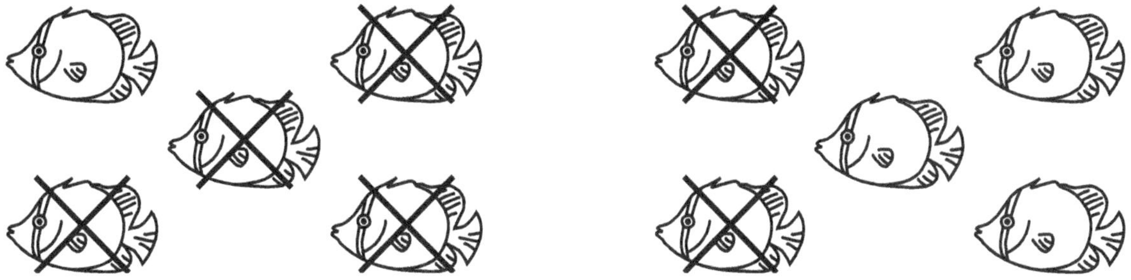

____ − ____ = ____

9.

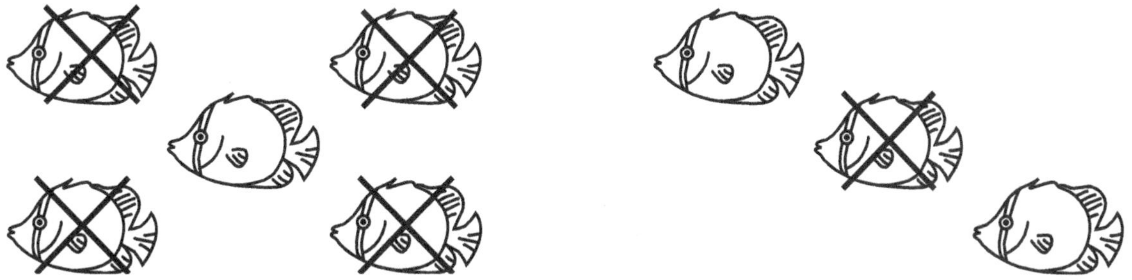

____ − ____ = ____

☐ Cross out  that the monkey eats.

☐ How many  are left?

☐ Write the subtraction.

**10.**

The monkey eats 2 bananas.

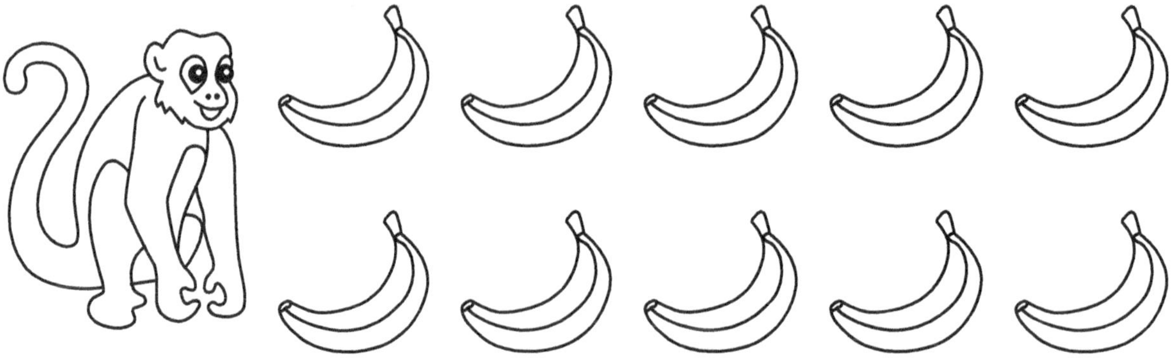

10 – ____ = ____

**11.**

The monkey eats 6 bananas.

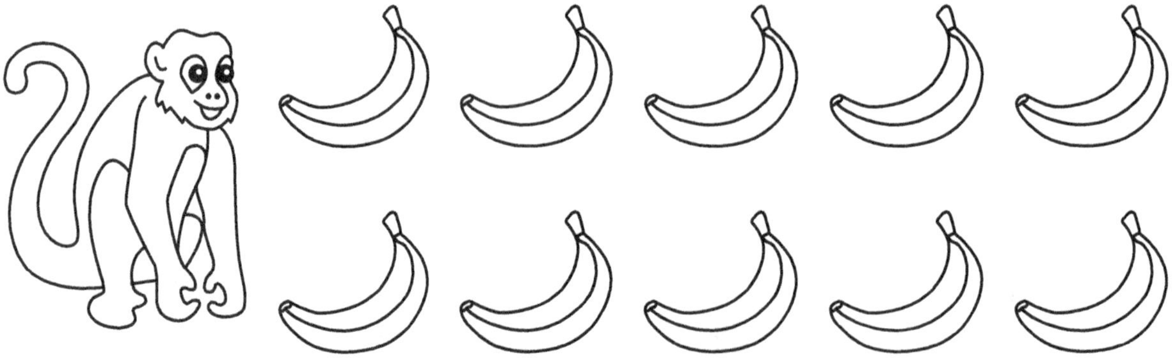

____ – ____ = ____

# OAK-4I Composing I0

☐ How many more make I0?

I.

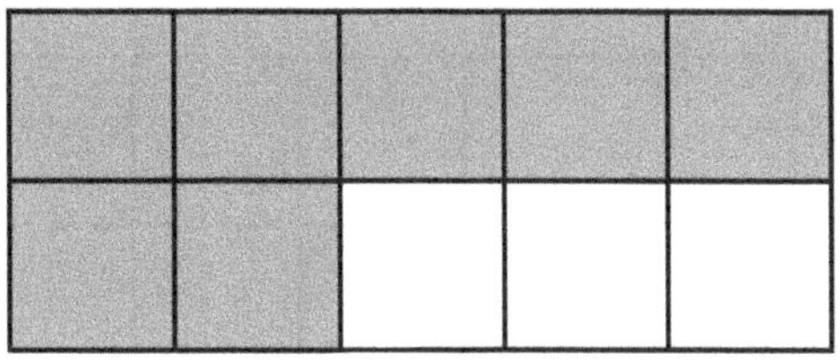

7 + ______ = I0

2.

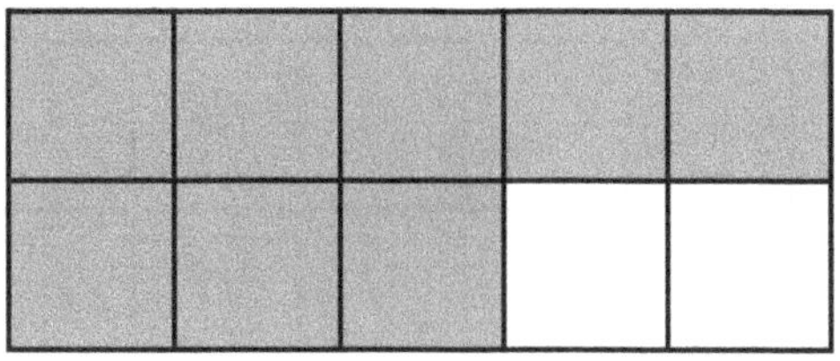

8 + ______ = I0

3.

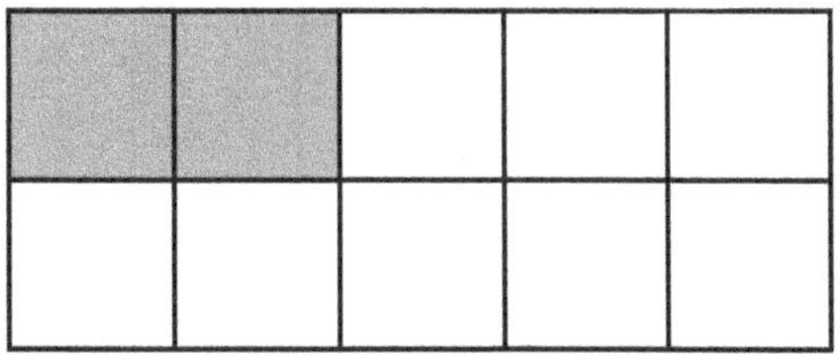

2 + ______ = I0

☐ Color the first number.

☐ How many more make 10?

**4.**

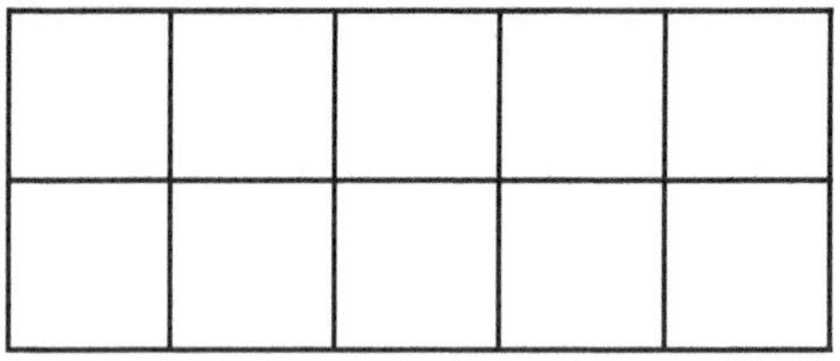

6 + ______ = 10

**5.**

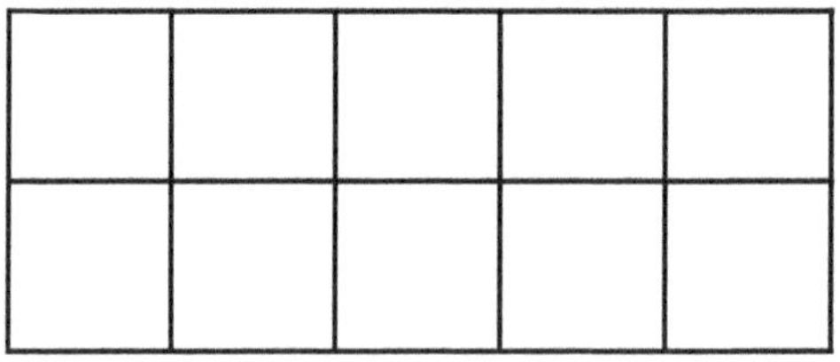

5 + ______ = 10

**6.**

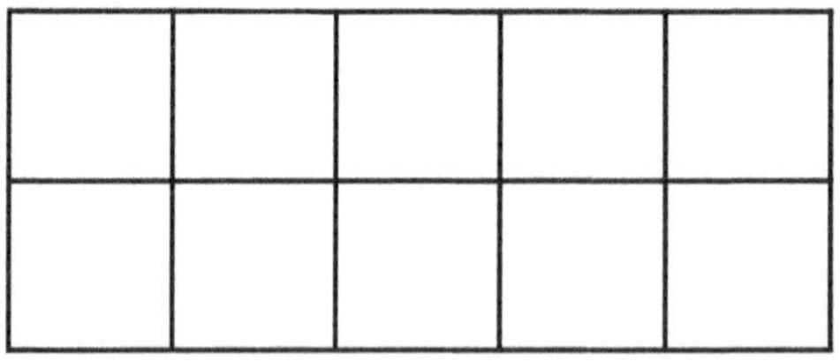

3 + ______ = 10

☐ Color the first number.

☐ How many more make 10?

7.

4 + _____ = 10

8.

9 + _____ = 10

9.

2 + _____ = 10

10.

3 + _____ = 10

# OAK-42 Counting On to 100

☐ Count on to 35.

1.

| | | | | |
|---|---|---|---|---|
| 1 | 2 | 3 | 4 | 5 |
| 6 | 7 | 8 | 9 | 10 |
| 11 | 12 | 13 | 14 | 15 |
| 16 | 17 | 18 | 19 | 20 |
| 21 | 22 | 23 | 24 | 25 |
| 26 | 27 | 28 | 29 | 30 |
| 31 | 32 | 33 | 34 | 35 |

Count on to 70.

2.

36 37 38 39 40

41 42 43 44 45

46 47 48 49 50

51 52 53 54 55

56 57 58 59 60

61 62 63 64 65

66 67 68 69 70

Count on to 100.

**3.**

| | | | | |
|---|---|---|---|---|
| 71 | 72 | 73 | 74 | 75 |
| 76 | 77 | 78 | 79 | 80 |
| 81 | 82 | 83 | 84 | 85 |
| 86 | 87 | 88 | 89 | 90 |
| 91 | 92 | 93 | 94 | 95 |
| 96 | 97 | 98 | 99 | 100 |

# OAK-43 Adding Small Numbers

☐ What addition do you see?

1.

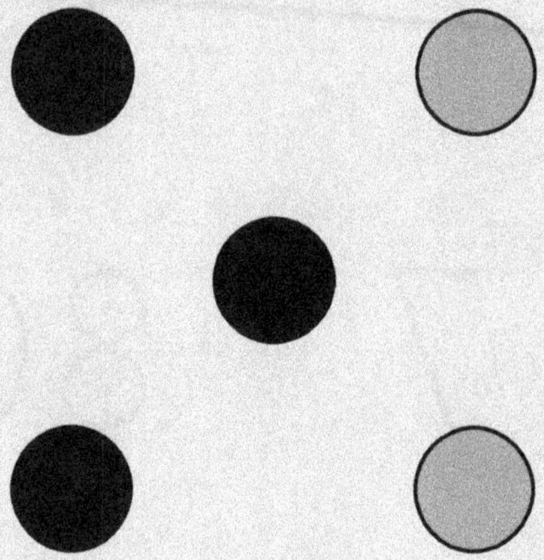

3 + 2

2.

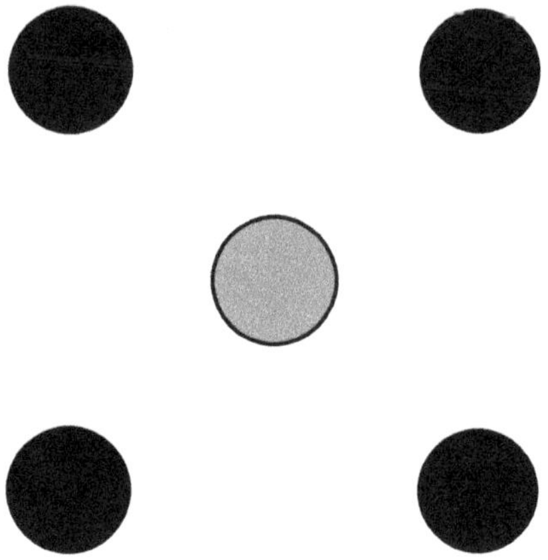

______ + ______

3.

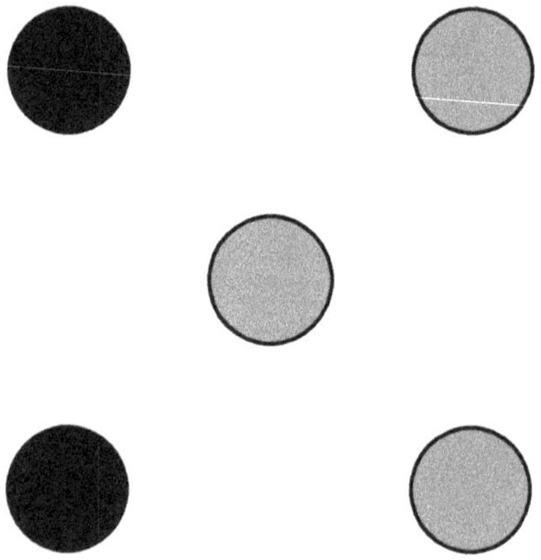

______ + ______

4.

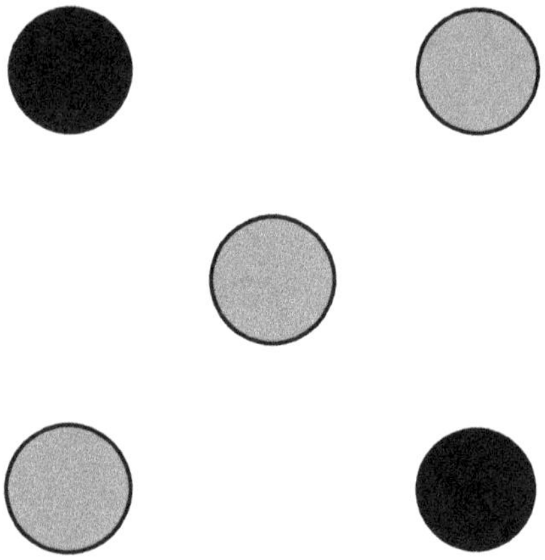

______ + ______

## ☐ What addition do you see?

5.

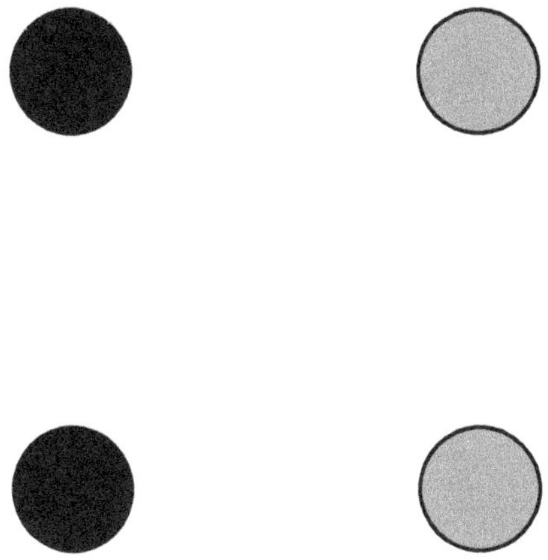

______ + ______

6.

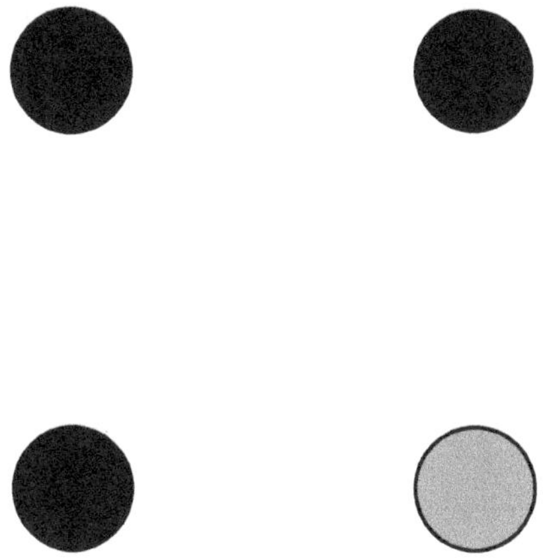

______ + ______

7.

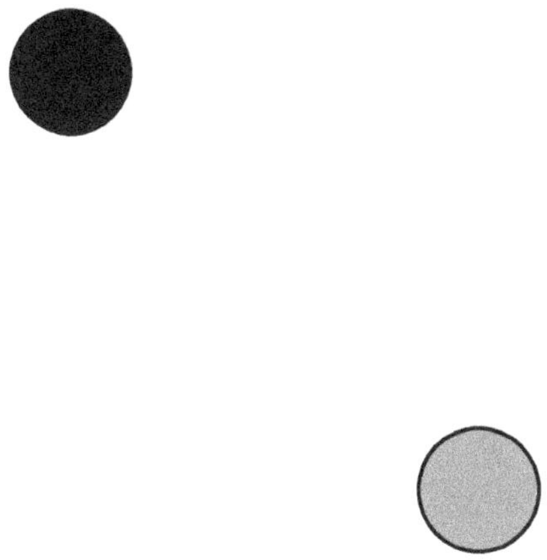

______ + ______

8.

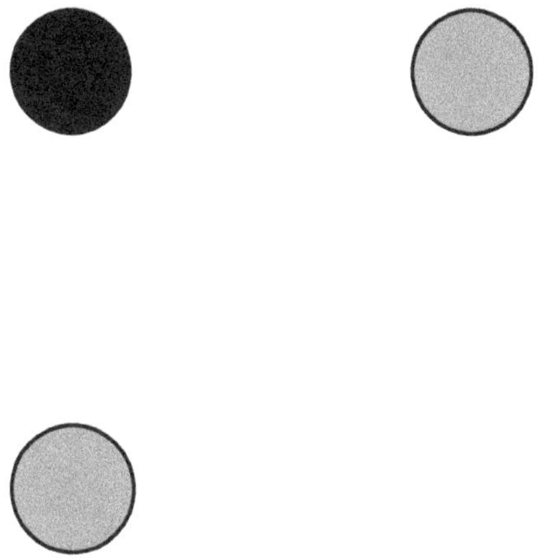

______ + ______

Draw dots to add.

**9.**

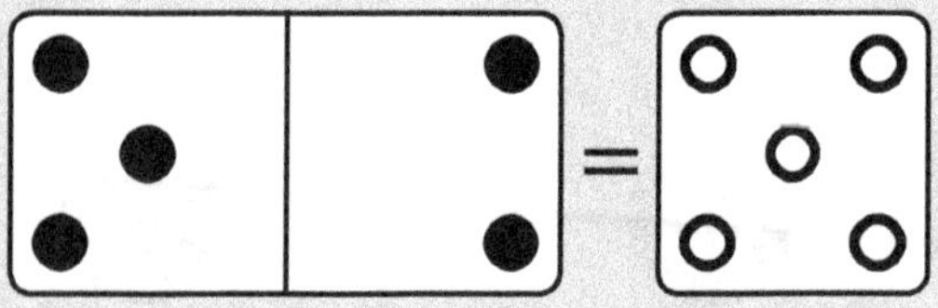

3 + 2 = 5

**10.**

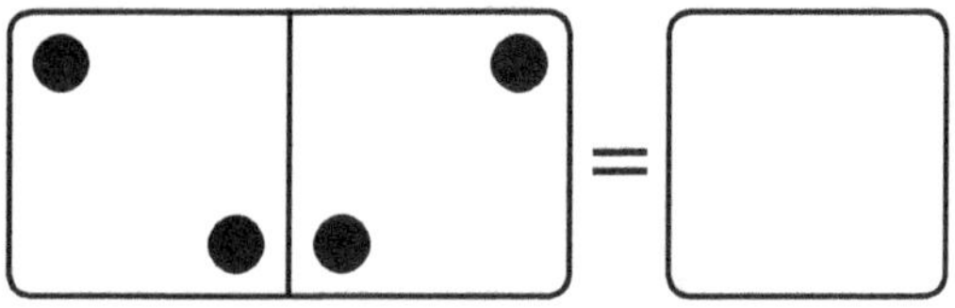

2 + 2 = ______

**11.**

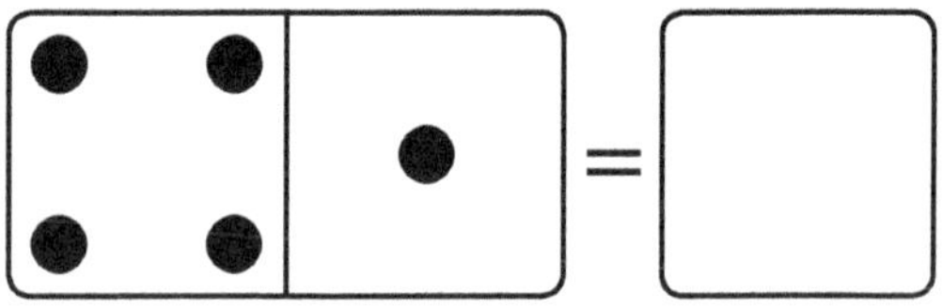

4 + 1 = ______

**12.**

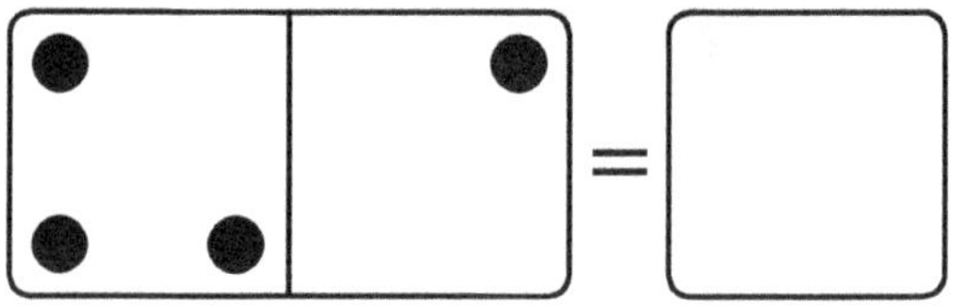

3 + 1 = ______

**13.**

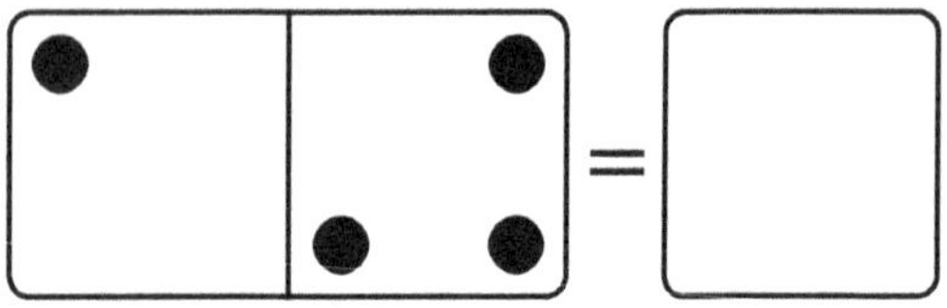

1 + 3 = ______

**14.**

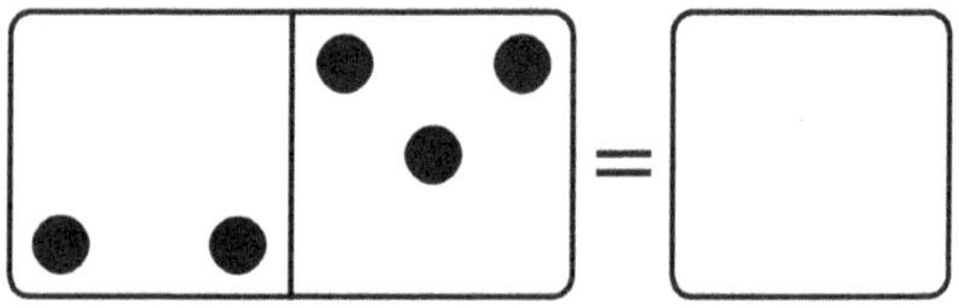

2 + 3 = ______

**15. BONUS**

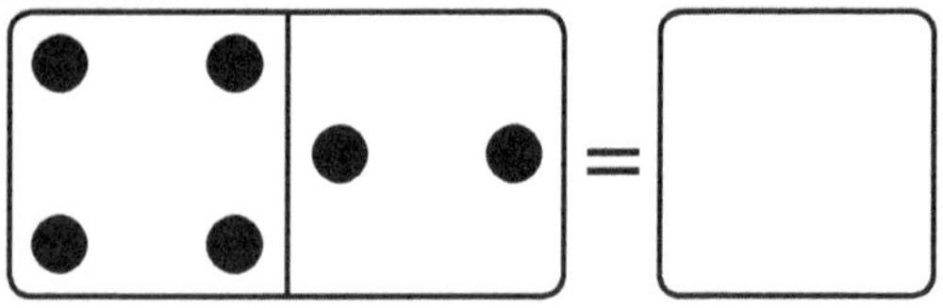

4 + 2 = ______

**16. BONUS**

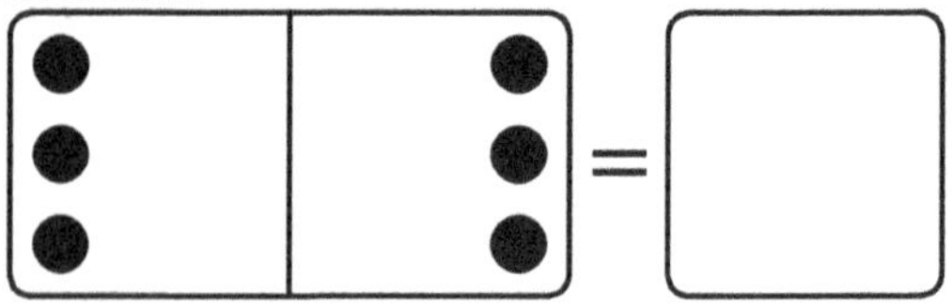

3 + 3 = ______

☐ Add.

**17.**

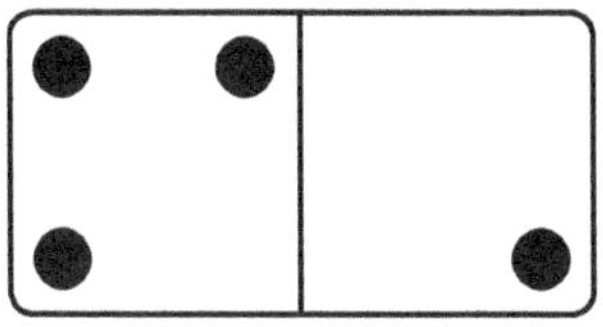

3 + 1 = ______

**18.**

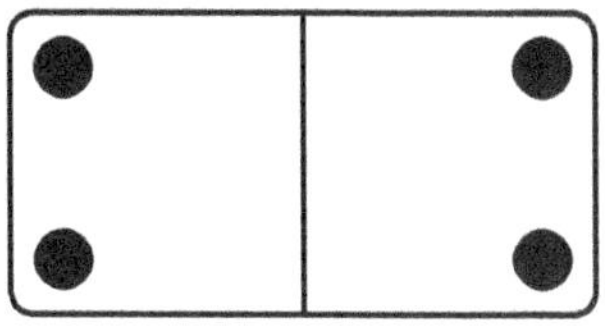

2 + 2 = ______

**19.**

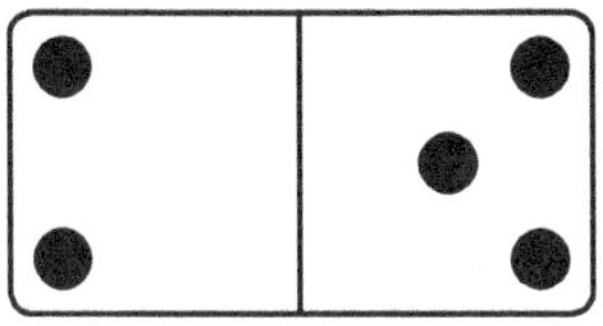

2 + 3 = ______

**20.**

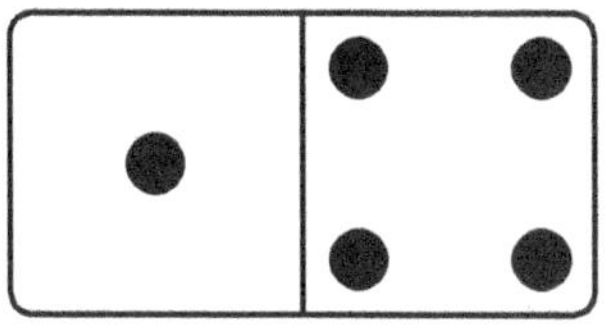

1 + 4 = ______

**21.**

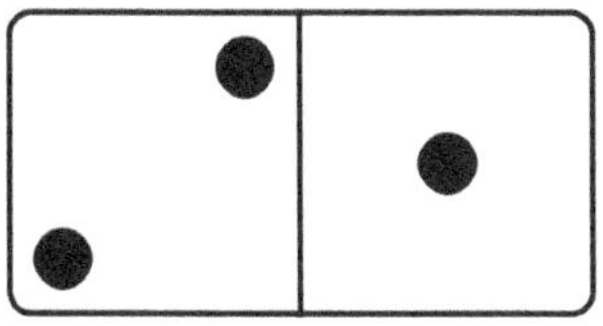

2 + 1 = ______

**22.**

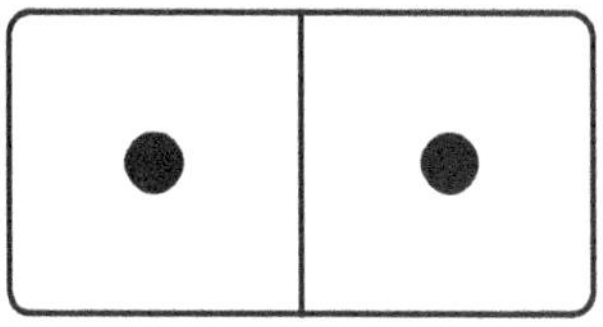

1 + 1 = ______

**23. BONUS**

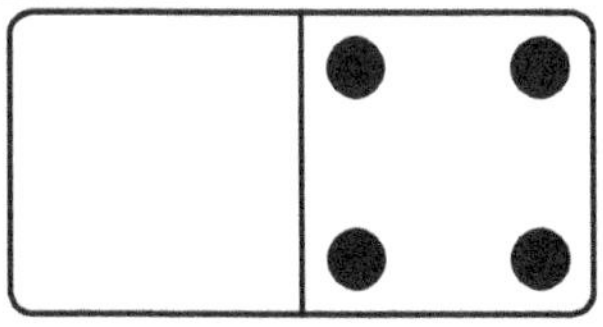

0 + 4 = ______

**24. BONUS**

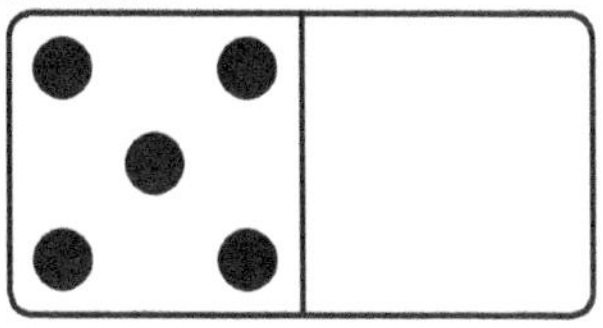

5 + 0 = ______

# OAK-44 Fluency in Addition

☐ Add.

1. $2 + 3 =$ ______

2. $1 + 2 =$ ______

3. $4 + 1 =$ ______

4. $2 + 1 =$ ______

5. $1 + 1 =$ ______

6. $3 + 2 =$ ______

7. $3 + 0 =$ ______

8. $1 + 4 =$ ______

9. $1 + 3 =$ ______

10. $3 + 1 =$ ______

11. $2 + 2 =$ ______

12. $0 + 3 =$ ______

13. $5 + 0 =$ ______

14. $2 + 0 =$ ______

☐ Add.

**15.**

3  chase a ball. 2  chase a ball.

How many pets in total?

3 + 2 = ______

**16.**

2  walk by. 2 more  walk by.

How many ants in total?

2 + 2 = ______

**17.**

3 bunnies hop by. I more bunny hops by.

How many bunnies in total?

3 + I = ______

☐ Add.

18.

4  run. I more  runs.

How many horses in total?

_____ + _____ = _____

19.

I boy reads. 2 girls read.

How many children in total?

_____ + _____ = _____

20.

Kim sees 2 trees. Rob sees I tree.

How many trees in total?

_____ + _____ = _____

# OAK-45 Subtracting Small Numbers

☐ What subtraction do you see?

1.

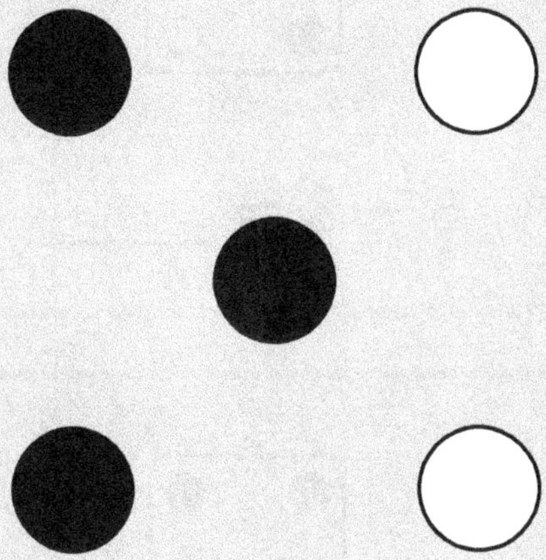

5 – 2

2.

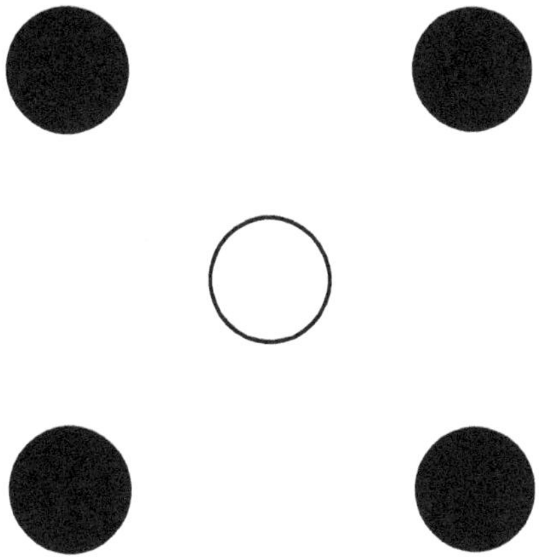

_____ – _____

3.

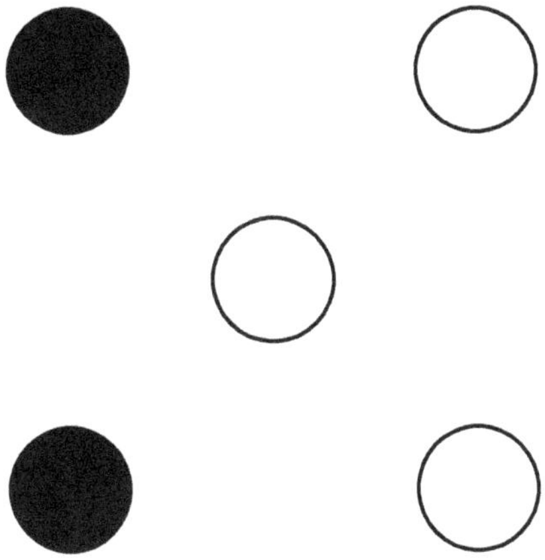

_____ – _____

4.

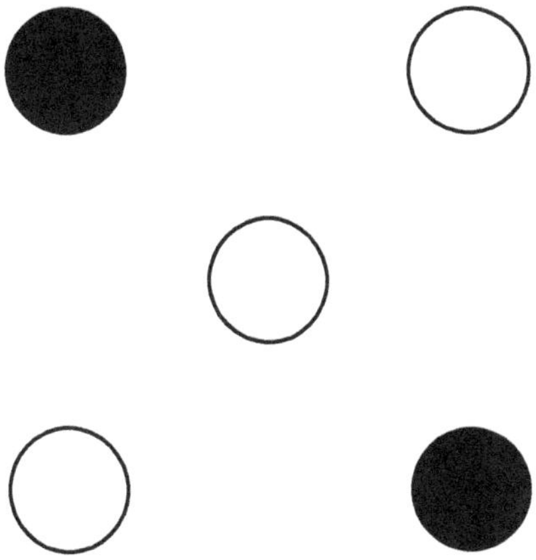

_____ – _____

☐ Subtract.

5.

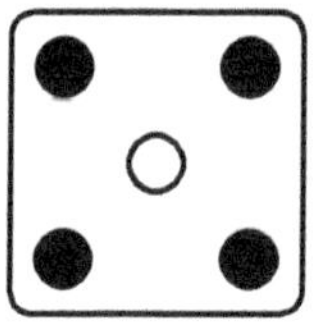

5 − 1 = ______

6.

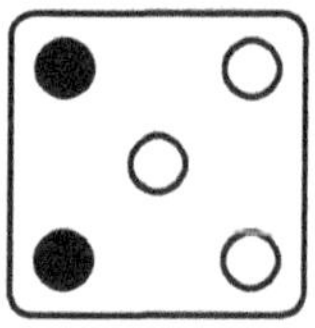

5 − 3 = ______

7.

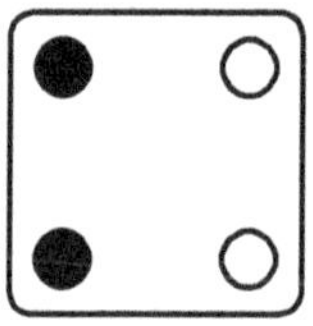

4 − 2 = ______

8.

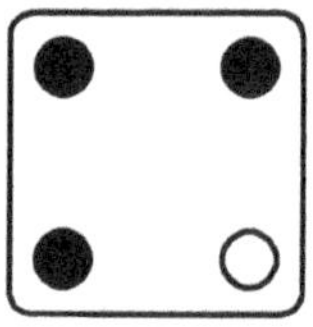

4 − 1 = ______

9.

3 − 2 = ______

10.

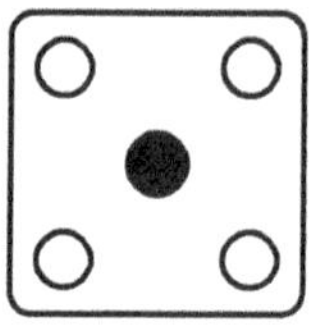

5 − 4 = ______

11.

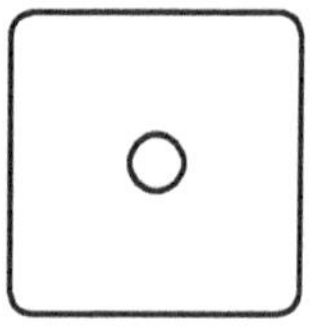

1 − 1 = ______

12.

3 − 0 = ______

## ☐ Subtract.

**13.**

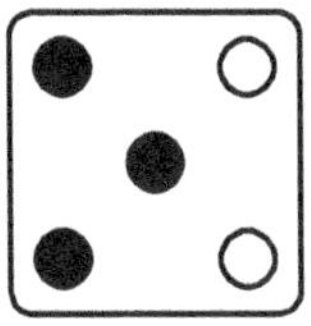

$5 - 2 =$ ______

**14.**

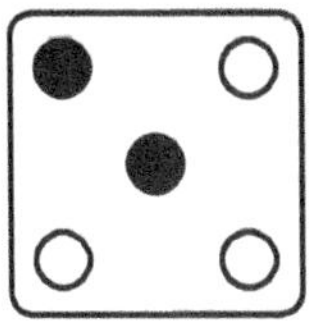

$5 - 3 =$ ______

**15.**

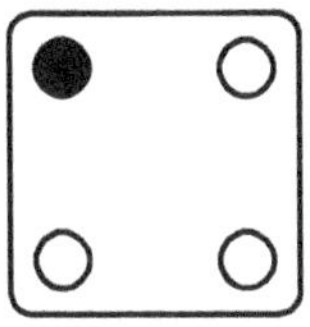

$4 - 3 =$ ______

**16.**

$3 - 1 =$ ______

**17.**

$3 - 3 =$ ______

**18.**

$5 - 0 =$ ______

**19.**

$4 - 4 =$ ______

**20.**

$2 - 1 =$ ______

# OAK-46 Fluency in Subtraction

☐ Subtract.

1. $3 - 2 =$ ______

2. $2 - 1 =$ ______

3. $4 - 1 =$ ______

4. $4 - 2 =$ ______

5. $1 - 1 =$ ______

6. $5 - 1 =$ ______

7. $3 - 0 =$ ______

8. $4 - 3 =$ ______

9. $5 - 3 =$ ______

10. $3 - 1 =$ ______

11. $2 - 2 =$ ______

12. $5 - 2 =$ ______

13. $5 - 0 =$ ______

14. $5 - 4 =$ ______

☐ Subtract.

**15.**

3  climb a wall. 2  fall down.

How many ants are on the wall now?

3 − 2 = ______

**16.**

4  hop on a log. 3  hop off.

How many frogs are on the log now?

4 − 3 = ______

**17.**

4 boys play tag. 1 boy leaves.

How many boys are playing tag now?

4 − 1 = ______

Subtract.

18.

5  are sleeping. 2  wake up.

How many cats are sleeping now?

_____ – _____ = _____

19.

4 girls are running. 2 girls stop running.

How many girls are running now?

_____ – _____ = _____

20.

5 birds are flying. I bird takes a rest.

How many birds are flying now?

_____ – _____ = _____

# OAK-47 Number Families

☐ How many in total?

1.

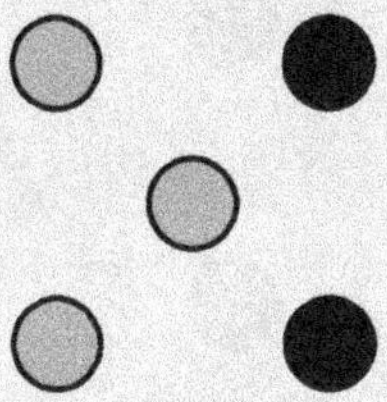

5

2.

____

3.

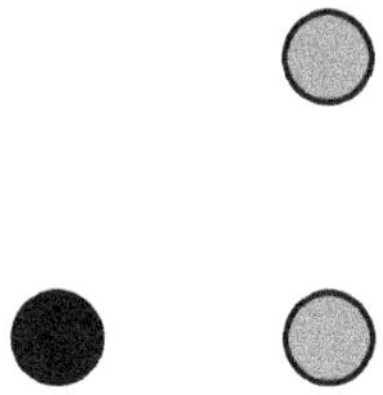

____

☐ How many  ?

4.

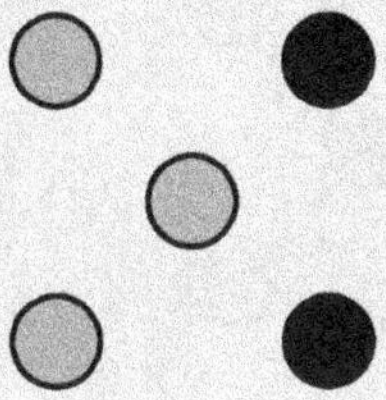

3

5.

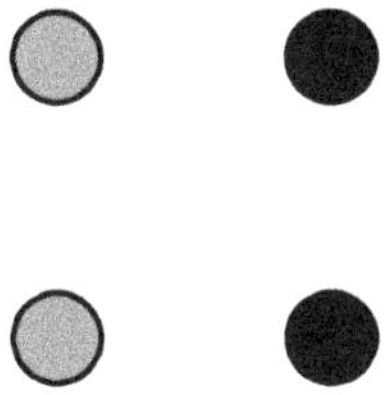

____

6.

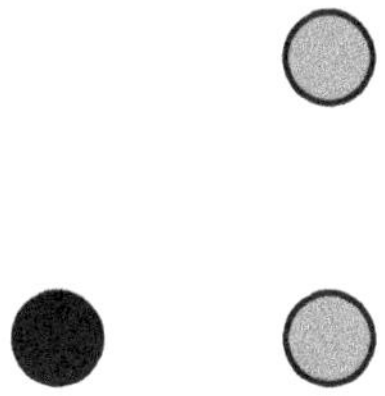

____

☐ How many  ?

7.

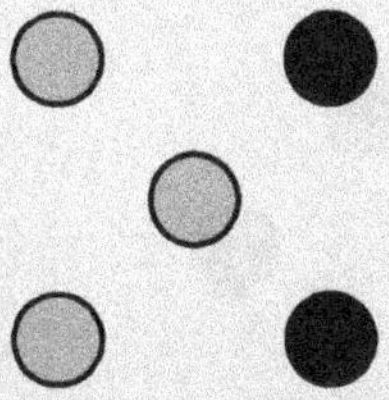

2

8.

____

9.

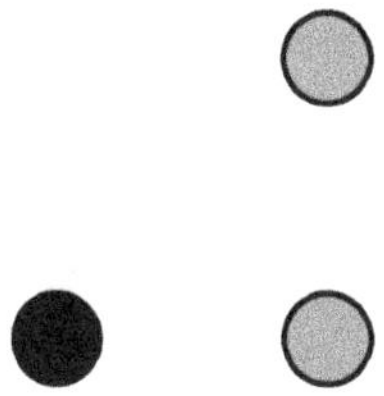

____

Write the addition.

10.

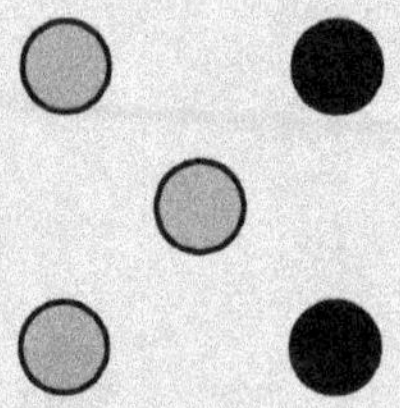

5 = 3 + 2

11.

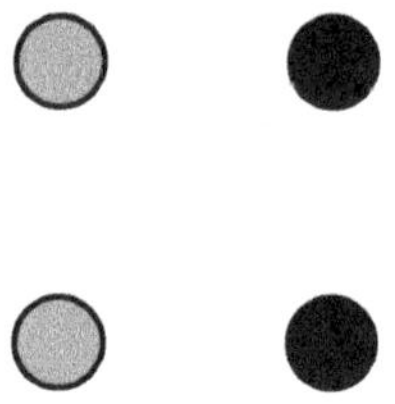

4 = ___ + ___

12.

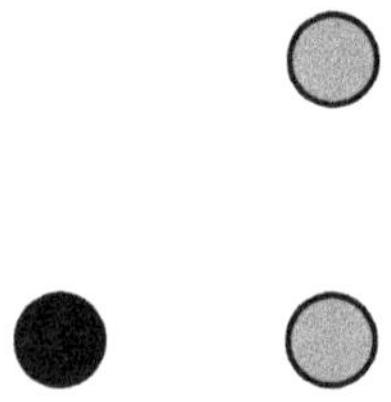

___ = ___ + ___

13.

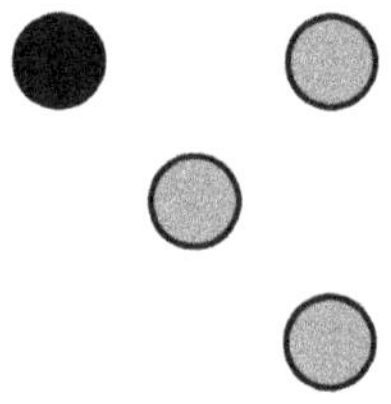

___ = ___ + ___

14.

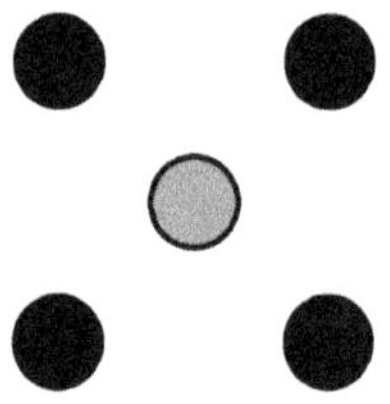

___ = ___ + ___

15.

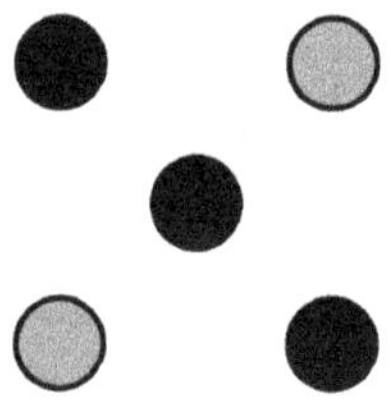

___ = ___ + ___

☐ Write the subtraction.

16.

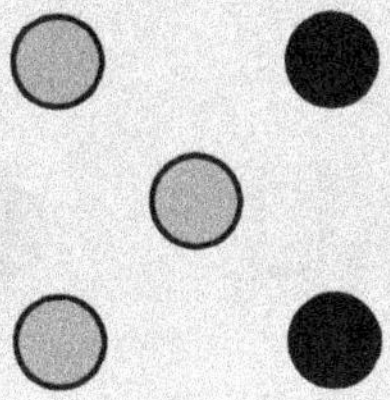

5 − 3 = 2

17.

4 − ____ = ____

18.

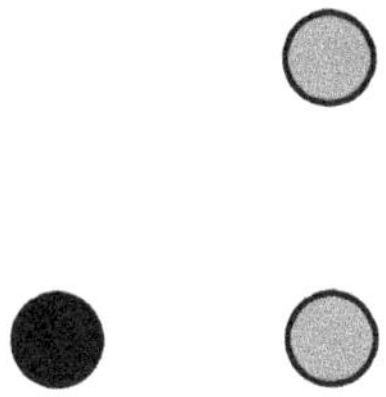

____ − ____ = ____

19.

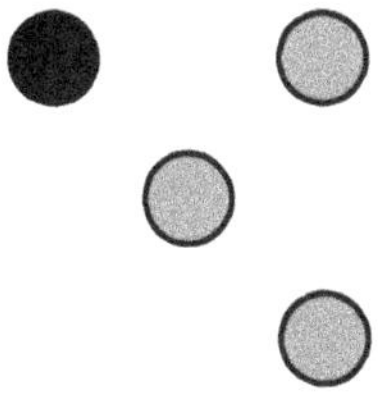

____ − ____ = ____

20.

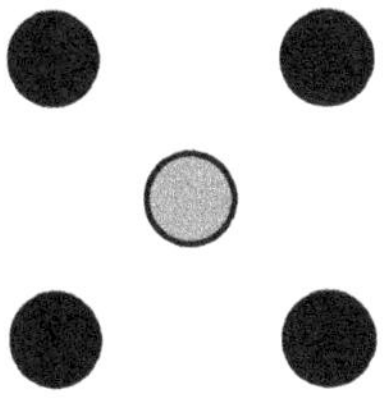

____ − ____ = ____

21.

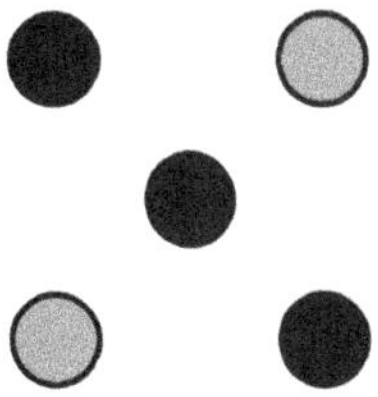

____ − ____ = ____

## ☐ Write the addition and the subtraction.

**22.**

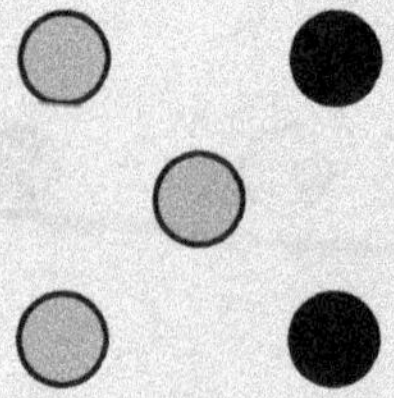

5 = 3 + 2

5 − 3 = 2

**23.**

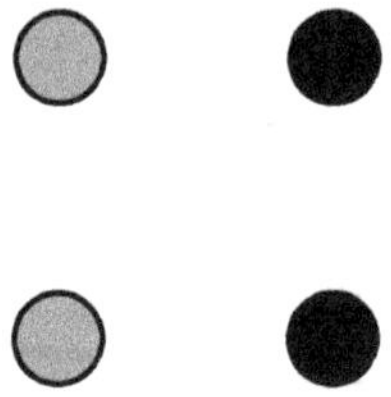

4 = ___ + ___

4 − ___ = ___

**24.**

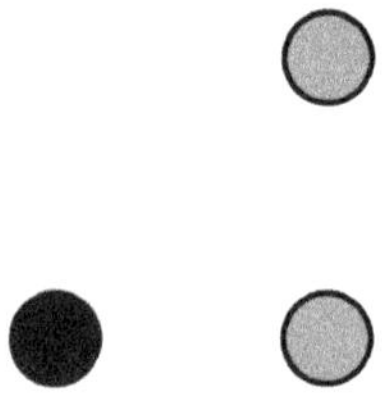

___ = ___ + ___

___ − ___ = ___

**25.**

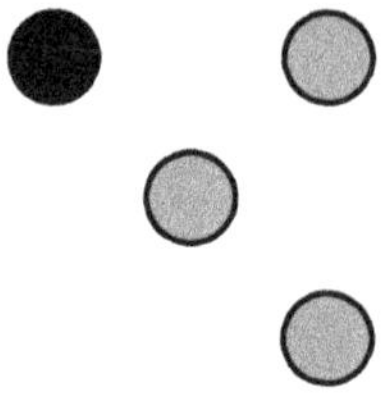

___ = ___ + ___

___ − ___ = ___

**26.**

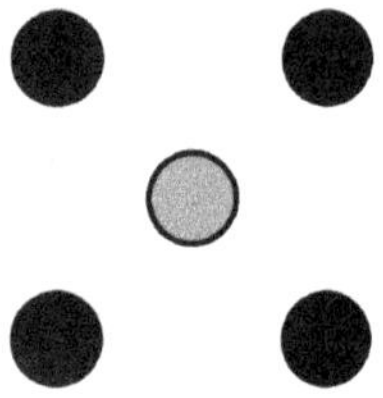

___ = ___ + ___

___ − ___ = ___

**27.**

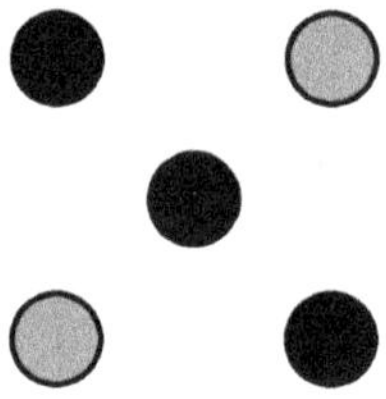

___ = ___ + ___

___ − ___ = ___

# OAK-48 Adding Numbers to 5

☐ Draw dots to make the number.

1.

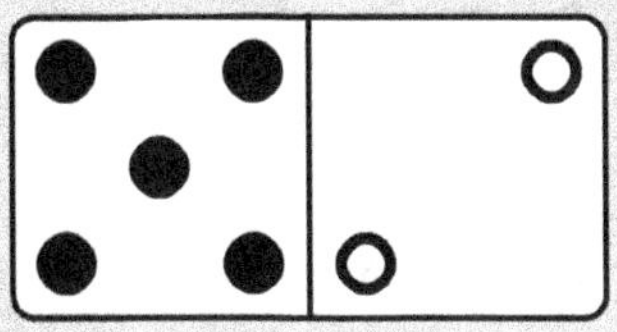

7

2.

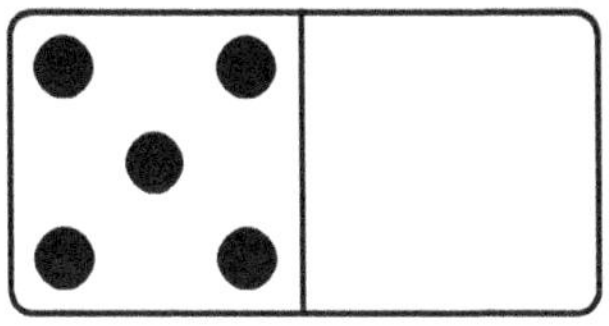

8

3.

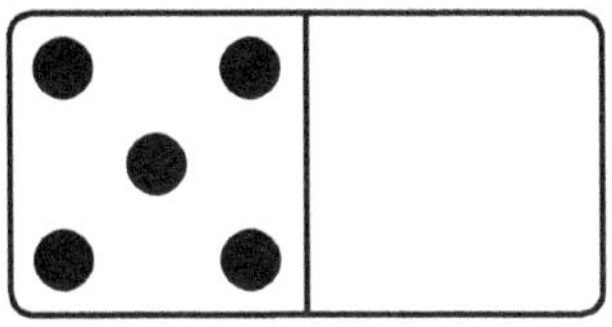

9

4.

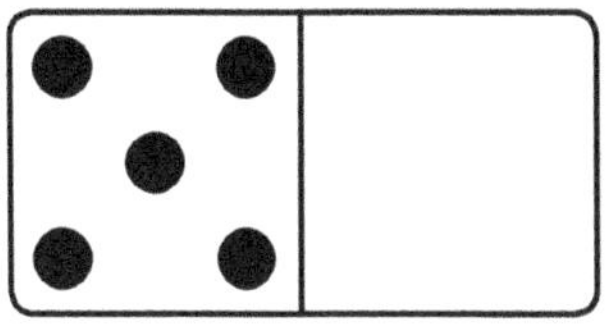

10

5.

6

6.

7

7.

8

8.

9

Write the missing number.

9.

$5 + 0 = \_\_\_\_$

$5 + 1 = \_\_\_\_$

$5 + 2 = \_\_\_\_$

$5 + 3 = \_\_\_\_$

$5 + 4 = \_\_\_\_$

$5 + 5 = \_\_\_\_$

10.

$5 = 5 + \_\_\_\_$

$6 = 5 + \_\_\_\_$

$7 = 5 + \_\_\_\_$

$8 = 5 + \_\_\_\_$

$9 = 5 + \_\_\_\_$

$10 = 5 + \_\_\_\_$

11.

$5 + 2 = \_\_\_\_$

$5 + 4 = \_\_\_\_$

$5 + 1 = \_\_\_\_$

$5 + 5 = \_\_\_\_$

$5 + 3 = \_\_\_\_$

$5 + 0 = \_\_\_\_$

12.

$8 = 5 + \_\_\_\_$

$6 = 5 + \_\_\_\_$

$10 = 5 + \_\_\_\_$

$9 = 5 + \_\_\_\_$

$5 = 5 + \_\_\_\_$

$7 = 5 + \_\_\_\_$

# MDK-6 Capacity

☐ Circle the one that **holds more**.

1.

2.

3.

4.

5.

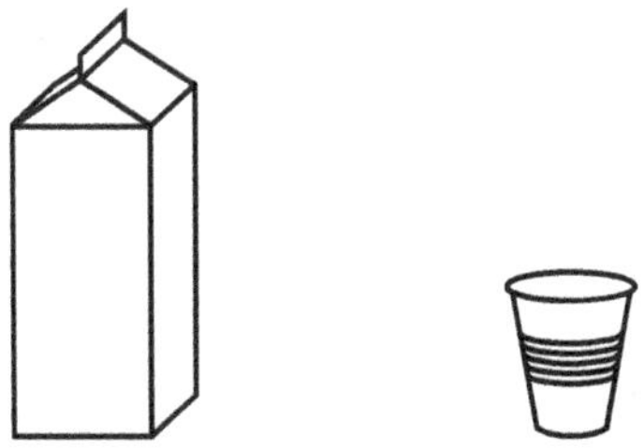

6.

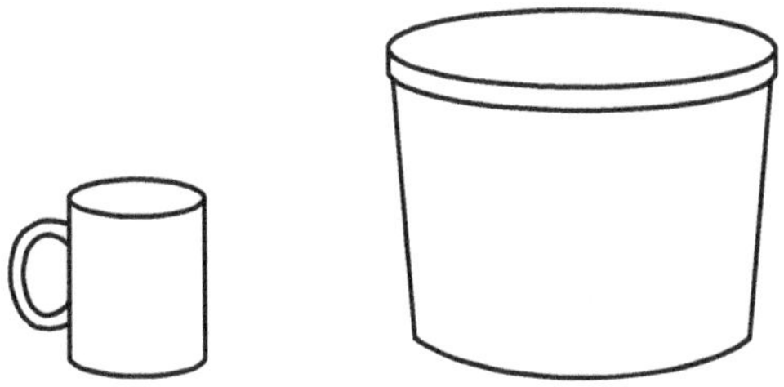

☐ Circle the one that **holds less.**

7.

8.

9.

10.

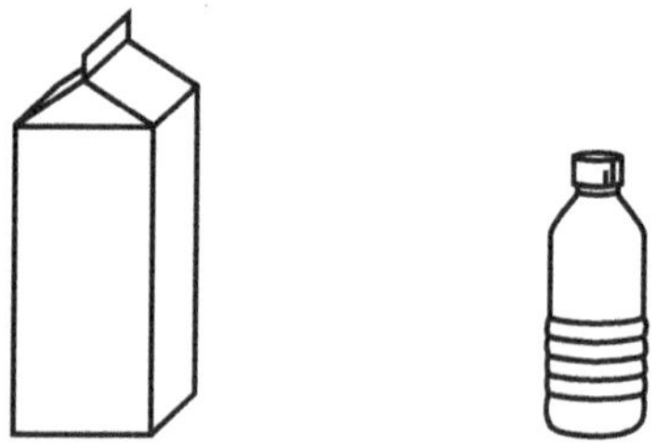

11.

12. BONUS

# MDK-7 Height

☐ Circle the **taller** one.

1.

2.

3.

4.

5.

6. BONUS

☐ Circle the **shorter** one.

7.

8.

9.

10.

11.

12. BONUS

☐ Circle 2 that are the **same height**.

13.

14.

15.

16.

17. BONUS

 **Length**

☐ Circle the **longer** one.

1.

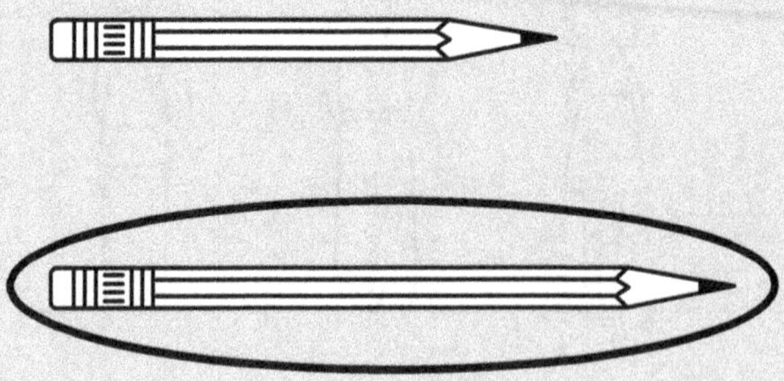

2.

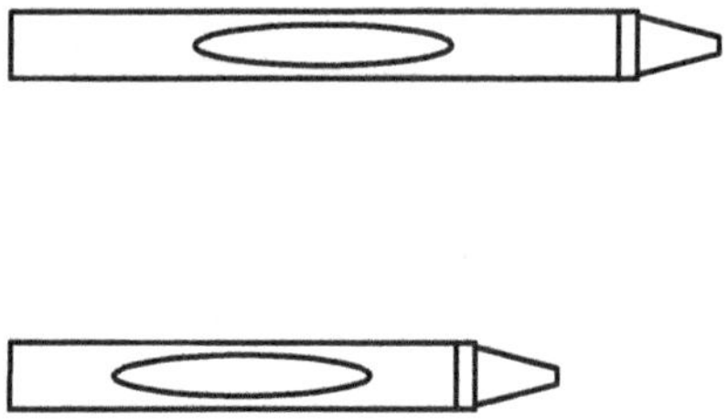

3.

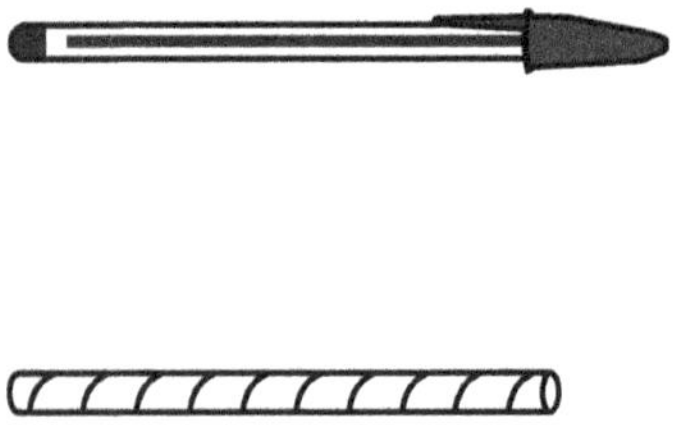

4.

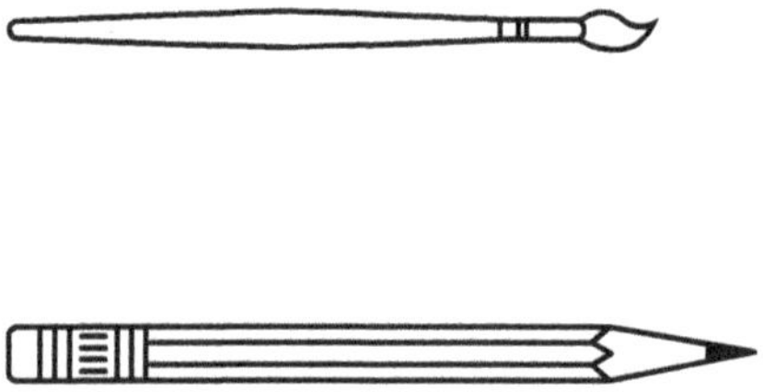

5.

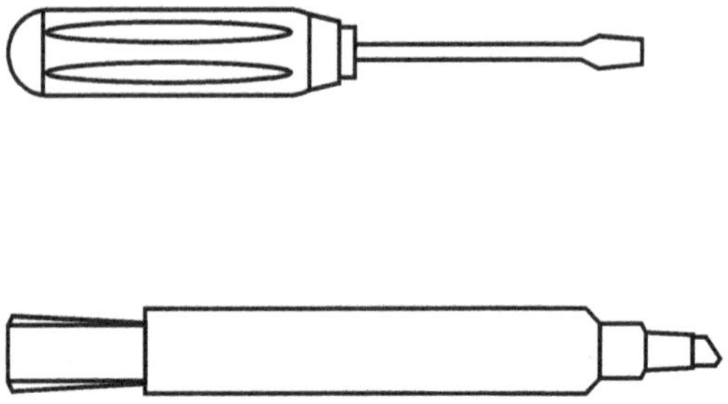

6. BONUS

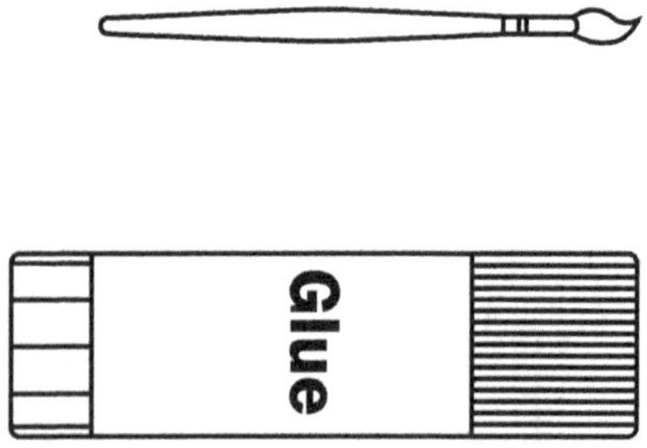

☐ Circle the **shorter** one.

7.

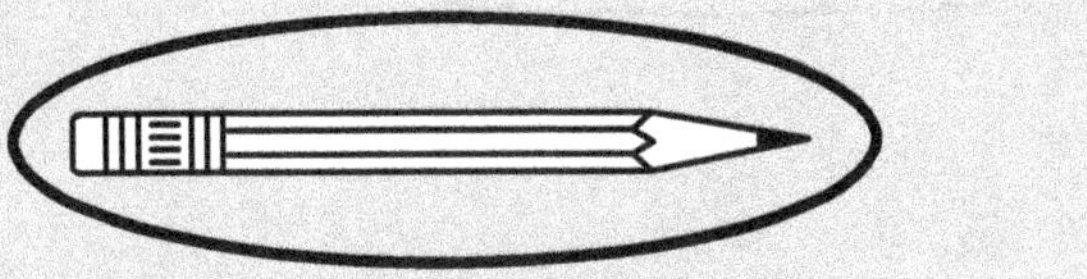

8.

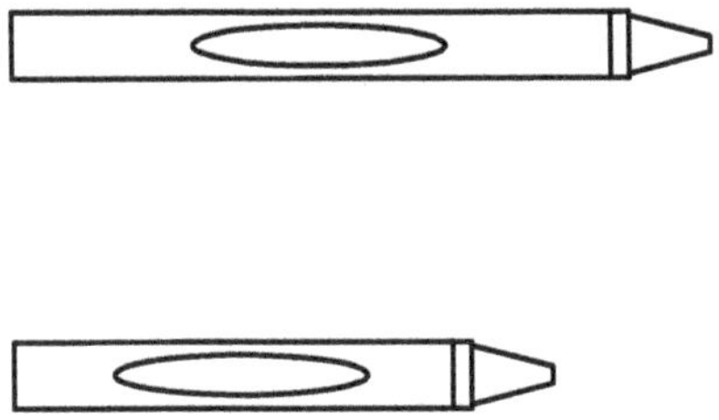

9.

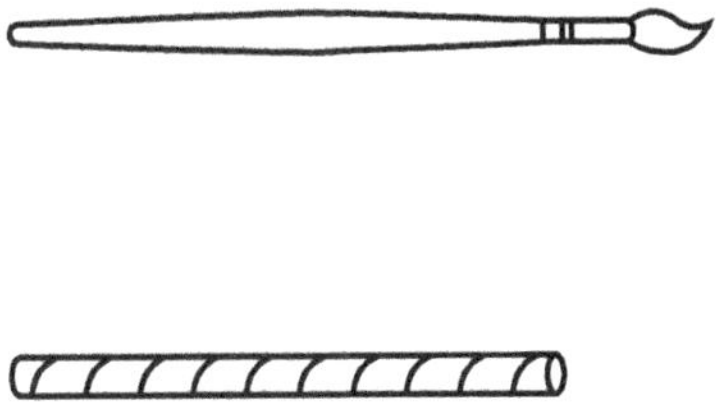

10.

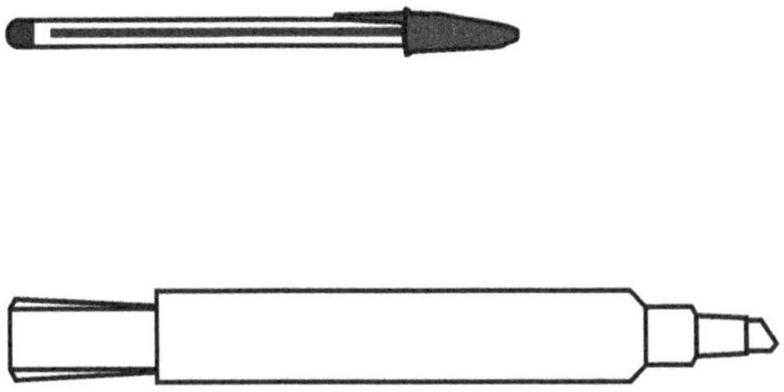

11.

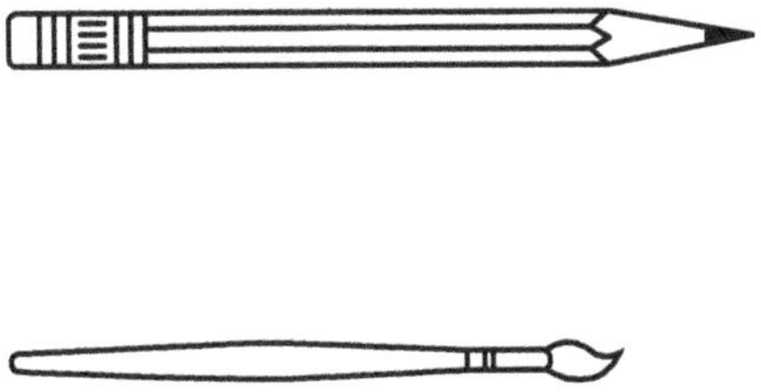

12. BONUS

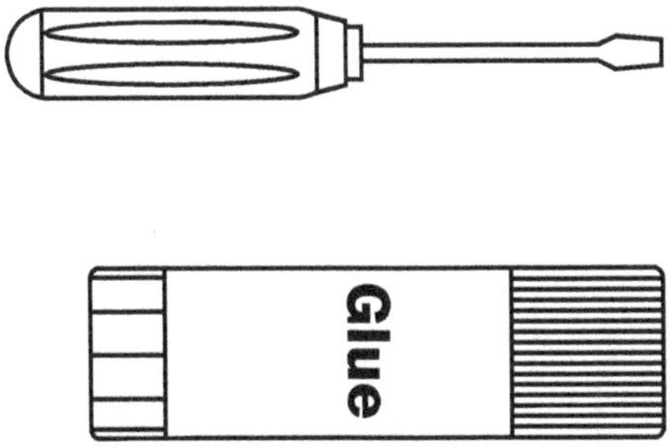

☐ Circle 2 that are the **same length**.

13.

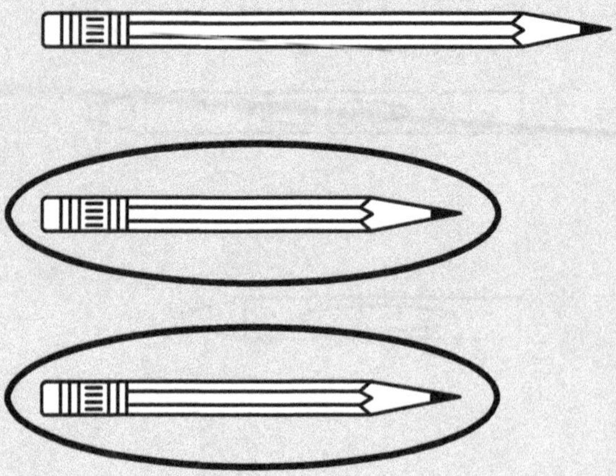

14.

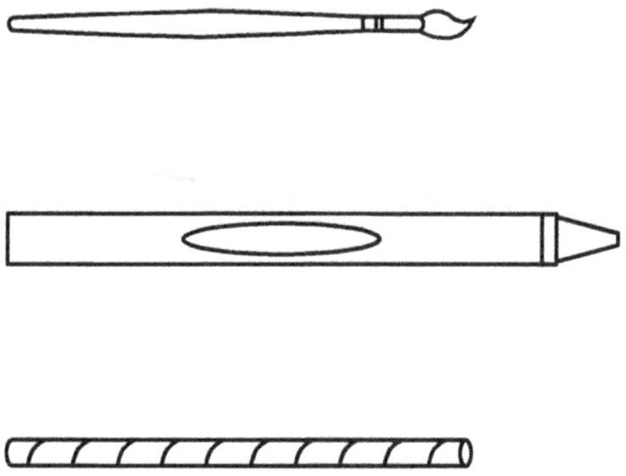

15.

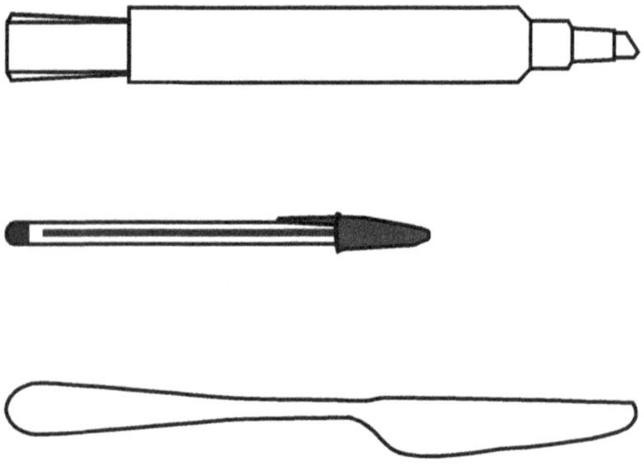

16.

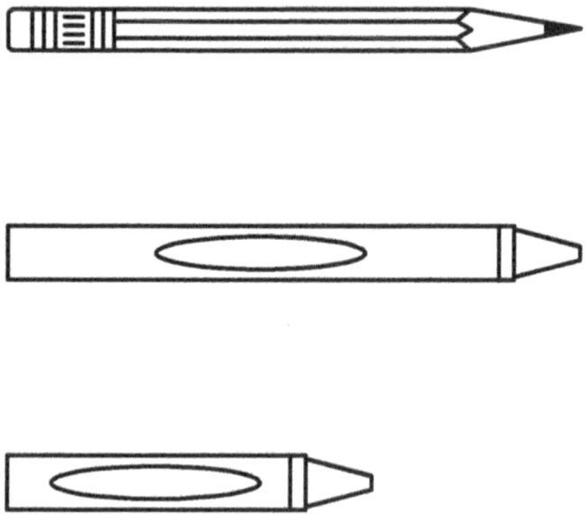

17.

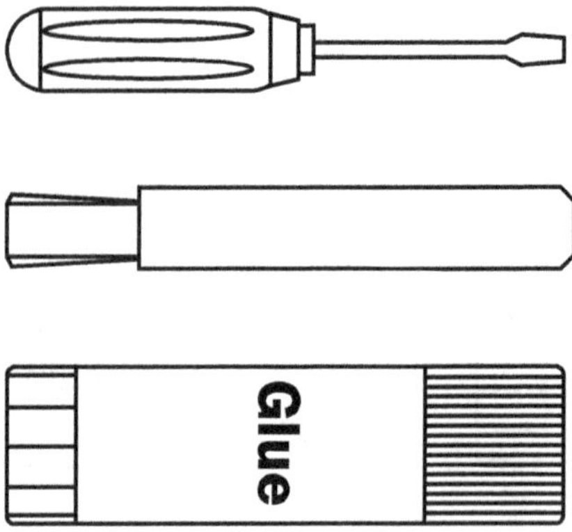


18. BONUS

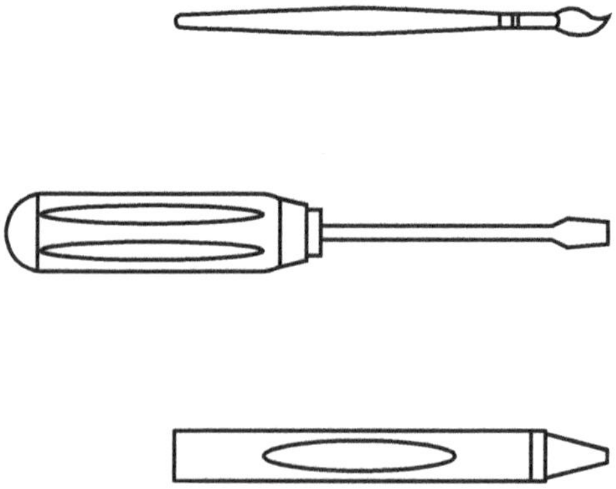

# MDK-9 Weight

☐ Circle the **heavier** one.

1.

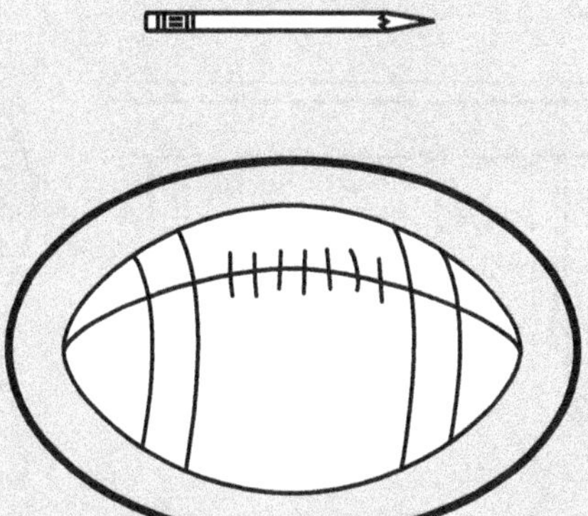

2.

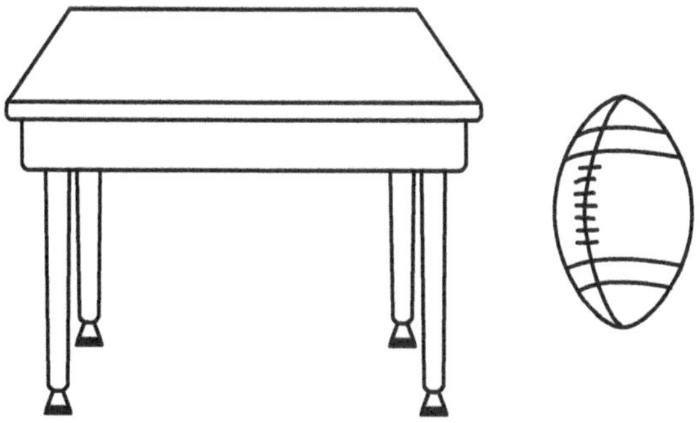

3.

4.

5.

6.

☐ Circle the **lighter** one.

7.

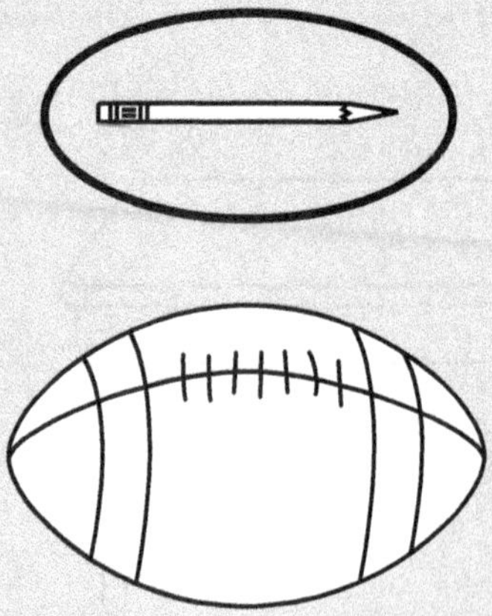

8.

9.

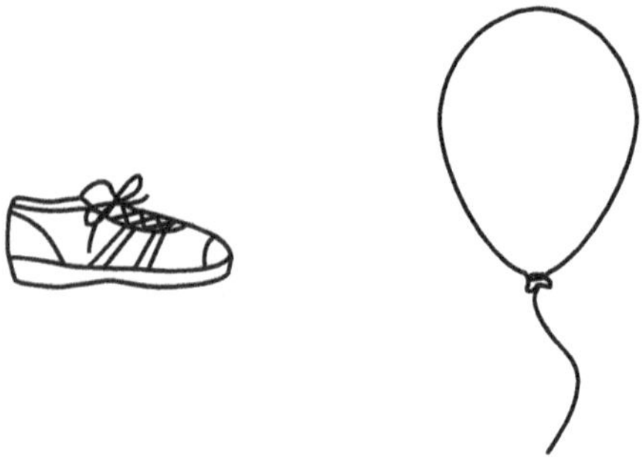

10.

11.

12.

# MDK-10 Many Ways to Be Bigger or Smaller

☐ Circle the **taller** one.

1.

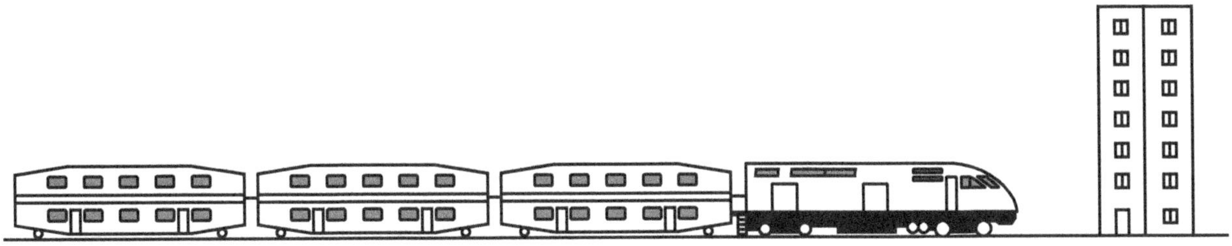

2.

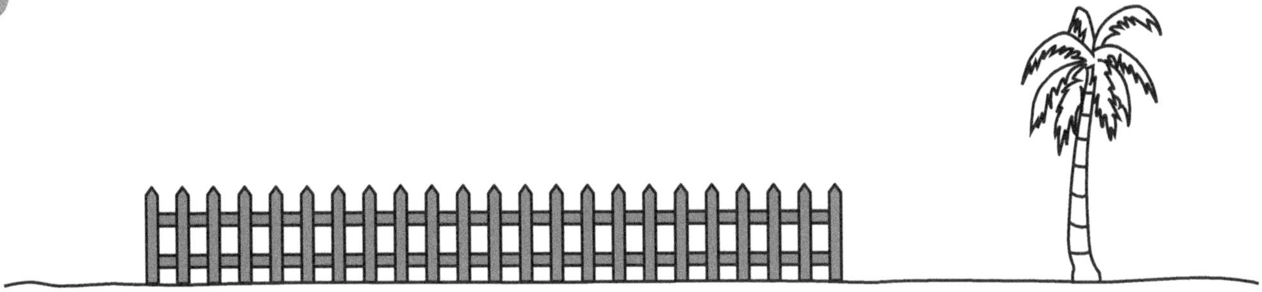

☐ Circle the **longer** one.

3.

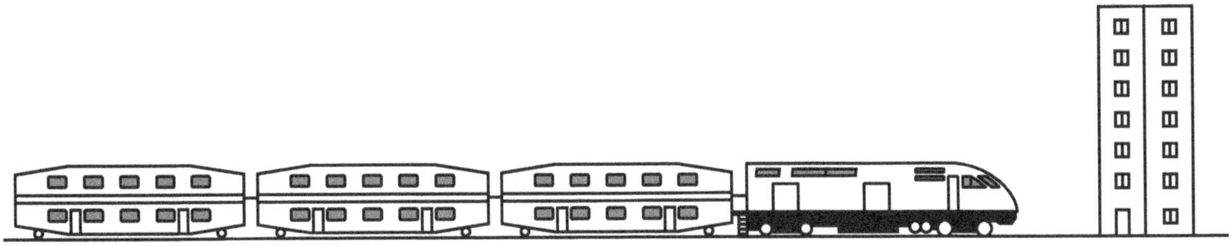

4.

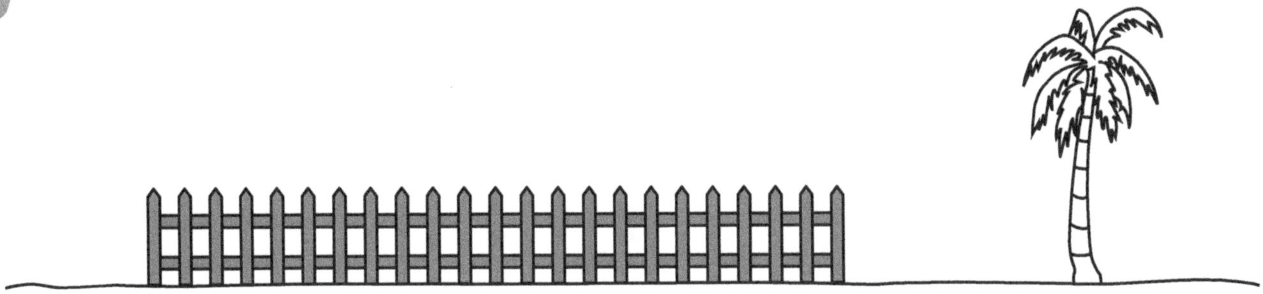

☐ Circle the **taller** one.

5.

6.

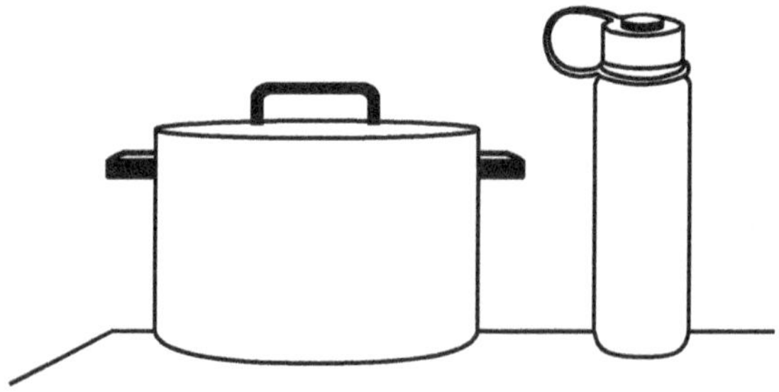

☐ Circle the one that **holds more**.

7.

8.

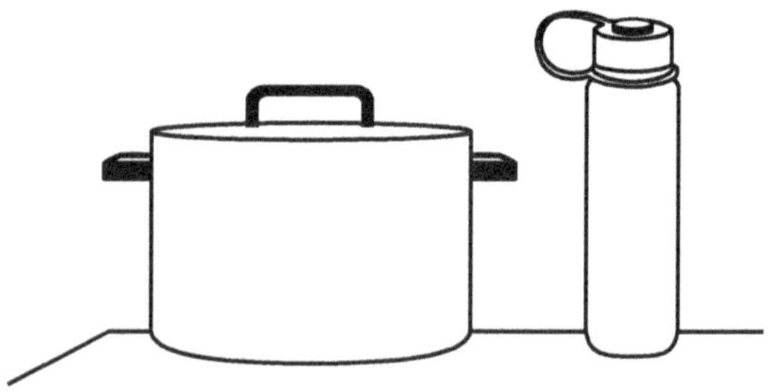

☐ Circle the **longer** one.

9.

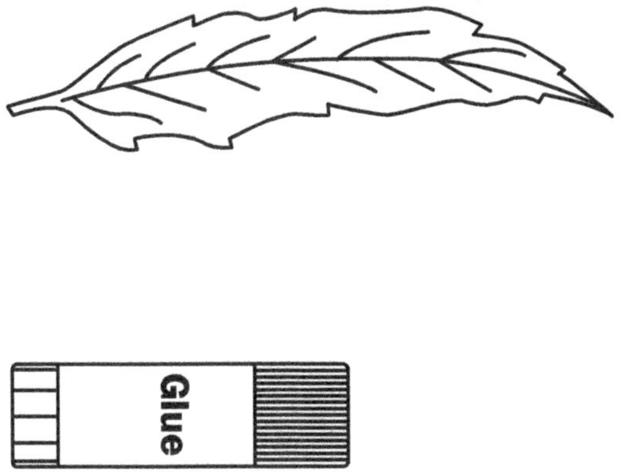


10.

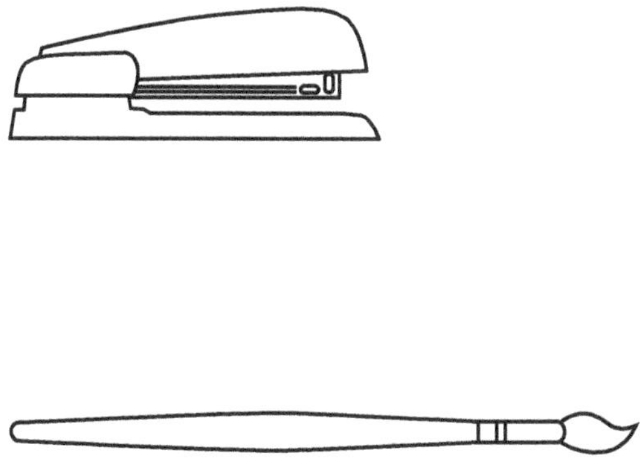

☐ Circle the **heavier** one.

11.

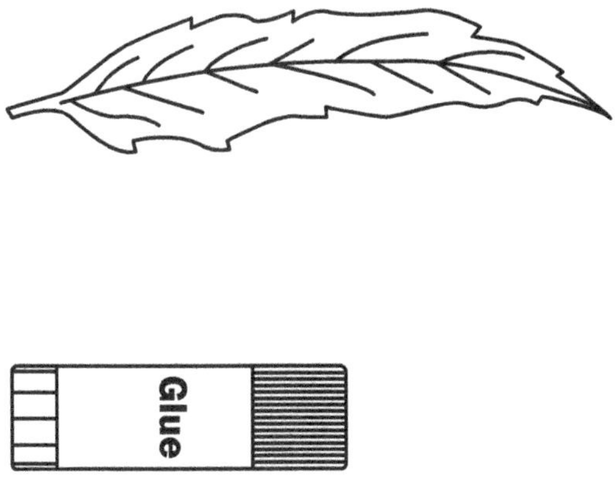


12.

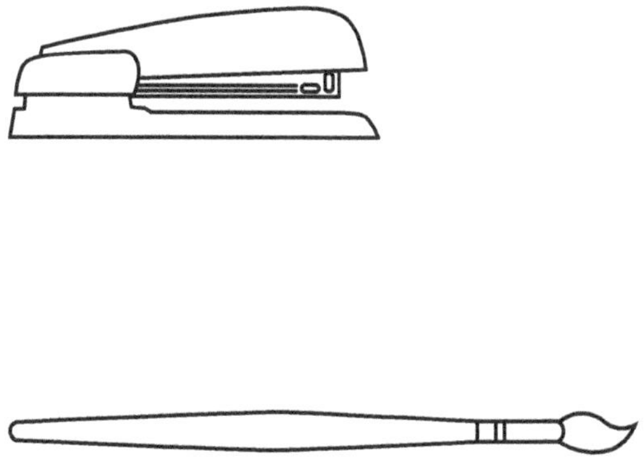

# MDK-11 More Combining Shapes

☐ Use pattern blocks to cover the shape.

1.

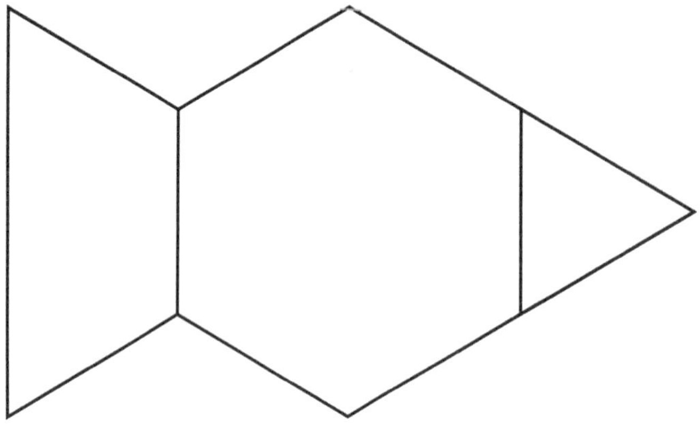

2.

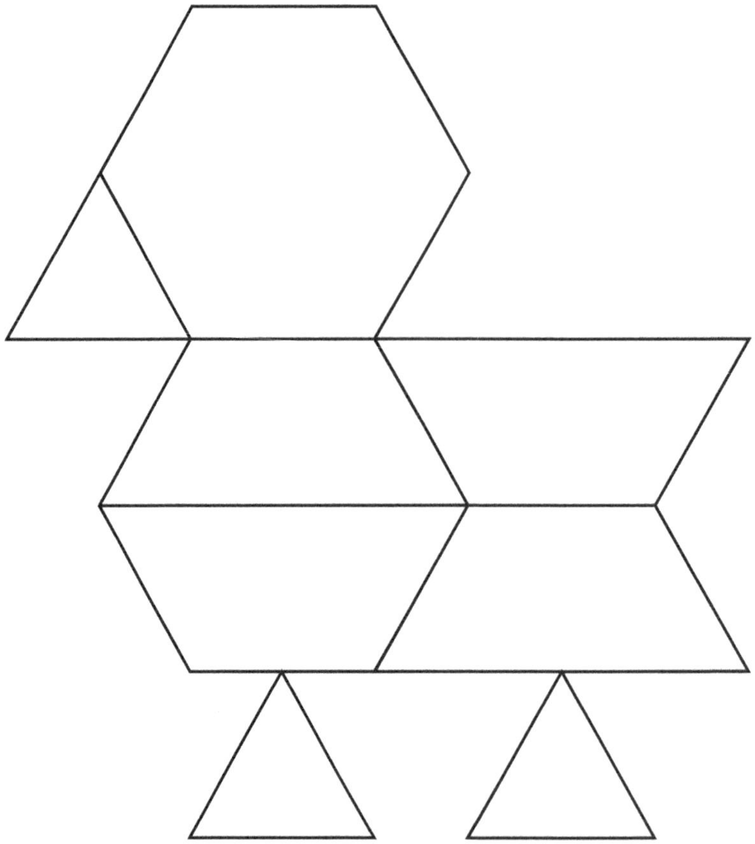

☐ Use pattern blocks to cover the shape.

3.

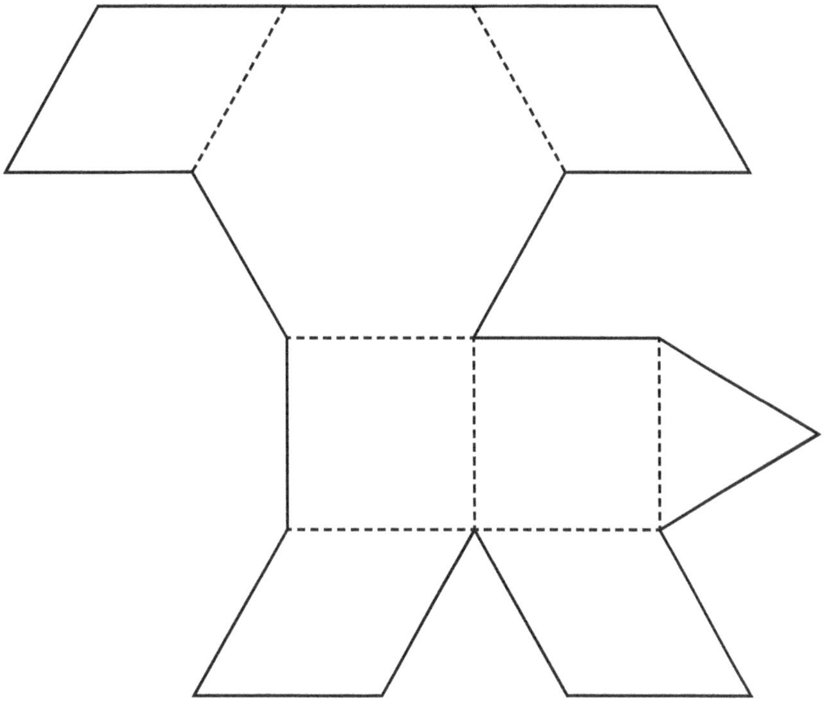

4.

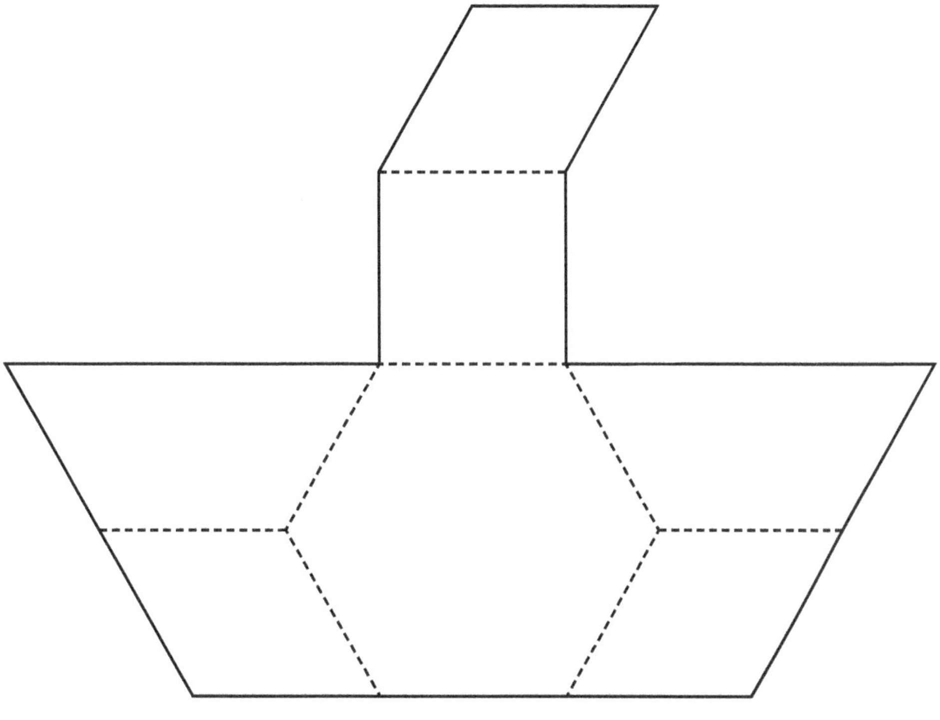

☐ Use pattern blocks to cover the shapes.

5.